基础 强化 冲刺

雅思阅读
教程

主　编：许　婷
副主编：付建强　龚柏岩
参　编：薛红刚　耿　雪　董　雪　唐责凯

IELTS
Reading

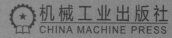

机械工业出版社
CHINA MACHINE PRESS

雅思阅读是通过复杂巧妙的题型设计来考查考生对文章细节及整体的多角度理解的一种考试。具体说来，雅思阅读对考生的能力考查更深入、更全面，既要求其能够准确理解文章细节，又要求其能够熟练概括文章段落大意。

本书正是依据雅思阅读考试特点来详解及训练如何应对各种问题的，旨在帮助考生摆脱解题思路困扰，了解不同题型的特点、要点，掌握题型破解方法，熟练运用各种解题技巧。

同时，本书还提供了高频阅读词汇和阅读必备语法知识讲解，帮助考生在提升应试技能的同时全面提升阅读能力。

本书配有雅思考试真题语料、讲解视频，能够帮助考生熟悉真题题型及考查内容，同时在经验丰富的老师指导下更为高效地提分。

图书在版编目（CIP）数据

雅思阅读教程／许婷主编. —北京：机械工业出版社，2024.1
ISBN 978－7－111－75142－7

Ⅰ.①雅…　Ⅱ.①许…　Ⅲ.①IELTS－阅读教学－自学参考资料
Ⅳ.①H319.4

中国国家版本馆CIP数据核字（2024）第003024号

机械工业出版社（北京市百万庄大街22号　邮政编码100037）
策划编辑：尹小云　　责任编辑：尹小云
责任校对：苏筛琴　　责任印制：郜　敏
三河市宏达印刷有限公司印刷
2024年1月第1版第1次印刷
184mm×260mm·13.5印张·1插页·335千字
标准书号：ISBN 978－7－111－75142－7
定价：62.00元

电话服务　　　　　　　网络服务
客服电话：010-88361066　　机　工　官　网：www.cmpbook.com
　　　　　010-88379833　　机　工　官　博：weibo.com/cmp1952
　　　　　010-68326294　　金　书　网：www.golden-book.com
封底无防伪标均为盗版　　机工教育服务网：www.cmpedu.com

前 言
Preface

雅思考试是世界上最受欢迎的英语语言测试之一，其阅读部分是考生必须面对的难点之一。与口语、写作部分（中国考生普遍在6.0分以下）相比，雅思阅读往往更容易在短时间内显著提高分数。可以说，雅思阅读分数的高低在一定程度上决定了雅思考试总分的高低。因此，通过有效的方法学习来提高雅思阅读能力是非常有必要的。

本书由平均教龄在15年以上、具有丰富雅思教学经验的优秀教师精心编写，旨在帮助考生熟悉雅思阅读中的各种题型及解题技巧，并且能熟练运用各种技巧来快速解题，在提升阅读能力的基础上提高雅思阅读分数。

本书具备以下特色：

一、由易到难：在难度方面，本书将雅思阅读备考内容按照对应的能力分为三个部分，即基础（词汇＋长难句）、题型精讲、真题同源文章精读。这三个部分的学习完整地涵盖了考生从较为基础的水平向高分水平进阶的过程。

二、针对性强：本书词汇部分收录了雅思阅读真题中的高频核心学术词汇与必备学科分类词汇，方便考生快速掌握针对性强的雅思阅读高频词汇并进行自我检测。长难句部分提供了精选于剑桥真题的丰富示例，教授考生通过提取主干的方法快速抓住文章信息点，讲练结合，能帮助考生快速提升句子分析能力及阅读能力。此外，夯实词汇及语法基础也是考生提升整体阅读速度、准确度进而突破高分的关键。

三、技巧独到高效：本书将雅思阅读分为判断题、填空题、匹配题、段落标题题和选择题等五个题型，分享了教出众多8.0分和满分学员的老师的教学"精华"。简化题型后能使重点更为突出，同时也能让学习更为高效。

四、20篇精读范本：为了提升考生对全文的解读能力，本书精选了20篇涵盖雅思阅读常见话题的文章，供考生学习如何抓住长难句的句子主干、如何分析上下文之间的逻辑关系以及如何把握文章的结构和主旨。

备考雅思阅读虽然劳心劳力，但好的方法犹如浩瀚大海中的灯塔、无垠夜空中的守护星，将指引你走向正确的方向，避免弯路和踩坑，顺利到达彼岸。最后，祝愿参加雅思考试的你取得优异的成绩，奔赴理想的学校！

编　者

雅思阅读需要掌握的预备知识

雅思考试作为一项标准化考试，有其相应的答题方法和技巧。但是，解题方法和技巧的应用都不能脱离词汇和语法等基础知识。因此，有必要先了解雅思考试的词汇量要求与语法常考点。

根据下表中的雅思官方信息可知，雅思 7.0 ~ 8.0 分对应 CEFR（Common European Framework of Reference for Languages，即欧洲共同语言参考标准）体系的 C1 阶段，该阶段的词汇量要求是 10000 词；雅思 5.5 ~ 6.5 分对应 CEFR 体系的 B2 阶段，该阶段的词汇量要求是 5500 词；雅思 4.0 ~ 5.0 分对应 CEFR 体系的 B1 阶段，该阶段的词汇量要求是 2500 词。一般而言，阅读词汇难度明显高于听力词汇难度，而雅思阅读要想拿到理想的成绩，需要掌握大约 7000 词。相比较而言，国内的标准化考试对词汇量的要求分别是：高考约 3500 词；大学英语四级考试约 4500 词；大学英语六级考试和考研约 5500 词。备考考生可以根据自己目前的词汇水平，集中掌握不足的部分。比如，大学英语四级考试及格的考生可以重点记忆缺乏的 2500 词。

CEFR Level	Active Vocabulary	Passive Vocabulary
A1	300	600
A2	600	1200
B1	1200	2500
B2	2500	5000
C1	5000	10000
C2	10000	20000

本书附录部分包含"雅思阅读高频核心学术词汇"和"雅思阅读必备学科分类词汇"。前者包含 10 个 list，是从真题中提取的高频词汇，是考生必须优先掌握的。鉴于雅思考试阅读文章涉及生物、环境、心理学、历史、考古、语言、教育等自然学科和社会科学的题材，考生需要对各学科的专业词汇有一定的了解。这部分内容考生可根据自身需求来学习掌握。

雅思考试阅读部分的另一个"拦路虎"是长难句。由于雅思考试阅读文章是学术性题材，用词多抽象且句式严谨，考生在阅读过程中会遇到并列句和从句套从句的复杂长句，这时考查的是考生能否理清句子之间的逻辑关系并抓取主要信息点。此时，想要在考场上有限的时间里"翻译"全文是费时费力且可能无效的方法。正确的方法是区分句子中的主要信息（主句的主谓宾）、次要信息（形容词、副词、介词短语、从句、部分非谓语、同位语、插入语等）。考生可以通过长难句的句型练习来训练这种能力。

目 录
Contents

第1章 雅思阅读语法基础

本章主要以英语句子种类为切入点来介绍简单句、并列句及三大从句（形容词性从句、名词性从句、副词性从句）的用法。在此，我们将教会大家通过拆分句子的方式，将嵌套有多个简单句的长难句简化并提出主句的主干部分，先掌握句子的主体结构及含义，然后在此基础上实现对整个句子的理解。

1.1 简单句

1.1.1 简单句定义及基本句型

简单句是只含有一个主谓结构且句子中各成分都是由单词或短语构成的独立句子或分句。在简单句中，主语和谓语是句子的核心。简单句有五种基本句型：

> ◇ 主谓（SV）
> ◇ 主谓宾（SVO）
> ◇ 主系表（SVP）
> ◇ 主谓宾宾（SVOO）
> ◇ 主谓宾补（SVOC）
> 说明：主语（S）、谓语（V）、宾语（O）、表语（P）、补语（C）

1.1.2 简单句句型练习

1 According to archaeological evidence, at least 5000 years ago, and long before the advent of the Roman Empire, the Babylonians[S] began to measure[V] time[O], introducing calendars to co-ordinate communal activities, to plan the shipment of goods and, in particular, to regulate planting and harvesting.

句子主干： the Babylonians began to measure time

极简翻译： 巴比伦人开始测量时间

原文翻译： 根据考古证据，至少在5000年前，在罗马帝国出现之前很久，巴比伦人就开始测量时间，引入日历来协调公共活动、计划货物运输，特别是调节种植和收获。

2 Centuries before the Roman Empire, the Egyptians^S had formulated^V a municipal calendar^O having 12 months of 30 days, with five days added to approximate the solar year.

句子主干： the Egyptians had formulated a municipal calendar

极简翻译： 埃及人制定了市政日历

原文翻译： 在罗马帝国之前的几个世纪，埃及人就制定了一种市政历法：一年有 12 个月，每个月 30 天，再加上 5 天，等于一个太阳年。

3 The idea^S of an autonomous discipline called "philosophy", distinct from and sitting in judgment on such pursuits as theology and science turns out^V, on close examination, to be of quite recent origin^O.

句子主干： The idea turns out to be of recent origin

极简翻译： 这个概念是最近才产生的

原文翻译： 经过仔细研究，一个被称为"哲学"的自主学科的概念——它与神学和科学等学科追求不同，而且对其他学科进行评判——是最近才产生的。

4 At various points in evolutionary history, enterprising individuals^S within many different animal groups moved out^V onto the land^O, sometimes even to the most parched deserts.

句子主干： individuals moved out onto the land

极简翻译： 动物迁徙到了陆地上

原文翻译： 在进化史上的不同时期，许多不同动物群体中有冒险精神的个体迁徙到了陆地上，有时甚至移居到了最干燥的沙漠。

5 On wide major roads, the guard rails^S often guide^V pedestrians^O to specific crossing points and slow down^V their progress^O across the road by using staggered access points to divide the crossing into two — one for each carriageway.

句子主干： the guard rails guide pedestrians and slow down their progress

极简翻译： 护栏引导行人并减缓他们的前进速度

原文翻译： 在宽阔的主干道上，护栏经常引导行人去往特定的十字路口，并通过交错的入口将十字路口分成两部分（每条车道一个）来减缓他们穿过马路的速度。

6 According to another legend, monks^S working for the Byzantine emperor Justinian smuggled^V silkworm eggs^O to Constantinople in 550 AD, concealed inside hollow bamboo walking canes.

句子主干： monks smuggled silkworm eggs

极简翻译： 僧侣走私蚕卵

原文翻译： 根据另一个传说，公元 550 年，为拜占庭皇帝查士丁尼工作的僧侣将蚕卵藏在空心的竹手杖中走私到了君士坦丁堡。

1.2 复合句

在简单句的基础之上可组装复合句和并列句，以表达更加复杂的意思。复合句中包含三种基本从句：

> ◇ **形容词从句（定语从句）**
> ◇ **名词性从句（主语从句、宾语从句、表语从句、同位语从句）**
> ◇ **副词性从句（状语从句：表时间、地点、原因、条件、目的、让步、比较、方式、结果）**

1.2.1 形容词性从句（定语从句）定义及句型练习

● 定义

定语从句（Attributive Clause，AC）指由关系词引导的从句，句法功能多是用作定语。在英语中，定语从句通常位于它所修饰的词（组）之后。被定语从句修饰的词（组）叫作先行词，引导定语从句的词称为关系词，关系词指代先行词，并在从句中充当一定的成分。

● 句型练习

1 To be at their most effective in their self-regulation, all children can be helped to identify their own ways of learning — **metacognition** — [which^{AC} will include strategies of planning, monitoring, evaluation, and choice of what to learn].

　　定语从句：which will...learn，修饰先行词 metacognition

　　句子主干：all children can be helped to identify their own ways of learning

　　极简翻译：所有儿童可以被帮助去确定他们自己的学习方法

　　原文翻译：为了最有效地进行自我调节，可以帮助所有儿童确定他们自己的学习方式——元
　　　　　　　　认知，其中包括计划、监控、评估和选择学习内容的策略。

2 Temporal hours, {which^{AC} were first adopted by the Greeks and then the Romans, [who^{AC} disseminated them through Europe]}, remained in use for more than 2,500 years.

　　定语从句①：which were...Europe，修饰先行词 Temporal hours

　　定语从句②：who disseminated...Europe，修饰先行词 Romans

　　句子主干：Temporal hours remained in use

　　极简翻译：时间制仍在使用

　　原文翻译：时间制首先被希腊人采用，然后被罗马人采用并推广到欧洲各地，沿用了2500
　　　　　　　　多年。

3 The **guard rails** {that^{AC} will be familiar to **anyone** [who^{AC} has attempted to cross the British road]}, for example, were an engineering solution to pedestrian safety based on **models** [that^{AC} prioritise the smooth flow of traffic].

定语从句①：that will...road，修饰先行词 guard rails

定语从句②：who has...road，修饰先行词 anyone

定语从句③：that prioritise...traffic，修饰先行词 models

句子主干：The guard rails were an engineering solution

极简翻译：护栏是一种工程解决方案

原文翻译：例如，任何试图穿越英国道路的人都熟悉的护栏是一种行人安全工程解决方案，其模式基于优先考虑交通畅通。

4 Travelling around Thailand in the 1990s, William Janssen was impressed with the basic rooftop **solar heating systems** {that^{AC} were on many **homes**, [where^{AC} energy from the sun was absorbed by a plate and then used to heat water for domestic use]}.

定语从句①：that were...use，修饰先行词 solar heating systems

定语从句②：where energy...use，修饰先行词 homes

句子主干：William Janssen was impressed with the solar heating systems

极简翻译：威廉·杨森对太阳能供暖系统印象深刻

原文翻译：20世纪90年代，威廉·杨森在泰国旅行时，对许多家庭屋顶的基础太阳能供暖系统印象深刻，在那里，太阳能被一块板吸收，然后用来加热家庭用水。

5 Many critics of Emily Brontë's novel *Wuthering Heights* see its second part as a **counterpoint** {that^{AC} comments on the **first part**, [where^{AC} a romantic reading receives more confirmation]}.

定语从句①：that...confirmation，修饰先行词 counterpoint

定语从句②：where a...confirmation，修饰先行词 first part

句子主干：critics see its second part as a counterpoint

极简翻译：批评家们认为第二部分是一种对立

原文翻译：艾米莉·勃朗特的小说《呼啸山庄》的许多评论家认为第二部分与第一部分的观点对立，在第一部分中，浪漫主义得到了更多的证实。

6 It is like a **drawing** (that)^{AC} [a child might make by sticking indivisible discs of color onto a canvas].

关系代词用作宾语时的省略：当关系代词 who，whom，which 和 that 在定语从句中用作动词宾语时可以省略

定语从句：省略 that，a child...canvas 修饰先行词 drawing

句子主干：It is like a drawing

极简翻译：它像一幅图画

原文翻译：这就像一个孩子把不可分割的彩色圆盘粘在画布上绘制的图画。

7 That **sex ratio** will be favoured { which^(AC) maximises the **number of descendants** (that)^(AC) [an individual will have] and hence the number of gene copies transmitted }.

定语从句①： which maximises...transmitted，修饰先行词 sex ratio

定语从句②： 省略 that，an individual...have，修饰先行词 number of descendants

句子主干： That sex ratio will be favoured

极简翻译： 那种性别比例将会是有利的

原文翻译： 那种性别比例将会是有利的，它会使个体拥有的后代数量最大化，从而使基因复制的数量最大化。

8 A few years ago, in one of the most fascinating and disturbing experiments in behavioural psychology, Stanley Milgram of Yale University tested 40 subjects from all walks of life for their willingness to obey instructions given by a "leader" in a **situation** { in which^(AC) the subjects might feel a personal distaste for the **actions** (that)^(AC) [they were called upon to perform] }.

定语从句①： in which...perform，修饰先行词 situation

定语从句②： 省略 that，they were...perform 修饰先行词 actions

句子主干： Stanley Milgram tested 40 subjects

极简翻译： 斯坦利·米尔格林姆测试了 40 名受试者

原文翻译： 几年前，来自耶鲁大学的斯坦利·米尔格林姆进行了一项在行为心理学中最有趣也最令人不安的实验，他测试了来自各行各业的 40 名受试者，看受试者是否愿意在他们可能会对被要求执行的行为感到厌恶的情况下服从"领导者"的指示。

9 Managers often fail to recognise the less obvious but profound **ways** (by which)^(AC) [these trends are influencing consumers' aspirations, attitudes, and behaviours].

定语从句中的省略： 以 way 为先行词的限制性定语从句，通常由 by which 或 that 引导，但通常省略 by which 或 that。

定语从句： 省略 by which，these trends...behaviours 修饰先行词 ways

句子主干： Managers fail to recognise the less obvious but profound ways

极简翻译： 管理人员没有意识到这些不这么明显却深刻的方式

原文翻译： 管理人员往往没有意识到这些趋势正在以不太明显却深刻的方式影响着消费者的愿望、态度和行为。

1.2.2 名词性从句（主语从句）定义及句型练习

定义

主语从句（Subject Clause，SC）是在复合句中充当主语的从句，通常放在主句谓语动词之前，有时为避免头重脚轻，会用形式主语 it 引导从句。

➡️ **句型练习**

1 What highly creative artistic activity produces^{SC} is not a new **generalisation** [that^{AC} transcends established limits], but rather an aesthetic particular.

主语从句：What highly...produces

定语从句：that transcends...limits 修饰先行词 generalisation

句子主干：What highly creative artistic activity produces is not a new generalisation, but rather an aesthetic particular.

极简翻译：极具创造性的艺术活动产生的不是一种新的概括，而是一种美学上的特殊性

原文翻译：极具创造性的艺术活动产生的不是一种新的超越既定界限的概括，而是一种美学上的特殊性。

2 That each large firm will act with consideration of its own needs and thus avoid selling its products for more than its competitors' charge^{SC} is commonly recognised by advocates of free-market economic theories.

主语从句：That each large firm...competitors charge

句子主干：That large firm will act with consideration and avoid selling its products for more than its competitors' charge is commonly recognised

极简翻译：这种观点被普遍承认

原文翻译：每个大公司都会考虑自己的需求，从而避免以高于竞争对手的价格销售产品，这是自由市场经济理论的倡导者普遍承认的。

3 It is one of nature's great ironies that the availability of nitrogen in the soil frequently sets an upper limit on plant growth even though the plants' leaves are bathed in a sea of nitrogen gas^{SC}.

主语从句：that the availability...nitrogen gas，it 为形式主语

句子主干：It is one of nature's great ironies

极简翻译：这是大自然最大的讽刺之一

原文翻译：大自然最大的讽刺之一是，尽管植物的叶子沐浴在氮气的海洋中，但土壤中氮的可用性往往会给植物的生长设定上限。

4 By the late 1970s, it was recognised in most societies that people have a right to health-care (though there has been considerable resistance in the United States to the idea that there is formal right to health-care)^{SC}.

主语从句：that people...health-care，it 为形式主语

句子主干：It was recognised in most societies

极简翻译：大多数社会都承认这一点

原文翻译：到 20 世纪 70 年代末，大多数社会都承认人们享有医疗保健权（尽管在美国，人们对享有正式医疗保健权的想法有相当大的抵制）。

1.2.3 名词性从句（宾语从句）定义及句型练习

➡ 定义

置于动词、介词等后面起宾语作用的从句叫作宾语从句（Object Clause，OC）。宾语从句的语序必须是陈述句语序。

➡ 句型练习

1 Neuroscience has revealed[V] which brain circuits are responsible for functions like understanding what other people think, empathy, fairness, and social identity[OC].

宾语从句：which brain…social identity（省略了引导词 that）

句子主干：Neuroscience has revealed which brain circuits are responsible for functions

极简翻译：神经科学揭示了一些大脑回路负责的功能

原文翻译：神经科学揭示了哪些大脑回路负责理解他人的想法、同理心、公平和社会认同等功能。

2 Studies conducted by Carolyn DeClerck of the University of Antwerp, Belgium, revealed[V] that people [who[AC] had received a dose of oxytocin] actually became less cooperative when dealing with complete strangers[OC].

宾语从句：that people…strangers

定语从句：who had…oxytocin，修饰先行词 people

句子主干：Studies revealed that people became less cooperative when dealing with complete strangers

极简翻译：研究表明，人们在与陌生人打交道时，会变得不那么合作

原文翻译：比利时安特卫普大学的卡罗利恩·德克拉克进行的研究显示，服用过一定剂量催产素的人在与完全陌生的人打交道时，实际上会变得不那么合作。

3 The FAA realised[V] that the airspace over the United States would at any time have many different kinds of planes, flying for many different purposes, in a variety of weather conditions[OC], and the same kind of structure was needed to accommodate all of them[OC].

宾语从句①：that the airspace…conditions

宾语从句②：the same…them（and 之后的宾语从句省略了引导词 that）

句子主干：The FAA realised that the airspace have many different kinds of planes, and the structure was needed to accommodate them

极简翻译：FAA 意识到，领空中有许多不同类型的飞机，需要有结构来容纳它们

原文翻译：美国联邦航空管理局意识到，在任何时候，美国领空中都会有许多不同类型的飞机，它们在各种各样的天气条件下出于许多不同的目的飞行，需要同一种结构来容纳所有这些飞机。

1.2.4 名词性从句（表语从句）定义及句型练习

➡ 定义

表语是用来说明主语的身份、性质、品性、特征和状态的，常位于系动词之后。如果句子的表语是由一个句子充当的，那么这个充当表语的句子就叫作表语从句（Predicative Clause，PC）。

➡ 句型练习

1 One of the **reasons** [**why**^AC the enthusiasm for rewilding is spreading so quickly in Britain] is that it helps to create a more inspiring vision than the green movement's usual promise of "Follow us and the world will be slightly less awful than it would otherwise have been"^PC.

表语从句：that it...have been，说明 reasons

定语从句：why...Britain，修饰先行词 reasons

句子主干：One of the reasons is that it helps to create a more inspiring vision than a usual promise

极简翻译：原因之一是这有助于创造一个比普通承诺更鼓舞人心的愿景

原文翻译：野外回归的热情在英国迅速蔓延的原因之一是，这有助于创造一个更鼓舞人心的愿景，而不是绿色运动通常所承诺的"跟随我们，世界将比不这么做的情况略好一些"。

2 What made matters worse^SC was that its proliferation coincided with sweeping changes in agriculture and a massive shift from sheep farming to dairying^PC.

表语从句：that its...dairying，说明主语

主语从句：What...worse

句子主干：What made matters worse was that its proliferation coincided with changes and a shift

极简翻译：更糟糕的是，它的扩散与变革及转变同时发生

原文翻译：更糟糕的是，它的扩散与农业的彻底变革以及从养羊业到奶牛业的大规模转变同时发生。

3 However, the difficulty with the evidence produced by these studies, fascinating as they are in collecting together anecdotes and apparent similarities and exceptions, is that they are not what we would today call norm-referenced^PC.

表语从句①：that they...norm-referenced，说明 difficulty

表语从句②：what we...norm-referenced，说明 they

句子主干：the difficulty is that they are not what we would today call norm-referenced

极简翻译：困难在于，它们不是我们今天所说的标准参照

原文翻译：然而，这些研究产生的证据的困难在于，它们并不是我们今天所说的标准参照，尽管它们收集了轶事、明显的相似之处和例外，令人着迷。

1.2.5　名词性从句（同位语从句）定义及句型练习

▶ 定义

同位语从句（Appositive Clause，AC）用来对其前面的抽象名词进行解释说明，被解释说明的词和同位语在逻辑上是主表关系。一个名词（或其他形式）对另一个名词或代词进行解释或补充说明，这个名词（或其他形式）是同位语（Appositive）。同位语与被它限定的词常常紧挨在一起。

▶ 句型练习

1 The conviction that historical relics provide infallible testimony about the past[AC] is rooted in the nineteenth and early twentieth centuries, when science was regarded as objective and value free.

同位语从句：that historical...past，补充说明 conviction

句子主干：The conviction is rooted in the nineteenth and early twentieth centuries

极简翻译：这种信念起源于 19 世纪和 20 世纪初

原文翻译：历史遗迹提供了关于过去的可靠证据，这一信念植根于 19 世纪和 20 世纪初，当时科学被认为是客观的、没有价值的。

2 In its most general sense, prescriptivism is the view that one variety of language has an inherently higher value than others[AC], and that this ought to be imposed on the whole of the speech community[AC].

同位语从句①：that one variety...others，补充说明 view

同位语从句②：that this ought...community，补充说明 view

句子主干：prescriptivism is the view

极简翻译：规范主义是一种观点

原文翻译：在最普遍的意义上，规范主义是这样一种观点，即一种语言本身就比其他语言具有更高的内在价值，而且这种价值应该被强加于整个语言社区。

3 However, Lewis and Brooks-Gunn（1979）suggest that infants' developing understanding that the movements they see in the mirror are contingent on their own[AC], leads to a growing awareness that they are distinct from other people[AC].

同位语从句①：that the movements...own，补充说明 understanding

同位语从句②：that they...people，补充说明 awareness

句子主干：Lewis and Brooks-Gunn suggest that infants' developing understanding leads to a growing awareness

极简翻译：刘易斯和布鲁克斯·古恩认为，婴儿理解能力的发展会导致意识的增强

原文翻译：然而，刘易斯和布鲁克斯·古恩（1979）认为，婴儿逐渐理解他们在镜子中看到的动作是由他们自己决定的，这导致他们越来越意识到自己与其他人不同。

4 Once out there, skilled seafarers would have detected abundant leads to follow to land: seabirds, coconuts and twigs carried out to sea by the tides, and the afternoon **pile-up** of clouds on the horizon [which^AC often indicates an island in the distance]^A.

同位语：seabirds, coconuts...distance，补充说明 leads

定语从句：which often...distance，修饰先行词 pile-up

句子主干：seafarers would have detected abundant leads

极简翻译：海员会发现大量线索

原文翻译：一旦到了那里，熟练的海员会发现大量可以追踪到陆地的线索：海鸟、椰子、被潮汐带到海上的树枝，以及下午地平线上堆积的云层，这通常表明远处有一座岛屿。

5 Meanwhile, Carsten De Dreu at the University of Amsterdam in the Netherlands discovered^V that volunteers given oxytocin showed favouritism: Dutch men became quicker to associate positive words with Dutch names than with foreign ones, for example^A/OC.

同位语：Dutch men...for example，补充说明 favouritism

宾语从句：that volunteers...for example

句子主干：Carsten De Dreu discovered that volunteers given oxytocin showed favouritism

极简翻译：卡斯滕·德德鲁发现，服用催产素的志愿者表现出了偏爱

原文翻译：与此同时，来自荷兰阿姆斯特丹大学的卡斯滕·德德鲁发现，服用催产素的志愿者表现出了偏爱：例如荷兰男性将积极词汇与荷兰名字联系起来的速度比将其与外国名字联系起来的速度更快。

6 They based their calendars on three natural cycles: the solar day, marked by the successive periods of light and darkness as the earth rotates on its axis; the lunar month, following the phases of the moon as it orbits the earth; and the solar year, defined by the changing seasons [that^AC accompany our planet's revolution around the sun]^A.

同位语：solar day; lunar month; and solar year，补充说明 three natural cycles

定语从句：that accompany...the sun，修饰 seasons

句子主干：They based calendars on three natural cycles

极简翻译：他们的日历基于三个自然周期

原文翻译：他们的日历基于三个自然周期：太阳日，以地球绕地轴旋转时连续的光明和黑暗时期为标志；太阴月，跟随月球绕地球运行时的相位；太阳年，由季节的变化来定义，季节的变化随着地球绕太阳的公转而改变。

1.2.6 副词性从句 (状语从句) 定义及句型练习

→ 定义

状语从句（Adverbial Clause）指句子用作状语时，起副词作用的句子。状语从句根据其作用可

分为时间、地点、原因、条件、目的、结果、让步、方式和比较等从句。状语从句一般由连词（从属连词）引导，也可以由词组引起。从句位于句首或句中时通常用逗号与主句隔开。

→ 句型练习

1 If aspects of the category clash^V with undesired outcomes of a trend, <u>such as associations with unhealthy lifestyles</u>, there is^V an opportunity to counteract those changes by reaffirming the core values of your category.

条件状语：由从属连词 If 引导

插入语：such as...lifestyles，补充说明 undesired outcomes of a trend

句子主干：If aspects of the category clash with undesired outcomes, there is an opportunity to counteract those changes

极简翻译：如果该类别的某些方面与不希望的结果发生冲突，就有机会抵消这些变化

原文翻译：如果某一类别的某些方面与某一趋势的不期望结果相冲突，例如与不健康的生活方式相关联，则有机会通过重申该类别的核心价值观来抵消这些变化。

2 Once you have gained^V perspective on how trend-related changes in consumer opinions and behaviours impact on your category, you can determine^V <u>which of our three innovation strategies to pursue</u>^{OC}.

条件状语：由从属连词 Once 引导

宾语从句：which of...pursue

句子主干：Once you have gained perspective, you can determine

极简翻译：一旦你有了观点，你就能决定

原文翻译：一旦你了解与趋势相关的消费者观点和行为的变化如何影响你的类别，你就可以决定采用我们的三种创新战略中的哪一种。

3 Granted that the presence of these elements need not argue^V an authorial awareness of novelistic construction comparable to that of Henry James, their presence does encourage^V attempts to unify the novel's heterogeneous parts.

让步状语：由过去分词短语 granted that 引导

句子主干：Granted that these elements need not argue an authorial awareness, their presence does encourage attempts

极简翻译：尽管这些元素不能证明作者的意识，但是它们的确鼓励尝试

原文翻译：尽管这些元素的存在并不需要证明作者对小说结构的意识可以与亨利·詹姆斯相媲美，但它们的存在确实鼓励了将小说的不同部分统一起来的尝试。

4 By the mid-1960s, the situation took^V an alarming turn with the outbreak of four more new pests, necessitating pesticide spraying to such an <u>extent that 50% of the financial outlay on cotton production was accounted for by pesticides</u>^{AC}.

伴随状语：由现在分词 necessitating 引导

同位语从句：that 50% of...pesticides，补充说明 extent

句子主干：the situation took an alarming turn with the outbreak of four more new pests

极简翻译：随着另外四种新害虫的爆发，情况发生了惊人的变化

原文翻译：到了20世纪60年代中期，随着另外四种新害虫的爆发，形势出现了令人担忧的变化，这迫使杀虫剂的喷洒到了这样的程度：50%的棉花生产经费都是因为杀虫剂而花掉的。

5 These have been, quite properly, organised^V into a more serial, logical order so that the worth of the output may be evaluated^V independently of the **behavioural processes** ［by which^{AC} it was obtained］.

结果状语：由从属连词 so that 引导

定语从句：by which...obtained，修饰先行词 behavioural processes

句子主干：These have been organised into a...order

极简翻译：这些已经被组织成……的顺序

原文翻译：这些已经被非常恰当地组织成了一个更连续、更合乎逻辑的顺序，因此，输出的价值可以独立于获得输出的行为过程来评估。

1.3 并列句

1.3.1 并列句定义及分类

由并列连词把两个或两个以上的句子连在一起组成的句子叫并列句。不同的并列连词表示并列分句之间的不同关系。

> **并列关系**：常由并列连词 and，not only...but（also）...及分号等来连接，分句之间是顺承关系或并列关系。
>
> **转折关系**：常用 but，yet，while，whereas 等来连接，后面分句与前面分句之间有意义上的转折关系。
>
> **因果关系**：常用 so，for，since 等连接，后面分句与前面分句之间有因果关系。

1.3.2 并列句句型练习

▶ **并列关系**

1 Moreover, not only do time signals beamed down from Global Positioning System satellites calibrate^V the functions of precision navigation equipment, they do^V so as well for mobile phones, instant stock-trading systems and nationwide power-distribution grids.

并列连词：not only…as well

句子主干：not only time signals calibrate the functions, they do so as well

极简翻译：时间信号不仅可以用于校准功能，还可以校准其他

原文翻译：此外，全球定位系统卫星发出的时间信号不仅可以校准精确导航设备的功能，还可以校准移动电话、即时股票交易系统和全国范围内的配电网的功能。

2 Not only are liver transplants never rejected, but they even induce a state of donor-specific unresponsiveness [in which^{AC} subsequent transplants of other organs, (such as skin), from that donor are accepted permanently].

并列连词：not only…but

定语从句：in which…permanently, 修饰先行词 a state

插入语：such as skin, 补充说明 organs

句子主干：Not only are liver transplants never rejected, but they even induce a state

极简翻译：肝脏移植不仅从未被排斥，甚至还诱发了一种状态

原文翻译：肝脏移植不仅从来不会被排斥，甚至还会诱发一种供者特异性无反应状态，在这种状态下，随后来自该供者的其他器官移植，如皮肤，会被永久接受。

3 Bauxite is the richest of all those aluminous rocks [that^{AC} occur in large quantities], and it yields alumina, the intermediate product required for the production of aluminum^{A}.

并列连词：and

定语从句：that occur…quantities, 修饰先行词 aluminous rocks

同位语：the intermediate…aluminum, 补充说明 alumina

句子主干：Bauxite is the richest of all those aluminous rocks, and it yields alumina

极简翻译：铝土矿是所有含铝岩石中最丰富的，可以生产氧化铝

原文翻译：铝土矿是所有含铝岩石中最丰富的一种，它可以生产氧化铝，这是生产铝所需的中间产品。

4 Open acknowledgement of the existence of women's oppression was too radical for the United States in the fifties, and Beauvoir's conclusion, that change in women's economic condition, though insufficient by itself, "remains the basic factor" in improving women's situation^{AC}, was particularly unacceptable.

并列连词：and

同位语从句：that change…situation, 补充说明 conclusion

句子主干：acknowledgement of oppression was too radical, and Beauvoir's conclusion was unacceptable

极简翻译：承认压迫太激进了，波伏瓦的结论不能被接受

原文翻译：公开承认女性受压迫的存在，对20世纪50年代的美国来说太激进了，波伏瓦的

结论是，女性经济状况的变化虽然本身不够，但"仍然是改善女性状况的基本因素"，这是特别不可接受的。

5 Participants in the online debate argued^V that our biggest challenge is to address the underlying causes of the agricultural system's inability to ensure sufficient food for all^{OC}, and they identified^V as drivers of this problem our dependency on fossil fuels and unsupportive government policies.

并列连词：and

宾语从句：that our...for all

句子主干：Participants argued that biggest challenge is to address the underlying causes, and they identified drivers of this problem

极简翻译：与会者认为最大的挑战是解决根本问题，同时他们确定了这一问题的原因

原文翻译：在线辩论的参与者认为，我们面临的最大挑战是解决农业系统无法确保所有人都有足够食物的根本问题，他们认为这一问题的驱动因素是我们对化石燃料的依赖和缺乏政府政策的扶持。

6 They failed to take into account that purpose-built street cafes could not operate in the hot sun without the protective awnings common in older buildings, and would need energy-consuming air conditioning instead^{OC}, or that its giant car park would feel so unwelcoming that it would put people off getting out of their cars^{OC}.

并列连词：or

宾语从句①：that purpose-built...instead

宾语从句②：that its giant car...their cars

句子主干：They failed to take into account that①, or that②

极简翻译：他们没有考虑两点

原文翻译：他们没有考虑到，专门建造的街头咖啡馆如果没有旧建筑中常见的保护性遮阳篷，就无法在烈日下营业，而且需要耗能的空调来代替，或者它的巨大停车场会让人感到不受欢迎，以至于人们无法下车。

7 Tolstoi's magical simplicity is a product of these tensions；his work is a record of the questions (that)^{AC} [he put to himself] and of the answers (that)^{AC} [he found in his search].

分号并列

定语从句①：可省略 that, he put...himself 修饰先行词 questions

定语从句②：可省略 that, he found...search 修饰先行词 answers

句子主干：Tolstoi's simplicity is a product of tensions；his work is a record of the questions and of the answers

极简翻译：托尔斯泰的简洁性是张力的产物；他的作品是问题和答案的记录

原文翻译：托尔斯泰神奇的简洁性就是这些张力的产物；他的作品记录了他向自己提出的问题，以及他在寻找过程中找到的答案。

8 They developed strategies for surviving harsh drought cycles, decades of heavy rainfall or unaccustomed cold; adopted **agriculture and stock-raising**, [which[AC] revolutionised human-life]; and founded the world's first pre-industrial civilisations in Egypt, Mesopotamia and the Americas.

分号并列

定语从句：which revolutionised…life，修饰先行词 agriculture and stock-raising

句子主干：They developed strategies；adopted agriculture and stock-raising；and founded civilisations

极简翻译：他们制定策略；采用农业和畜牧业；建立文明

原文翻译：他们制定了在严酷的干旱周期、数十年的强降雨或是异常寒冷中生存的策略，采用了农业和畜牧业，这点彻底改变了人类生活，并在埃及、美索不达米亚和美洲建立了世界上第一个工业化前的文明。

➡ 转折关系

1 That is not to suggest[V] everyone should dance their way to work, however healthy and happy it might make us[OC], but rather that the techniques used by choreographers to experiment with and design movement in dance could provide engineers with tools to stimulate new ideas incity-making[OC].

并列连词：but

宾语从句①：everyone should…make us（省略了引导词 that）

宾语从句②：that the techniques…city-making

句子主干：That is not to suggest (that) ①，but rather that ②

极简翻译：这并不是建议……而是建议……

原文翻译：这并不是建议每个人都应当跳着舞去上班，无论这么做会让我们多么健康和快乐，而是说编舞者在尝试和设计舞蹈动作时所使用的这些技巧可以为工程师们提供一些工具，激发城市建设的新想法。

2 An alien civilisation could choose many different ways of sending information across the galaxy, but many of these either require too much energy, or else are severely attenuated while traversing the vast distances across the galaxy.

并列连词：but

句子主干：An alien civilisation could choose many different ways, but many of these either require too much energy, or else are severely attenuated

极简翻译：外星文明可以选择许多方式，但其中有的需要太多能量，有的会严重衰减

原文翻译：一个外星文明可以选择许多不同的方式在星系中发送信息，但其中许多要么需要太多的能量，要么在穿越银河系的遥远距离时会严重衰减。

3 With novels, the reader attends mainly to the meaning of words rather than **the way**（**by which**）^{AC}［they are printed on the page］, whereas the "reader" of a painting must attend just as closely to the material form of marks and shapes in the picture as to any **ideas**（**that**）^{AC}［they may signify］.

并列连词：whereas

定语从句①：可省略 by which, they are...page 修饰先行词 the way

定语从句②：可省略 that, they may signify 修饰先行词 ideas

句子主干：the reader attends to the meaning rather than the way, whereas the "reader" of a painting must attend just as closely to the form as to ideas

极简翻译：读者关注含义而不是方式，而一幅画的"读者"像关注意义一样关注形式

原文翻译：阅读小说时，读者关注的主要是文字的含义，而不是它们在页面上的印刷方式；而图画的"读者"必须密切关注画面中标记和形状的物质形式，以及它们可能代表的任何想法。

➡ 因果关系

1 The physicist rightly dreads precise argument, since an **argument**［**that**^{AC} is convincing only if it is precise］loses all its force if the **assumptions**［**on which**^{AC} it is based］are slightly changed.

并列连词：since

定语从句①：that is...precise, 修饰先行词 an argument

定语从句②：on which...based, 修饰先行词 assumptions

句子主干：The physicist rightly dreads precise argument, since an argument loses all its force if the assumptions are slightly changed

极简翻译：物理学家害怕精确的论证是有道理的，因为只要假设稍有改变，论证就失去了所有的力量

原文翻译：物理学家害怕精确的论证是有道理的，因为一个只有在精确的情况下才令人信服的论证，如果它所基于的假设稍有改变，它就会失去所有的力量。

第2章 雅思阅读判断题

2.1 判断题简介

判断题是雅思阅读中最有代表性的题目，甚至可以说是很多考生了解雅思阅读的第一扇窗。判断题是考查细节理解能力的题型，所以出题概率很高，一般三篇文章里至少两篇文章都会设置判断题，而最新的官方数据表明，2022年判断题的出题比例高达30%。所谓"抓住细节得天下"，大家一定要拿下判断题这种题型。

判断题都"天性专一"，一般一道题仅对应原文中的一两句话，甚至一句话的一部分，而不会对应多个句子、多个段落甚至全文。如果你在原文中很多地方都能找到一道判断题的出处，那么"恭喜"你，一定是定位出了问题，赶紧重新定位。

但是大家对判断题的感觉是既熟悉又陌生，熟悉是因为我们都很熟悉"正误"判断题，陌生是因为雅思阅读的判断题多了一个逻辑类型，即 NOT GIVEN。这意味着我们的思维不能非黑即白，非对即错。而模棱两可的 NOT GIVEN，通常是大多数考生面临的难点。

2.2 解题技巧

要想快速解答雅思阅读判断题，首先需要弄懂这种题型的逻辑。那么，如何区分判断题中的三种逻辑（TRUE/YES，FALSE/NO，NOT GIVEN）呢？我们借助下面的例子，快速把握逻辑要领，同时明确答题要求。

> 原文：Ricky can speak Shaanxi dialect.
> 译文：里基会说陕西方言。

判断方法：

- 如果题目表述和原文同义，那么答案就是 TRUE 或者 YES。比如：

  Ricky is able to speak Shaanxi local language. 里基能说陕西方言。

  这里只不过是把 can 变成了 is able to，dialect 变成了 local language。表述与原文同义。

- 如果题目表述与原文意思相悖，那么答案就是 FALSE 或者 NO。比如：

  Ricky is unable to communicate with Shaanxi natives. 里基不能和陕西当地人交流。

  这句话明显与原文信息相反。里基既然会说陕西方言，当然可以和老乡交流。

- 如果题目中某些信息与原文没有任何对应，那么就应该是 NOT GIVEN。比如：

  Ricky can sing Xintianyou. 里基会唱信天游。

  这里需要注意的是，不要根据常识"过度推理"。虽然里基会说陕西方言，但不代表他会唱信天游。这里既不是原文的同义表达，也不是驳斥原文，就只能是 NOT GIVEN。

> **特别提示**
>
> 注意看清答题要求，按照题目要求作答。题目中给出的是 TRUE/FALSE，就不要写成 YES/NO，必须大写，必须写全称，不要简写。

弄懂判断题的逻辑之后，我们再来看看解题步骤。大家可以遵循以下三个通用步骤：

> 读题，找出题目中的定位词（阿拉伯数字、大写专有名词、特殊词汇等）；
>
> 预判考点信息（积极词汇、消极词汇、形容词、极端词汇、比较级等）。一般按照"名词、动词、形容词"的优先顺序去对照。
>
> 按照"顺序原则"去原文中定位句子。判断题是遵循"顺序原则"的友好题型。
>
> 提醒：考点也可以帮助定位。

解题时，大家可以运用"3 题分析原则"。如果一组题目的数量超过了 3 道题，建议 3 题 3 题做。如果题目数量是 6 道题甚至 10 道题，全部分析完再去做，估计前面的题目都忘得差不多了。一次做 3 道题既能让你保持清晰准确的记忆，又能提高定位的效率。因为很多时候第 1 题的定位句不好找，但第 2 题或第 3 题的定位句更容易找出，这样就可以抓住一道题目"上下求索"，然后"顺藤摸瓜"把所有题目的定位句都找出来。

2.3 真题再现

"知己知彼，百战不殆"，下面我们就结合雅思真题对三种逻辑（TRUE/YES，FALSE/NO，NOT GIVEN）进行细化，让大家一看到题目，马上就能根据逻辑分类快速对号入座，而不受知识背景和复杂句式的干扰。

(1) TURE/YES，其本质是"同义表达"。

最简单的形式就是对原文进行同义词或者同义短语的替换。

> 题目：Conserving energy may help to extend a human's life. 保存能量可能有助于延长人的寿命。
>
> 原文：It follows from the above that sparing use of energy reserves should tend to extend life. 由此可见，节约使用能源储备应该有助于延长寿命。

解析：energy, extend, life 都是原封不动的定位词。题目中的 Conserving energy 对应原文中的 sparing use of energy reserves。千万不要在 may 和 should 的语气上过度计较。雅思阅读考查的是科普说明文，不会对语气进行考查，也不要纠缠 help 和 tend to 是不是完全同义。提醒：雅思阅读中的同义是语境中的信息对应，不是咬文嚼字。

(2) 正话反说或反话正说。

> 题目：Bio-control is free from danger under certain circumstances. 生物控制在某些情况下没有危险性。
>
> 原文：When handled by experts, bio-control is safe, non-polluting and self-dispersing. 由专家处理时，生物控制是安全、无污染且自我消散的。

解析：bio-control 是原词定位，根据考点 free from danger 很容易找到原句（safe 就是 free from danger）。此外，题目中的 under certain circumstances 是对原文 When handled by experts 的概括。这里大家需要了解一种设题形式：原文中可能同时列出了数项信息，但是题目只考查其中一项信息，而其他信息不会影响对于此项信息的判断。比如原文中的 non-polluting 和 self-dispersing 这两项信息均未被考查，但它们不影响我们对于 safe 与否的判断。

(3) 归纳总结型。

题目是对原文内容的概括，一般会出现形容词或者名词，而这些词在原文中并没有同义词或者反义词（需要通过概括原文细节来得出）。

> 题目：The metal used in the float process had to have specific properties. 浮法工艺中使用的金属必须具有特定的性能。
>
> 原文：The metal had to melt at a temperature less than the hardening point of glass (about 600℃), but could not boil at a temperature below the temperature of the molten glass (about 1500℃). The best metal for the job was tin. 该金属必须在玻璃硬化的温度（约 600℃）以下熔化，但不能在熔化玻璃以下的温度（约 1500℃）沸腾。能完成任务的最佳金属就是锡。

解析：题目中的 metal 和 had to 都是原封不动的定位词，考点是形容词 specific，尽管在原文中找不到这个单词的同义词或者反义词，但是这句话中的数字足以说明这种金属的独特特征。property 意为"特性，特征"，常考同义词有 trait, characteristic, feature 等。

📌 **特别提示**

如果题目中有以下单词，那么答案是 TRUE/YES 的概率较大。

may/maybe/can/could/possible/perhaps/likely（也许/可能）；not all（不全是）；not always（并非总是）；not necessarily（不一定）；sometimes（有时）；seem/appear（似乎）

真题 1

In boxes 1–7 on your answer sheet, write

TRUE	if the statement agrees with the information
FALSE	if the statement contradicts the information
NOT GIVEN	if there is no information on this in the passage

第 1 题

题干：The FAA was created as a result of the introduction of the jet engine. 美国联邦航空管理局是由于引进喷气式引擎而成立的。

预判：FAA 为专有名词，可以作为定位词；as a result 表达了一种因果逻辑关系。

原文：An accident that occurred in the skies over the Grand Canyon in 1956 resulted in the establishment of the Federal Aviation Administration（FAA）to regulate and oversee the operation of aircraft in the skies over the United States, which were becoming quite congested. 1956 年发生在大峡谷上空的一次事故导致美国联邦航空管理局（FAA）成立，以管理监控美国上空日益拥挤的飞行状况。

解析：resulted in 对应 as a result，原文中给出的原因是一次事故，而题干中给的原因是引进喷气式引擎，这属于非常直接的驳斥。注意：不能因为原文没有提及 jet engine 就误判为 NOT GIVEN。只要原因错了，就是驳斥。

答案：FALSE

第 2 题

题干：Air Traffic Control started after the Grand Canyon crash in 1956. 航空管制是在 1956 年大峡谷空难后开始的。

预判：专有名词 Air Traffic Control 和数字 1956 都可以作为定位词。

原文：Rudimentary air traffic control（ATC）existed well before the Grand Canyon disaster. 初步的航空管制在大峡谷灾难之前就存在了。

解析：题干中的时间定位词 after 和原文中的 before 是相互驳斥的。

答案：FALSE

第 3 题

题干：Beacons and flashing lights are still used by ATC today. 如今，ATC 仍在使用信标和闪光灯。

预判：名词 Beacons 可以作为定位词；still...today 为时间定位词。

原文：...while beacons and flashing lights were placed along cross-country routes to establish the earliest airways. However, this purely visual system was useless in bad weather, and, by the 1930s, radio communication was coming into use for ATC. The first region to have something approximating today's ATC was New York City, with other major metropolitan areas following soon after. ……而信标和闪光灯则被放置在越野路线上，以建立最早的航线。然而，这种纯视觉系统在恶劣天气下毫无用处，到 20 世纪 30 年代，无线电通信已用于 ATC。第一个拥有类似今天 ATC 的地区是纽约市，不久之后其他主要大都市紧随其后。

解析：原文中关于 beacons 的描述均使用了一般过去时。注意转折词 however，原文中 However 之后介绍的也是过去的事情，因此，beacons 现在是否依然在使用，文中并没有提及。

答案：NOT GIVEN

第 4 题

题干：Some improvements were made in radio communication during World War II. 第二次世界大战期间，无线电通信取得了一些改进。

预判：World War II 为定位信息；improvement 之类的积极词汇为考点。

原文：In the 1940s, ATC centres could and did take advantage of the newly developed radar and improved radio communication brought about by the Second World War, but the system remained rudimentary. 在 20 世纪 40 年代，空中交通管制中心可以而且确实利用了第二次世界大战带来的新开发的雷达和改进的无线电通信，但该系统仍然很简陋。

解析：原文中的动词 improved 直接对应题干中的名词 improvements。虽然原文中出现了转折连词 but，但其后的内容不影响前面的判断。

答案：TRUE

第 5 题

题干：Class F airspace is airspace which is below 365m and not near airports. F 类空域指低于 365 米且不在机场附近的空域。

预判：数字（365）和专有名词（Class F airspace）为定位信息。and 前后的内容都是考点。

原文：In general, from 365m above the ground and higher, the entire country is blanketed by controlled airspace. In certain areas, mainly near airports, controlled airspace extends down to 215m above the ground, and, in the immediate vicinity of an airport, all the way down to the surface. Controlled airspace is that airspace in which FAA regulations apply. Elsewhere, in uncontrolled airspace, pilots are bound by fewer regulations. In this way, the recreational pilot who simply wishes to go flying for a while without all the restrictions imposed by the FAA has only to stay in uncontrolled airspace, below 365m. 一般来说，从距离地面 365 米以及更高的地方，整个国家都被受控空域所覆盖。在某些地区，主要是机场附近，受控空域延伸至地面 215 米以上，在机场外围，一直延伸至地面。受控空域是适用美国联邦航空管理局（FAA）法规的空域。在其他地方，在不受控制的空域，飞行员受到的法规约束更少。这样，只是希望在不受美国联邦航空管理局施加的所有限制的情况下飞行一段时间的休闲飞行员只需要待在 365 米以下的不受控制的空域。

解析：这道题是需要定位至两个段落（这种情况很少见），在实际答题过程中，如果一时做不出来，可以先跳过，最后再来做。根据原文的信息可知：越靠近机场越受管控。

答案：FALSE

第 6 题

题干：All aircraft in Class E airspace must use IFR. E 类空域的所有飞机都必须使用 IFR。

预判：专有名词作为定位词。考点是 All（极端逻辑）。

原文：The difference between Class E and A airspace is that in Class A, all operations are IFR, and pilots must be instrument-rated, that is, skilled and licensed in aircraft instrumentation. E 类和 A 类空域的区别在于，在 A 类空域，所有操作都是 IFR，飞行员必须拥有仪表等级，即熟练掌握飞机仪表并持有飞机仪表执照。

解析：题干与原文表达的意思完全相反。注意原文中的考点词 difference。

答案：FALSE

第 7 题

题干：A pilot entering Class C airspace is flying over an average-sized city. 一名进入 C 类空域的飞行员正在一个中等规模的城市上空飞行。

预判：Class C 为定位信息；形容词 average-sized 是考点。

原文：Three other types of airspace, Classes D, C and B, govern the vicinity of airports. These correspond roughly to small municipal, medium-sized metropolitan and major metropolitan airports respectively, and encompass an increasingly rigorous set of regulations. 另外三种类型的空域，D 类，C 类和 B 类，管理着机场附近。这些分别大致对应小型市政机场、中型大都市机场和大型大都市机场，并包含一套越来越严格的法规。

解析：原文中将 D 类、C 类和 B 类空域三者放在一起描述，而题干中仅考查了 C 类空域的相关信息，只是进行了同义替换：medium-sized 呼应 average-sized。提醒：大家可以积累一些与城市相关的单词（city/town/municipal/metropolis/metropolitan/urban）。

答案：TRUE

真题 2

In boxes 8 – 10 on your answer sheet, write

TRUE	if the statement agrees with the information
FALSE	if the statement contradicts the information
NOT GIVEN	if there is no information on this

第 8 题

题干：Modern-day plastic preparation is based on the same principles as that patented in 1907. 现代塑料制备的原理与 1907 年获得专利的原理相同。

预判：1907 和 patent 为定位信息；the same 是考点。

原文：On 13 July 1907，Baekeland took out his famous patent describing this preparation, the essential features of which are still in use today. 1907 年 7 月 13 日，贝克兰拿出了描述这种制剂的著名专利，其基本特征至今仍在使用。

解析：题干和原文表达的意思一致。题干中的 Modern-day 与原文中的 today 为同义替换；principles 与 features 指代的内容相同；the same 和 still in use 表达相同的含义。

答案：TRUE

第 9 题

题干：Bakelite was immediately welcomed as a practical and versatile material. 酚醛塑料作为一种实用且用途广泛的材料立即受到了欢迎。

预判：题干中没有明显的定位信息。可以将考点 immediately，welcome，practical，versatile 作为定位信息。

原文：Baekeland's invention, although treated with disdain in its early years, went on to enjoy an unparalleled popularity. 贝克兰的发明虽然在早期受到了蔑视，但后来却享有无与伦比的人气。

解析：题干和原文表达的意思完全相反。原文中 although 引导的让步状语提到这种发明在早期受到了蔑视，随后才强调这种发明后来大受欢迎（went on），驳斥了题干中的时间信息 immediately。welcomed 与 popularity 对应。

答案：FALSE

第 10 题

题干：Bakelite was only available in a limited range of colors. 酚醛塑料只有有限的颜色范围。

预判：colors 为定位词；only 和 limited 是考点。

原文：Consumers everywhere relished its dazzling array of shades, delighted that they were now, at last, no longer restricted to the wood tones and drab browns of the pre-plastic era. 各地的消费者都津津乐道于其令人眼花缭乱的色调，很高兴他们现在终于不再局限于前塑料时代的木质色调和单调的棕色。

解析：题干和原文表达的意思完全相反。原文中的否定部分 no longer restricted to 驳斥了题干中的 only limited。colors 和 shades 是同义词；limited 和 restricted 是同义词。

答案：FALSE

第 3 章　雅思阅读填空题

3.1　填空题简介

与雅思阅读中的其他题型（如判断题、匹配题和选择题）相比，填空题是一种较为简单的题型。填空题包括 complete the notes，complete the summary，label the diagram，complete the table，complete the sentences 等细分题型。其中，complete the notes 和 complete the summary 是出现频率最高的两种题型。此外，由于简答题一般答案词数不超过 3 个，故也算在填空题之中。这些细分题型本质上是一致的，解题技巧也基本相同。

3.2　解题技巧

雅思阅读填空题有两个答题要点：首先，需要填写原文中的原词，即答案词来自原文，不可概括和改写；其次，大多数题的答案词具有顺序性，即答案词在原文中出现的先后顺序与其在题目中出现的先后顺序是一致的。如：第 3 题答案词所在原文的定位句会在第 2 题定位句之后、第 4 题定位句之前，该特征可以有效降低定位答案词的难度。

此外，雅思阅读中的填空题属于细节定位题。每道题考查的是原文中对应的一到两句话，并不涉及对整个段落或者全文的整体理解。因此，考生需注意不要被文章的知识背景束缚，掌握解题步骤和同义替换即可。

解题时，考生遵循以下步骤即可：

（1）确定答案词的个数。

如果题目指示语为 Choose *ONE WORD ONLY* from the passage for each answer，则答案词是一个词。依此类推即可。

（2）判断空格处需填入词的词性，并根据语义进行预判。

- 若空格处需要填入名词，则可以通过谓语或者修饰语考虑名词的单复数形式。比如：much

后面要填入不可数名词，many 后面要填入可数名词的复数形式。

- 若空格前面是主语，则需要填入谓语动词，此时要注意时态。
- 若空格前面是助动词 will/情态动词或不定式符号 to，则需要填入动词原形（do）。
- 若空格在名词前面，则通常需要填入形容词。
- 若空格在 be 动词后面，则通常需要填入形容词、被动语态或者名词。
- 有时还可以对空格处的内容进行预判。比如：_____ felt very confused about the results，根据句意及句子结构可知空格处需要填入"人"，这时可以有意识地在原文定位时搜索表示"人"的名词。

(3) 圈画题目中的关键词，特别关注空格前后的信息。对原文进行预判。

- 数字、特殊词汇、专有名词：这些通常可以在原文中直接找到。
- 单词的词性有所变化。比如题目中出现了 suggest，由此预判原文可能是 suggestion。
- 同义替换。比如题目中出现了 test，由此预判原文可能是 experiment/study 等。再如，题目中出现了 hard，可预判原文是 difficult/harsh。
- 重要的逻辑词，比如表达转折、因果、并列、假设、递进等关系的连接词。即使单词被改写了，但逻辑是不会变的。表示逻辑关系的连接词有可能与原文一致，但也有可能会换成同义表达。以下是常见的连接词：

因果关系	because/so/as/therefore/thus/hence
对比关系	in contrast/by contrast/on the contrary
并列关系	and/also/as well as/not only...but also
转折让步关系	but/however/although/though/despite/in spite of/while

值得注意的是，逻辑关系词不局限于同义连接词之间的替换，也可能会改变词性。以因果关系为例，名词（cause/reason/factor）、动词（短语）（lead to/trigger/cause/contribute to/result in）、介词短语（as a result）、副词（consequently）等均可以表示这种逻辑关系。

(4) 定位。

雅思阅读填空题设题的段落起点可以是文章中的任何一个段落，但一般多见于开头几段，或者末尾几段。可根据文章题目的顺序来判断：若是第一道大题，则可以从开头段定位；若是最后一道大题，则重点关注后面几段。若是第二道大题，则可以从第一道大题对应段落之后开始找。

在大多数情况下，可通过特殊词汇、数字、专有名词等不易改写的信息在原文相应段落中寻找定位线索。同时，要注意同义替换，因为题干中的关键词可能会被改写。

3.3 真题再现

下面，我们将结合雅思真题掌握如何运用以上讲解的技巧来快速解答填空题。

真题 1

Questions 1 – 5

Choose *ONE WORD ONLY* from the passage for each answer.

Write your answers in boxes 1 – 5 on your answer sheet.

Alexander Henderson

Early life

- was born in Scotland in 1831—father was a **1** _____
- trained as an accountant, emigrated to Canada in 1855

Start of a photographic career

- opened up a photographic studio in 1866
- took photos of city life, but preferred landscape photography
- people bought Henderson's photos because photography took up considerable time and the **2** _____ was heavy
- the photographs Henderson sold were **3** _____ or souvenirs

Travelling as a professional photographer

- travelled widely in Quebec and Ontario in 1870s and 1880s
- took many trips along eastern rivers in a **4** _____
- worked for Canadian railways between 1875 and 1897
- worked for CPR in 1885 and photographed the **5** _____ and the railway at Rogers Pass

注意：根据题目指示语可判断答案词个数为 1 个词。

第 1 题

题干：was born in Scotland in 1831—father was a 1 _____

解析：空格处前面是 father was a，故应该填入单数名词，且可能填入的是 "人"，注意表示人的名词后缀 -er/-or/-ist/-ant/-ent/-ee/-ian 等。题干中可以圈画的关键词有 Scotland，1831 和 father，通过这些词可以定位至文章第一段第一句话：Alexander Henderson was born in Scotland in 1831 and was the son of a successful merchant.（亚历山大·亨德森 1831 年出生于苏格兰，是一位成功商人的儿子。）根据这句话可知，Henderson 是一位成功商人的儿子，也就是说他的父亲是一位商人。

答案：merchant

第 2 题

题干：people bought Henderson's photos because photography took up considerable time and the 2 _____ was heavy

解析：空格处前面是定冠词 the，后面是系表结构 was heavy，所以空格处应该填入单数名词。题干中可以圈画的关键词有 considerable time，heavy，逻辑词 because 和 and 也可以帮助定位，通过这些词可以定位至文章中的句子：There was little competing hobby or amateur photography before the late 1880s because of the time-consuming techniques involved and the weight of the equipment.（在 19 世纪 80 年代末之前，由于所涉及的技术耗时和设备的重量，几乎没有竞争性爱好或业余摄影。）题干中的 considerable time 和 heavy 分别对应原文中的 time-consuming 和 weight。

答案：equipment

第 3 题

题干：the photographs Henderson sold were 3 _____ or souvenirs

解析：空格处前面是 were，后面是 or souvenirs，所以空格处应该是跟 souvenirs 并列的名词，且与 souvenirs 词义相近。题干中可以圈画的关键词有 souvenirs，可以定位至文章中的句子：People wanted to buy photographs as souvenirs of a trip or as gifts.（人们想买照片作为旅行的纪念品或礼物。）其中，souvenirs 与 gifts 并列。

答案：gifts

第 4 题

题干：took many trips along eastern rivers in a 4 _____

解析：空格处前面是 a，所以空格处应该填入单数名词。题干中可以圈画的关键词是 eastern rivers，通过它可以定位至文章中的句子：He was especially fond of the wilderness and often travelled by canoe on the Blanche, du Lievre, and other noted eastern rivers.（他特别喜欢荒野，经常乘独木舟在布兰奇河、杜利夫尔河和其他著名的东部河流上旅行。）题干中的 took many trips 对应原文中的 travelled，由此可精准定位答案句 travelled by canoe on the Blanche, du Lievre, and other noted eastern rivers，其中，具体名词只有 canoe。

答案：canoe

第 5 题

题干：worked for CPR in 1885 and photographed the 5 _____ and the railway at Rogers Pass

解析：空格处前面是冠词 the，后面是 and the railway，所以应该填入名词，且与 the railway 并列。题干中可以圈画的关键词有 CPR，in 1885，railway 和 Rogers Pass，通过这些词可以定位至文章中的句子：In 1885 he went west along the Canadian Pacific Railway (CPR) as far as Rogers Pass in British Columbia, where he took photographs of the mountains and the progress of construction.（1885 年，他沿着加拿大太平洋铁路向西行驶，直到不列颠哥伦比亚省的罗杰斯山口，在那里他拍摄了山脉和施工进度的照片。）题干中的 photographed 对应原文中的 took photographs of，故答案是拍摄内容。

答案：mountains

真题 2

Questions 6–9

Complete the summary below.

Choose *NO MORE THAN TWO WORDS* from the passage for each answer.

Write your answers in boxes 6–9 on your answer sheet.

The Impact of Driverless Cars

Figures from the Transport Research Laboratory indicate that most motor accidents are partly due to 6 _____, so the introduction of driverless vehicles will result in greater safety. In addition to the direct benefits of automation, it may bring other advantages. For example, schemes for 7 _____, will be more workable, especially in towns and cities, resulting in fewer cars on the road.

According to the University of Michigan Transportation Research Institute, there could be a 43 percent drop in 8 _____ of cars. However, this would mean that the yearly 9 _____ of each car would, on average, be twice as high as it currently is. This would lead to a higher turnover of vehicles, and therefore no reduction in automotive manufacturing.

注意：根据题目指示语可判断答案词个数为不能超过 2 个词。

第 6 题

题干：Figures from the Transport Research Laboratory indicate that most motor accidents are partly due to 6 _____, so the introduction of driverless vehicles will result in greater safety.

解析：空格处前面是介词短语 due to，所以应该填入名词，但不能是单数可数名词。题干中可以圈画的关键词有 Transport Research Laboratory，motor accidents，通过这些词可以定位至文章中的句子：...indeed, research at the UK's Transport Research Laboratory has demonstrated that more than 90 percent of road collisions involve human error as a contributor factor...（……事实上，英国交通研究实验室的研究表明，90% 以上的道路碰撞都是人为失误造成的……）在题干与原文中，most motor accidents 对应 90 percent of road collisions，due to 对应 as a contributor factor，故答案是事故原因。

答案：human error

第 7 题

题干：For example, schemes for 7 _____, will be more workable, especially in towns and cities, resulting in fewer cars on the road.

解析：空格处前面是介词 for，所以应该填入名词。题干中可以圈画的关键词有 schemes，towns and cities 和 road，通过这些词可以定位至文章中的句子：Automation means that initiatives for car-sharing become much more viable, particularly in urban areas with significant travel demand.（自动化意味着汽车共享计划变得更加可行，尤其是在出行需求巨大的城市地区。）在题干与原文中，towns and cities 对应 urban areas，workable 对应 viable，schemes 对应 initiatives，故答案是 car-sharing。

答案：car-sharing

第 8 题

题干：According to the University of Michigan Transportation Research Institute, there could be a 43 percent drop in 8 _____ of cars.

解析：空格处前面是介词 in，所以应该填入名词。题干中可以圈画的关键词有 University of Michigan Transportation Research Institute 和 43 percent drop，通过这些词可以定位至文章中的句子：Modelling work by the University of Michigan Transportation Research Institute suggests automated vehicles might reduce vehicle ownership by 43 percent.（密歇根大学交通研究所的建模工作表明，自动化车辆可能会减少 43% 的车辆保有量。）在题干与原文中，drop 对应 reduce，cars 对应 vehicle，故答案为 reduce 的对象。

答案：ownership

第 9 题

题干：However, this would mean that the yearly 9 _____ of each car would, on average, be twice as high as it currently is.

解析：空格处前面是形容词 yearly，后面是介词短语 of each car，所以应该填入一个名词。题干中可以圈画的关键词有 yearly，twice，通过这些词可以定位至文章中的句子：…but that vehicles' average annual mileage would double as a result.（……但汽车的平均年里程将因此翻一番。）在题干与原文中，However 对应 but，yearly 对应 annual，twice 对应 double，故答案是被 yearly 修饰的名词。

答案：mileage

真题3

Questions 1–3

Complete the sentences below.

Choose *ONE WORD ONLY* from the passage for each answer.

Write your answers in boxes 1–3 on your answer sheet.

1   As a captain and _____ , Woodget was very skilled.

2   Ferreira went to Falmouth to repair damage that a _____ had caused.

3   Between 1923 and 1954, Cutty Sark was used for _____ .

4   Cutty Sark has twice been damaged by _____ in the 21st century.

注意：根据题目指示语可判断答案词个数为 1 个词。

第 1 题

题干：As a captain and _____ , Woodget was very skilled.

解析：空格处前面是 As a captain and，所以应该填入单数名词，且语义上是与 captain 并列的某一类 "人"。题干中可以圈画的关键词有 captain，Woodget，skilled，通过这些词可以定位至文章中的句子：The ship's next captain, Richard Woodget, was an excellent navigator, who got the best out of both his ship and his crew. （该船的下一任船长理查德·伍德杰是一位出色的领航员，他让这艘船和船员的能力都发挥到了极致。）由此可知，Richard Woodget 是一名出色的领航员。

答案：navigator

第 2 题

题干：Ferreira went to Falmouth to repair damage that a _____ had caused.

解析：空格处前面是 a，所以应该填入单数名词。题干中可以圈画的关键词有 Ferreira，Falmouth，damage，通过这些词可以定位至文章中的句子：She was sold to a Portuguese firm, which renamed her Ferreira. For the next 25 years, she again carried miscellaneous cargoes around the world. Badly damaged in a gale in 1922, she was put into Falmouth harbour in southwest England, for repairs. （它被卖给了一家葡萄牙公司，该公司将它改名为 "费雷拉"。在接下来的 25 年里，它再次在世界各地运送各种货物。1922 年，它在一次大风中严重受损，被送入英格兰西南部的法尔茅斯港进行维修。）故答案是导致损害的原因。

答案：gale

第 3 题

题干：Between 1923 and 1954, Cutty Sark was used for _____.

解析：空格处前面是介词 for，所以应该填入名词。题干中可以圈画的关键词有 1923，1954，通过这些词可以定位至文章中的句子：Badly damaged in a gale in 1922…the ship returned to Falmouth the following year and had her original name restored. Dowman used Cutty Sark as a training ship, and she continued in this role after his death. When she was no longer required, in 1954, she was transferred to dry dock at Greenwich to go on public display. （1922 年，这艘船在大风中严重受损……第二年，它返回法尔茅斯，并恢复了原名。道曼使用 "卡蒂萨克" 号作为训练船，在他死后，它继续担任这一

角色。1954 年，当它不再被需要时，就被转移到了格林尼治的干船坞进行公开展示。）题干中的 1923 对应原文中 1922 之后的 the following year，题干为"在 1923 年至 1954 年期间，'卡萨蒂克'号被用于_____"，通过精准定位答案句 Dowman used Cutty Sark as a training ship，可知答案是 training。

答案：training

第 4 题

题干：Cutty Sark has twice been damaged by _____ in the 21st century.

解析：空格处前面是介词 by，所以应该填入名词。题干中可以圈画的关键词有 twice，21st century，damaged，通过这些词可以定位至文章中的句子：The ship suffered from fire in 2007, and again, less seriously, in 2014, but now Cutty Sark attracts a quarter of a million visitors a year.（该船在 2007 年遭遇火灾，在 2014 年再次遭遇火灾，但情况并不那么严重，但现在"卡蒂萨克"号每年吸引 25 万游客。）在题干与原文中，21st century 对应 2007 和 2014，twice 对应 again，damaged 对应 suffered，故答案是造成损害的原因。

答案：fire

第4章 雅思阅读匹配题

4.1 段落信息匹配题

4.1.1 段落信息匹配题简介

段落信息匹配题指题干中给出若干项信息，要求考生找出文中分别对应这些信息的段落。段落信息匹配题主要考查信息的定位和对同义表达的理解，重点考查在原文中查找细节信息的能力，因此，通常情况下，找到了"定位信息"，就找到了同义转换内容，根据这些定位信息就可以正确解答题目。该题型的判断标志是：Which paragraph/section contains the following information?

段落信息匹配题虽然只是匹配题型中的一个分支，但是其重要性、难度和出题概率都不亚于文章标题题和判断题。对大多数考生来说，这是最耗费时间、失分最多、最难的题型。

该题型具有以下特点：
(1) 题目中所给出的信息为原文中的细节内容；
(2) 题目中的信息是原文中对应段落句子的同义替换，所以题目中的定位词在原文中很少以原词的形式出现；
(3) 题目是无序的，与原文内容无出现先后顺序上的对应；
(4) 题目中有时会出现提示"NB: You may use any letter more than once."以加大解题难度。

综上所述，该题型的解题难点之一是：定位困难。考生往往找不到题目中的定位词或关键词。因此，这种题型很难像其他题型一样，先找出题目中的关键词，然后去原文中定位，解答该题型时要求考生对同义表达的理解更加深刻、更加敏锐。

4.1.2 解题技巧

下面我们来看段落信息匹配题的解题技巧：
(1) 阅读该题型的所有题目信息，找出题目中的关键词，并且预判可能出现的对应同义转换。
(2) 回到原文从首段开始阅读，如果某段落中出现了题目中关键词的同义表达，即可确定答案。
(3) 注意"NB: You may use any letter more than once."如果出现这句话，那么有些段落可能会被选中两次。

4.1.3 真题再现

下面我们以雅思真题为例，在具体的解题过程中看看以上题型特点和解题技巧是如何体现的，从而熟悉该题型和解题方法。

真　题

Plant "Thermometer" Triggers Springtime Growth by Measuring Night-Time Heat

A photoreceptor molecule in plant cells has been found to have a second job as a thermometer after dark—allowing plants to read seasonal temperature changes. Scientists say the discovery could help breed crops that are more resilient to the temperatures expected to result from climate change.

A An international team of scientists led by the University of Cambridge has discovered that the "thermometer" molecule in plants enables them to develop according to seasonal temperature changes. Researchers have revealed that molecules called phytochromes—used by plants to detect light during the day—actually change their function in darkness to become cellular temperature gauges that measure the heat of the night. The new findings, published in the journal *Science*, show that phytochromes control genetic switches in response to temperature as well as light to dictate plant development.

B At night, these molecules change states, and the pace at which they change is "directly proportional to temperature", say scientists, who compare phytochromes to mercury in a thermometer. The warmer it is, the faster the molecular change—stimulating plant growth.

C Farmers and gardeners have known for hundreds of years how responsive plants are to temperature: warm winters cause many trees and flowers to bud early, something humans have long used to predict weather and harvest times for the coming year. The latest research pinpoints for the first time a molecular mechanism in plants that reacts to temperature—often triggering the buds of spring we long to see at the end of winter.

D With weather and temperatures set to become even more unpredictable due to climate change, researchers say the discovery that this light-sensing molecule also functions as the internal thermometer in plant cells could help us breed tougher crops. "It is estimated that agricultural yields will need to double by 2050, but climate change is a major threat to achieving this. Key crops such as wheat and rice are sensitive to high temperatures. Thermal stress reduces crop yields by around 10% for every one degree increase in temperature," says lead researcher Dr Philip Wigge from

第 4 章 雅思阅读匹配题

Cambridge's Sainsbury Laboratory. "Discovering the molecules that allow plants to sense temperature has the potential to accelerate the breeding of crops resilient to thermal stress and climate change. "

E   In their active state, phytochrome molecules bind themselves to DNA to restrict plant growth. During the day, sunlight activates the molecules, slowing downgrowth. If a plant finds itself in shade, phytochromes are quickly inactivated—enabling it to grow faster to find sunlight again. This is how plants compete to escape each other's shade. "Light-driven changes to phytochrome activity occur very fast, in less than a second," says Wigge.

   At night, however, it's a different story. Instead of a rapid deactivation following sundown, the molecules gradually change from their active to inactive state. This is called "dark reversion". "Just as mercury rises in a thermometer, the rate at which phytochromes revert to their inactive state during the night is a direct measure of temperature," says Wigge.

F   "The lower the temperature, the slower the rate at which phytochromes revert to inactivity, so the molecules spend more time in their active, growth-suppressing state. This is why plants are slower to grow in winter. Warm temperatures accelerate dark reversion, so that phytochromes rapidly reach an inactive state and detach themselves from the plant's DNA—allowing genes to be expressed and plant growth to resume. " Wigge believes phytochrome thermo-sensing evolved at a later stage, and co-opted the biological network already used for light-based growth during the downtime of night.

G   Some plants mainly use day length as an indicator of the season. Other species, such as daffodils, have considerable temperature sensitivity, and can flower months in advance during a warm winter. In fact, the discovery of the dual role of phytochromes provides the science behind a well-known rhyme long used to predict the coming season: oak before ash we'll have a splash, ash before oak we're in for a soak.

   Wigge explains: "Oak trees rely much more on temperature, likely using phytochromes as thermometers to dictate development, whereas ash trees rely on measuring day length to determine their seasonal timing. A warmer spring, and consequently a higher likeliness of a hot summer, will result in oak leafing before ash. A cold spring will see the opposite. As the British know only too well, a colder summer is likely to be a rain-soaked one. "

H   The new findings are the culmination of twelve years of research involving scientists from Germany, Argentina and the US, as well as the Cambridge team. The work was done in a model system, using a mustard plant called Arabidopsis, but Wigge says the phytochrome genes necessary for temperature sensing are found in crop plants as well. "Recent advances in plant genetics now mean that scientists are able to rapidly identify the genes controlling these processes in crop plants, and even alter their activity using precise molecular 'scalpels,'" adds Wigge. "Cambridge is uniquely well-positioned to do this kind of research as we have outstanding collaborators nearby who work on more applied aspects of plant biology, and can help us transfer this new knowledge into the field."

Questions 1 – 5

Reading Passage 1 has eight sections, A – H.

Which section contains the following in formation?

Write the correct letter, A – H, in boxes 1 – 5 on your answer sheet.

1 mention of specialists who can make use of the research findings

2 a reference to a potential benefit of the research findings

3 scientific support for a traditional saying

4 a reference to people traditionally making plans based on plant behaviour

5 a reference to where the research has been reported

第 1 题

解析：题干中关键词包括 specialists。该词在原文中可能会对应具体的专家姓名，也有可能以某特定领域的专家出现，如 biologists, chemists 等。H 段最后一句中的 outstanding collaborators 对应题干中的 specialists，后半句中的 help us transfer this new knowledge into the field 对应题干中的 make use of the research findings。

答案：H

第 2 题

解析：题干中的关键词包括 potential benefit。该短语在原文中可能会对应将来的某个具体的好处或优点。D 段最后一句中的 Discovering the molecules that allow plants to sense temperature 对应题干中的 the research findings，最后一句中的 has the potential 对应题干中的 potential，最后一句中的 accelerate the breeding of crops 对应题干中的 benefit。

答案：D

第 3 题

解析：题干中的关键词包括 scientific support 和 a traditional saying，两者之间是相互支持的关系，并且会以相对具体的表达呈现出来。G 段第一小段第二句中的 provides the science 对应题干中的 scientific support，第三句中的 a well-known rhyme long used 对应题干中的 a traditional saying。

答案：G

第 4 题

解析：题干中的关键词 people 可能对应具体的某一类人，关键词 plans 在原文中可能对应某项
　　　具体的活动。C 段第一句中的 Farmers and gardeners 和 humans 对应题干中的 people，
　　　第一句中的 have known for hundreds of years 和 long 对应题干中的 traditionally，第一
　　　句中的 used to predict weather and harvest times for the coming year 对应题干中的
　　　making plans。

答案：C

第 5 题

解析：题干中的关键词包括 research，题干中的 where 在原文中对应具体的地点。A 段最后一
　　　句中的 The new findings 对应题干中的 the research，最后一句中的 published 对应题干
　　　中的 reported，最后一句中的 in the journal *Science* 对应题干中的 where。

答案：A

4.2　人名匹配题

4.2.1　人名匹配题简介

人名匹配题属于匹配题中的一种，在雅思阅读考试中属于中等难度题型。人名匹配题要求将研
究发现、言论、观点或成就等与对应的研究者进行匹配。该题型通常不按题目对应内容在原文
中出现的顺序出题。

4.2.2　解题技巧

解答人名匹配题时，建议考生先找出原文中的所有大写人名，然后将人名出现处上下文所有表
达观点的句子与题目进行对比，最后得出答案。需要注意的是，有些人名在原文中只出现了一
次，而有些人名会多次出现。人名还有可能以简称和代词的形式出现。

下面我们来看人名匹配题的解题步骤：

(1) 找出该题型所有题目（或选项）中的关键词；

(2) 阅读原文时标记人名出现的位置；

(3) 看到原文句子中出现了题目内容的同义表达，即可确定答案。

4.2.3 真题再现

下面我们将结合雅思真题运用以上技巧及步骤解题，进而熟练掌握这种题型的解题方法。

真　题

Motivational Factors and the Hospitality Industry

A critical ingredient in the success of hotels is developing and maintaining superior perform-ance from their employees. How is that accomplished? What Human Resource Management (HRM) practices should organisations invest in to acquire and retain great employees?

Some hotels aim to provide superior working conditions for their employees. The idea origina-ted from workplaces—usually in the non-service sector—that emphasised fun and enjoyment as part of work-life balance. By contrast, the service sector, and more specifically hotels, has traditionally not extended these practices to address basic employee needs, such as good working conditions.

Pfeffer (1994) emphasises that inorder to succeed in a global business environment, organi-sations must make investment inHuman Resource Management (HRM) to allow them to acquire employees who possess better skills and capabilities than their competitors. This in-vestment will be to their competitive advantage. Despite this recognition of the importance of employee development, the hospitality industry has historically been dominated by underde-veloped HR practices (Lucas, 2002).

Lucas also points out that "the substance of HRM practices does not appear to be designed to foster constructive relations with employees or to represent a managerial approach that enables developing and drawing out the full potential of people, even though employees may be broadly satisfied with many aspects of their work" (Lucas, 2002). In addition, or maybe as a result, high employee turnover has been a recurring problem throughout the hospitality industry. Among the many cited reasons are low compensation, inadequate benefits, poor working conditions and compromised employee morale and attitudes (Maroudas et al., 2008).

Ng and Sorensen (2008) demonstrated that when managers provide recognition to employees, motivate employees to work together, and remove obstacles preventing effective performance, employees feel more obligated to stay with the company. This was succinctly summarised by Michel et al. (2013): "Providing support to employees gives them the confidence to perform their jobs better and the motivation to stay with the organisation." Hospitality organisations can therefore enhance employee motivation and retention through the development and improvement of their working conditions. These conditions are inherently linked to the working environment.

While it seems likely that employees' reactions to their job characteristics could be affected by a predisposition to view their work environment negatively, no evidence exists to support this hypothesis (Spector et al., 2000). However, given the opportunity, many people will find something to complain about in relation to their workplace (Poulston, 2009). There is a strong link between the perceptions of employees and particular factors of their work environment that are separate from the work itself, including company policies, salary and vacations.

Such conditions are particularly troubling for the luxury hotel market, where high-quality service, requiring a sophisticated approach to HRM, is recognised as a critical source of competitive advantage (Maroudas et al., 2008). Ina real sense, the services of hotel employees represent their industry (Schneider and Bowen, 1993). This representation has commonly been limited to guest experiences. This suggests that there has been a dichotomy between the guest environment provided in luxury hotels and the working conditions of their employees.

It is therefore essential for hotel management to develop HRM practices that enable them to inspire and retain competent employees. This requires an understanding of what motivates employees at different levels of management and different stages of their careers (Enz and Siguaw, 2000). This implies that it is beneficial for hotel managers to understand what practices are most favourable to increase employee satisfaction and retention.

Herzberg (1966) proposes that people have two major types of needs, the first being extrinsic motivation factors relating to the context in which work is performed, rather than the work itself. These include working conditions and job security. When these factors are unfavourable, job dissatisfaction may result. Significantly, though, just fulfilling these needs does not result in satisfaction, but only in the reduction of dissatisfaction (Maroudas et al., 2008).

Employees also have intrinsic motivation needs or motivators, which include such factors as achievement and recognition. Unlike extrinsic factors, motivator factors may ideally result in job satisfaction (Maroudas et al., 2008). Herzberg's (1966) theory discusses the need for a "balance" of these two types of needs.

The impact of fun as a motivating factor at work has also been explored. For example, Tews, Michel and Stafford (2013) conducted a study focusing on staff from a chain of themed restaurants in the United States. It was found that fun activities had a favourable impact on performance and manager support for fun had a favourable impact in reducing turnover. Their findings support the view that fun may indeed have a beneficial effect, but the framing of that fun must be carefully aligned with both organisational goals and employee characteristics.

"Managers must learn how to achieve the delicate balance of allowing employees the freedom to enjoy themselves at work while simultaneously maintaining high levels of performance. " (Tews et al. , 2013)

Deery (2008) has recommended several actions that can be adopted at the organisational level to retain good staff as well as assist in balancing work and family life. Those particularly appropriate to the hospitality industry include allowing adequate breaks during the working day, staff functions that involve families, and providing health and well-being opportunities.

Questions 1–5

Look at the following statements (Questions 1–5) and the list of researchers below.

Match each statement with the correct researcher, A–F.

Write the correct letter, A–F, in boxes 1–5 on your answer sheet.

NB: You may use any letter more than once.

1 Hotel managers need to know what would encourage good staff to remain.

2 The actions of managers may make staff feel they shouldn't move to a different employer.

3 Little is done in the hospitality industry to help workers improve their skills.

4 Staff are less likely to change jobs if cooperation is encouraged.

5 Dissatisfaction with pay is not the only reason why hospitality workers change jobs.

List of Researchers

A Pfeffer

B Lucas

C Maroudas et al.

D Ng and Sorensen

E Enz and Siguaw

F Deery

第 1 题

题干：Hotel managers need to know what would encourage good staff to remain.

原文：It is therefore essential for hotel management to develop HRM practices that enable them to inspire and retain competent employees. This requires an understanding of what motivates employees at different levels of management and different stages of their careers (Enz and Siguaw, 2000). (第 8 段第 1、2 句)

解析：题干中的关键词是 Hotel managers 和 good staff。第 8 段第 1 句指出：因此，酒店管理层必须制订人力资源管理实践，使其能够激励和留住有能力的员工。这是 Enz 和 Siguaw 的观点。第 8 段中的 competent employees 对应题干中的 good staff；management 对应题干中的 managers。

答案：E

第 2 题

题干：The actions of managers may make staff feel they shouldn't move to a different employer.

原文：Ng and Sorensen（2008）demonstrated that when managers provide recognition to employees, motivate employees to work together, and remove obstacles preventing effective performance, employees feel more obligated to stay with the company.（第 5 段第 1 句）

解析：题干中的关键词是 actions of managers，feel 和 different employer。原文第 5 段第 1 句指出：Ng 和 Sorensen 证明，当经理们认可员工，激励员工互相合作，并且消除他们有效业绩的障碍时，员工们会感到更有义务留在公司。第 5 段中的 provide recognition to employees 对应题干中的 make staff feel；feel more obligated to stay with the company 对应题干中的 shouldn't move to a different employer。

答案：D

第 3 题

题干：Little is done in the hospitality industry to help workers improve their skills.

原文：Lucas also points out that "the substance of HRM practices does not appear to be designed to foster constructive relations with employees or to represent a managerial approach that enables developing and drawing out the full potential of people, even though employees may be broadly satisfied with many aspects of their work"（Lucas, 2002）.（第 4 段第 1 句）

解析：题干中的关键词是 workers 和 skills。原文第 4 段第 1 句提到：Lucas 还指出，人力资源管理实践的实质似乎并不是为了培养与员工的建设性关系，也不是为了代表一种能够充分开发和发挥员工潜力的管理方法，尽管员工可能对其工作的许多方面普遍满意。第 4 段中的 drawing out the full potential 对应题干中的 help workers improve their skills；does not appear 对应题干中的 Little。

答案：B

第 4 题

题干：Staff are less likely to change jobs if cooperation is encouraged.

原文：Ng and Sorensen（2008）demonstrated that when managers provide recognition to employees, motivate employees to work together, and remove obstacles preventing effective performance, employees feel more obligated to stay with the company.（第 5 段第 1 句）

解析：题干中的关键词是 change jobs 和 cooperation。原文第 5 段第 1 句指出：Ng 和 Sorensen 证明，当经理们认可员工，激励员工互相合作，并且消除他们有效业绩的障碍时，员工们 会感到更有义务留在公司。第 5 段第 1 句中的 motivate 对应题干中的 encouraged；work together 对应题干中的 cooperation。

答案：D

第 5 题

题干：Dissatisfaction with pay is not the only reason why hospitality workers change jobs.

原文：Among the many cited reasons are low compensation, inadequate benefits, poor working conditions and compromised employee morale and attitudes (Maroudas et al., 2008). （第 4 段最后一句）

解析：题干中的关键词是 pay，reason 和 change jobs。第 4 段最后一句列举的是一些酒店行业 高离职率的原因，其中包括补偿金少、福利不足、工作条件差、员工士气低落、态度不 好等。由此可见，对收入的不满并不是离职的唯一原因。第 4 段中的 inadequate benefits 对应题干中的 Dissatisfaction with pay。

答案：C

第 5 章　雅思阅读段落标题题

5.1　段落标题题简介

段落标题题是一种考查全文浏览能力及文章意思归纳与概括的题型，在 3 篇阅读文章中都有可能出现（最有可能出现在第 1 篇和第 2 篇阅读文章中）。段落标题题要求掌握泛读能力，也是阅读部分所有题型中需要花费较多时间的题型，因此，考生只有掌握解题方法才能快速作答。

段落标题题是唯一出现在文章内容之前的题型，解题时需要往后浏览文章内容。题号是段落编号，标题框内的段落标题备选项用罗马数字（i, ii, iii, iv, v, vi, vii...）列出。框内标题个数多于段落数，有些备选标题是混淆项。

考生可能对于标题题的解法并不陌生，因为很多考试中都有类似概括段落大意的这种题型。但是需要注意的是，雅思阅读中的段落标题题有一定的难度，所给出的备选标题词数很少，大多数标题只有五六个单词。因此，将内容全面的句意概括缩减成与之匹配的短语概括，这是考生需要练习的重点。

5.2　解题技巧

解答雅思阅读段落标题题时，需要注意遵循以下步骤及技巧：

（1）翻译并分析框内备选标题，找出每个标题中的关键词。

由于该题型考查的是概括能力，不同于细节题，它对于理解能力提出了更高的要求。考生在翻译框内的备选标题时，不能只是简单浏览，一定要精准翻译，同时结合文章的大标题深入理解这些标题，只有这样才有可能事半功倍。

接下来结合一道真题来进行分析。

文章题目：The Meaning and Power of Smell

以下为方框内的备选标题：

List of Headings

i   The difficulties of talking about smells

ii   The role of smell in talking about smells

iii Future studies into smell

iv   The relationship between the brain and the nose

v   The interpretation of smell as a factor in defining groups

vi   Why our sense of smell is not appreciated

vii Smell is our superior sense

viii The relationship between smell and feelings

✔ 备选标题分析：

i The difficulties of talking about smells 讨论气味的困难

这篇文章的主题是气味的意义和力量。但这个标题说的是讨论气味的困难。我们分析标题时要从它本身入手，同时合理展开。"讨论"就意味着要描述气味。而"困难"则意味着不容易描述，原因可能是气味是看不见、摸不到的。

ii The role of smell in personal relationships 气味在人际关系中的作用

这个标题比较容易理解。"气味"是文章大标题中包含的词，而人际关系是这个段落的中心内容，既然是概括，我们就要思考：人际关系具体对应哪些词呢？常见的人际关系有：亲人、伴侣、朋友等。

iii Future studies into smell 关于气味的未来研究

注意这个标题的中心词不是"气味"，而是"研究"。此段不再介绍气味的作用以及它的特点，而更多是针对气味的学术探讨。学术研究方面的词汇可能会出现在此段中，具体有哪些，大家可以预测一下。

iv The relationship between the brain and the nose 大脑与鼻子之间的关系

这个标题的内容与气味本身关系不大。此段侧重身体两个器官之间关系的客观描述和分析。大家注意不要进行引申。在学术文章中，不能把大脑这个器官引申为精神，也不能把鼻子引申为嗅觉。

v The interpretation of smells as a factor in defining groups 气味作为定义群体的一个因素的解释

这个标题可以说是所有标题中最抽象、最难理解的一个。首先，标题中的"解释""因素"等词没有具体的含义，可以弱化。因此，这个标题里中最重要的部分是"定义群体"。其次，大家需要理解"定义群体"是什么（也就是对群体进行定义，即各群体是怎样的）。

vi Why our sense of smell is not appreciated 为什么我们的嗅觉不被欣赏

这个标题是一个表原因的疑问句，因而此段主要是回答一个问题。这个问题的陈述句是：嗅觉是不被欣赏的。此段应该是先阐述这种现象，然后解释出现该现象的原因。

vii Smell is our superior sense 嗅觉是我们的高级感觉

这个备选标题带有非常明确的指示作用。此段应该主要是介绍嗅觉的优点，并且此段中会出现表示积极含义的修饰语，尤其是形容词。

viii The relationship between smell and feelings 嗅觉与情感之间的关系

这个标题有两个中心词：嗅觉和情感。对应段落中除了"嗅觉"这个文章中心词以外，情感、情绪之类的词汇也会占一定比重。大家可以想一下表达情感、情绪的词有哪些呢（比如喜欢、不喜欢等）？

（2）对备选标题进行简单的归纳和分类。

以上文提及的关于"气味"的文章为例，当大家翻译完备选标题并确定标题关键词之后，可以做一些简单的归纳和分类。

iv 和 viii 相似，探讨的都是二者之间的关系。前者是大脑与鼻子之间的关系；后者是嗅觉与情感之间的关系。

ii 和 v 介绍的都是气味的作用。前者是气味在人际关系中起作用；后者是气味在定义群体时起作用。

vi 和 vii 的观点相反。前者指出嗅觉不被欣赏；后者指出嗅觉是我们的高级感觉。

i 和 iii 是比较特殊的两项。前者指出讨论气味有困难；后者的中心词是"研究"。

特别提示

方框内的备选标题中虽然含有混淆项，但是大多数是对文章各段落意思的正确概括。其中正确的标题会共同构成一篇文章。而文章是有完整性和连贯性的，所以在分析备选标题时，不要把它们当作独立的个体去分析，而要将其中段落意思上有关联的放在一起分析。经过归纳和分类后，大家从方框内备选标题中选择答案时，就不再是"8 选 1"或"9 选 1"了，而是"2 选 1"或"3 选 1"了，这样一来，正确率就会有很大提升。

（3）看段落。

在此，首先要指出解答段落标题题的一个误区。通常情况下，一篇学术文章的各段落都是有中心句的，且多为所在段落的第一句话，因此，不少考生认为只要看每段的首句就可以得出答案了。但实际上这么做是行不通的。近年来，由于雅思考试的难度不断增加，当一篇文章要考查段落标题题时，出题人会把大部分段落的中心句删掉。这样一来，有些段落内容看起来会特别松散，这并不是因为此文不符合学术文章的要求，而是因为出题人将某些关键句（或者是答案句直接对应的句子）删掉了。这就对考生的概括能力有了更高的要求，同时也意味着考生需要阅读更多内容，而不能仅根据某个句子得到答案。

当然，多阅读，并不意味着每个句子都要读，也不意味着每个词都要翻译，弄清什么该读什么不该读才是快速正确地解答段落标题题的关键。简单来说，想要做好段落标题题，大家需要记住三点：

> （1）主干部分最重要，修饰部分可不读（句子层面）；
>
> （2）论点句最重要，举例、数据部分可不读（段落层面）；
>
> （3）不断重复的内容就是中心内容（段落层面）。

接下来我们将结合雅思真题对以上三点进行细致的讲解。

（1）主语是非常重要的。

学术文章倾向于多用意思较为明确的"主谓宾"，这样会使文章的观点看上去思路更清晰。一篇文章大部分段落的主语通常都是此段的中心词。解题时，如果某个段落的主语比较多样，只需要对每句话的主语进行归类，就能很快找到答案了。

请找出以下段落中每句话的主语部分。

Most of the research on smell undertaken to date has been of a physical scientific nature. Significant advances have been made in the understanding of the biological and chemical nature of olfaction, but many fundamental questions have yet to be answered. Researchers have still to decide whether smell is one sense or two—one responding to odours proper and the other registering odourless chemicals in the air. Other unanswered questions are whether the nose is the only part of the body affected by odours, and how smells can be measured objectively given the nonphysical components. Questions like these mean that interest in the psychology of smell is inevitably set to play an increasingly important role for researchers.

解析：这篇文章的中心词是"气味"，但此段各句子的主语中却不见"气味"的身影，而都是与问题以及研究相关的词，因而要选择的标题也应该是与研究相关的。此段对应的标题是：Future studies into smell。标题中的 studies 对应此段中的 research，researcher，questions 等词。

（2）论点句是非常重要的，而论点句之后列举的大量数据和例子可以不看。

数据和例子都是用来具体解释论点的。在细节题中，这些解释句有可能是出题点，但是在概括段意的题型中，这些解释句对解题不起作用，是可以忽略的。

请找出以下段落中列举数据和例子的部分。

The strong economic growth expected in countries which are candidates for entry to the EU will also increase transport flows, in particular road haulage traffic. In 1998, some of these countries already exported more than twice their 1990 volumes and imported more than five times their 1990 volumes. And although many candidate countries inherited a transport system which encourages rail, the distribution between modes has tipped sharply in favour of road transport since the 1990s. Between 1990 and 1998, road haulage increased by 19.4%, while during the same period rail haulage decreased by 43. 5% , although — and this could benefit the enlarged EU — it is still on average at a much higher level than in existing member states.

解析：此段中第 1 句为论点句，除此之外都是详细的数据说明，这些数据是用来支持论点的。在这种段落中，只需要弄懂论点句，其他部分可以忽略。此段只需要读懂第 1 句话就可以选出对应的标题了。第 1 句的意思是：有望加入欧盟的国家的强劲经济增长也将增加运输流量，特别是公路运输流量。其对应的标题是：Transport trends in countries awaiting EU admission。

(3) 一个段落中不断重复的内容就是此段的主要内容。

各段落的内容应该是与文章大标题相关的，因此，除了大标题的重复外，另外一个重复出现的词应该是段落的中心词。如果出现这种情况，可以把此段概括成大标题与重复中心词之间的关系，再对照备选标题找出答案。

请找出以下段落中不断重复的内容。

Uncontrolled airspace is designated Class F, while controlled airspace below 5, 490m above sea level and not in the vicinity of an airport is Class E. All airspace above 5, 490m is designated Class A. The reason for the division of Class E and Class A airspace stems from the type of planes operating in them. Generally, Class E airspace is where one finds general aviation aircraft (few of which can climb above 5, 490m anyway) , and commercial turboprop aircraft. Above 5, 490m is the realm of the heavy jets. The difference between Class E and A airspace is that in Class A, all operations are IFR, and pilots must be instrument-rated, that is, skilled and licensed in aircraft instrumentation. Three other types of airspace, Classes D, C and B, govern the vicinity of airports. These correspond roughly to small municipal, medium-sized metropolitan and major metropolitan airports respectively. To enter Class B airspace, such as on approach to a major metropolitan airport, an explicit ATC clearance is required. The private pilot who cruises without permission into this airspace risks losing their license.

解析：此段的篇幅虽然很长，但很明显的是其中出现了不断重复的内容，即 Class A/B/C/D/E/F。结合文章的大标题"空中交通管制"，不难看出此段内容是针对某种情况的几种分类。因而此段对应的答案标题是：Defining airspace categories. 其中，categories 是 class 的同义词（均表示"种类，类别"）。

5.3　真题再现

我们已经详细讲解了解答段落标题题的步骤，大家只需要遵循"分析标题、归纳标题、理解段落主要内容"这三点就可以快速解题了。接下来我们将结合雅思真题来熟练掌握该题型的解题方法。

真题
i   The areas and artefacts with in the pyramid itself
ii   A difficult task for those involved
iii   A king who saved his people
iv   A single certainty among other less definite facts
v   An overview of the external buildings and areas
vi   A pyramid design that others copied
vii   An idea for changing the design of burial structures
iii   An incredible experience despite the few remains
ix   The answers to some unexpected questions

请根据下列所给段落内容选择方框内对应的标题。

第 1 题

题目： **A**   The pyramids are the most famous monuments of ancient Egypt and still hold enormous interest for people in the present day. These grand, impressive tributes to the memory of the Egyptian kings have become linked with the country even though other cultures, such as the Chinese and Mayan, also built pyramids. The evolution of the pyramid form has been written and argued about for centuries. However, there is no question that, as far as Egypt is concerned, it began with one monument to one king designed by one brilliant architect：the Step Pyramid of Djoser at Saqqara.

解析： 此段的标题是 A single certainty among other less definite facts，原因在于这个标题突出了段落中的一个重要主题：在讨论金字塔的起源和演化时，有很多不确定的事实，但有一个事实是确定的。这个确定的事实是：在埃及，它始于一座由一位杰出建筑师设计的国王纪念碑，即位于塞加拉的左塞尔阶梯金字塔。此标题通过使用 single certainty（一种确定性）这一表达，强调了在众多不确定事实中的唯一确定观点。这个标题概括了整个段落的主旨，即金字塔的演变虽然充满争议，但在埃及，金字塔始于一座特定的纪念碑。

答案： iv

第 2 题

题目： **B**   Djoser was the first king of the Third Dynasty of Egypt and the first to build in stone. Prior to Djoser's reign, tombs were rectangular monuments made of dried clay brick, which covered underground passages where the deceased person was buried. For reasons which remain unclear, Djoser's main official, whose name was Imhotep, conceived of building a taller, more impressive tomb for his king by stacking stone slabs on top of one another, progressively making them smaller, to form the shape now known as the Step Pyramid. Djoser is thought to have reigned for 19 years, but some historians and scholars attribute a much longer time for his rule, owing to the number and size of the monuments he built.

解析：此段的标题是 An idea for changing the design of burial structures，因为此段介绍了埃及第三王朝国王左塞尔统治时期，由他的主要官员伊姆霍特普提出的一种改变墓葬结构设计的创意。在左塞尔之前，陵墓通常是用干燥的黏土砖建造的矩形建筑，覆盖着地下通道，用于埋葬亡者。然而，伊姆霍特普提出了他的设想：为国王建造一座更高、更令人印象深刻的陵墓，将石板叠在一起，逐渐变小，形成了现在被称为"阶梯金字塔"的形状。而该标题强调了埃及墓葬结构的一种新创意，也就是说，标题强调了此段的主题。

答案：vii

第 3 题

题目：C The Step Pyramid has been thoroughly examined and investigated over the last century, and it is now known that the building process went through many different stages. Historian Marc Vande Mieroop comments on this, writing "Much experimentation was involved, which is especially clear in the construction of the pyramid in the centre of the complex. It had several plans...before it became the first Step Pyramid in history, piling six levels on top of one another... The weight of the enormous mass was a challenge for the builders, who placed the stones at an inward incline inorder to prevent the monument breaking up."

解析：此段的标题是 A difficult task for those involved，因为它突出了建造阶梯金字塔的过程中面临的巨大挑战。此段介绍了建造阶梯金字塔经历的多个不同阶段，以及在此过程中经历的多次实验。历史学家马克·范·德·米罗普在评论中提到："这涉及大量实验，建造建筑群中心金字塔时尤为明显。它在成为历史上第一座阶梯金字塔之前有过几种计划……它一层一层地堆积了六层。巨大石块的重量对建造者来说是一种挑战，他们将石块向内倾斜，以防止纪念碑破裂。"而该标题强调了参与建造金字塔的人们面临的艰巨任务。

答案：ii

第 4 题

题目：D When finally completed, the Step Pyramid rose 62 meters high and was the tallest structure of its time. The complex in which it was built was the size of a city in ancient Egypt and included a temple, courtyards, shrines, and living quarters for the priests. It covered a region of 16 hectares and was surrounded by a wall 10.5 meters high. The wall had 13 false doors cut into it with only one true entrance cut into the south-east corner; the entire wall was then ringed by a trench 750 meters long and 40 meters wide. The false doors and the trench were incorporated into the complex to discourage unwanted visitors. If someone wished to enter, he or she would have needed to know in advance how to find the location of the true opening in the wall. Djoser was so proud of his accomplishment that he broke the tradition of having only his own name on the monument and had Imhotep's name carved on it as well.

解析：此段的标题是 An overview of the external buildings and areas，因为它是对阶梯金字塔外部建筑及区域的概述。此段详细介绍了阶梯金字塔建成后的规模和结构，包括其高度、建筑群的规模以及周围的墙壁和护城河。阶梯金字塔高 62 米，是当时最高的建筑物。除了阶梯金字塔本身，此段中还提到了整个建筑群，包括寺庙、庭院、神殿和牧师的生活区。建筑群的规模有古埃及一座城市那么大，占地 16 公顷，周围有一堵高达 10.5 米的墙壁，而整个墙壁被一条长 750 米、宽 40 米的沟渠环绕。假门和沟渠被纳入建筑群，以阻止不受欢迎的游客。而标题是对阶梯金字塔外部建筑及区域的概述，与段落内容是一致的。

答案：v

第 5 题

题目：E The burial chamber of the tomb, where the king's body was laid to rest, was dug beneath the base of the pyramid, surrounded by a vast maze of long tunnels that had rooms off them to discourage robbers. One of the most mysterious discoveries found inside the pyramid was a large number of stone vessels. Over 40,000 of these vessels, of various forms and shapes, were discovered in storerooms off the pyramid's underground passages. They are inscribed with the names of rulers from the First and Second Dynasties of Egypt and made from different kinds of stone. There is no agreement among scholars and archaeologists on why the vessels were placed in the tomb of Djoser or what they were supposed to represent. The archaeologist Jean-Philippe Lauer, who excavated most of the pyramid and complex, believes they were originally stored and then given a "proper burial" by Djoser in his pyramid to honor his predecessors. There are other historians, however, who claim the vessels were dumped into the shafts as yet another attempt to prevent grave robbers from getting to the king's burial chamber.

解析：此段的标题是 The areas and artifacts with in the pyramid itself，因为它介绍了金字塔的内部区域及文物。此段着重介绍了金字塔的墓室，这是国王尸体的安葬之处。此外，此段还提到了金字塔内部的神秘发现之一，即大量石制器皿。在金字塔地下通道附近的储藏室中发现了 40000 多个形状各异的器皿，上面刻有埃及第一和第二王朝统治者的名字，这些器皿由不同种类的石头制成。学者和考古学家对于这些器皿被放置在墓穴内的原因以及它们代表着什么没有达成一致的意见。考古学家让·菲利普·劳尔认为，它们最初被存放起来，然后由左塞尔在金字塔内进行了"合适的埋葬"，以向他的前任致敬。然而，也有其他历史学家声称这些器皿被倒入通道，是为了阻止盗墓者进入国王的墓室。而标题介绍了金字塔的内部区域及文物，与段落内容是一致的。

答案：i

第 6 章 雅思阅读选择题

6.1 选择题简介

选择题（Multiple Choice）是大家都很熟悉的题型，因为这种题型几乎会出现在各种英语考试之中。但是，需要注意的是，雅思阅读选择题除了传统的"3 选 1"，还有"多选多"。雅思阅读选择题通常也会遵守"顺序"原则，出题顺序与所对应原文信息出现的顺序基本一致，一般来说，一个题目出自一个段落（也可能一个段落对应 2 道题），有可能一段一段出题，也有可能跳过一两个段落再出下一道题。总体上看，只要把握"顺序"原则，答案句定位一般比较容易。

6.2 解题技巧

解答选择题时，有时答案可能只对应原文中的某一句话，很难快速定位，因此需要灵活使用"排除法"，首先排除容易判断的错误答案。选择题的各选项有时可能对应原文中的较多内容，大家在解题时通常需要阅读整个段落，因此，提高阅读速度、培养对考点以及同义替换内容的敏感度至关重要。

解答这类题型时，大家可遵循以下步骤：

（1）读题干，仔细看每一个选项的内容，找出定位词、考点，预判原文中可能出现的对应形式。

（2）通过题干或者选项中的名词、形容词、动词、数字、特殊词语等定位。

注意：解答选择题时，不要仅通过题干来定位。很多时候，根据选项内容可能更容易定位。选项中特殊词汇出现的段落一般就是与题目对应的段落。可以假定选项内容都是正确的，预判选项考点在文中可能出现的呼应形式。

（3）定位至原文中对应的段落，确定考点对应的句子。

一般来说，雅思阅读选择题的设题方式有以下四种：

（1）细节题。

这种题目很像判断题，需要认真审题，在原文中找准题目对应的句子，同时要善用排除法。

（2）主旨推理总结题。

这种题目的题干中一般会出现 suggest，conclude 等词，答案通常不是原文中的原词原句，需要推理判断得出。

（3）文章标题（title）或主旨大意题（main topic）。

这种题目考查对文章标题主旨或者段落主旨的理解，答案必须包含中心词，一般出自文章引言或者首尾段。

（4）多选题。

这种题目一般是从若干选项中选出符合题目要求的多个选项。题目要求中常包含 WHICH TWO，WHICH THREE 等词，选项数量多，4 ~10 个不等。出题点一般集中在一两个段落里，通常要求精读整个段落，题目均考查细节。

特别提示

由于很多选择题本质上是考查细节，所以判断题的解题技巧同样适用。
- 含有绝对意义词汇（如 must，always，all）的选项，一般为错误选项。
- 含有 can，may，sometimes，some，not always 等的选项，一般为正确答案。
- 与原文表述完全一致的选项一般不是正确答案。

6.3 真题再现

Choose the correct letter, A, B, C or D.

Write the correct letter in boxes 1–4 on your answer sheet.

第 1 题

题目：According to the introduction, we become aware of the importance of smell when

A we discover a new smell.

B we experience a powerful smell.

C our ability to smell is damaged.

D we are surrounded by odours.

预判：这道题出自文章的引言（introduction）部分，这点题干中已经明确指出了。题干中的

aware of 是考点，预判文中会对其进行改写。A 选项考点是形容词 new，B 选项考点是形容词 powerful，C 选项考点是 ability 和含有消极意义的 damaged，D 选项考点是 surrounded。

原文：The sense of smell, or olfaction, is powerful. Odours affect us on a physical, psychological and social level. For the most part, however, we breathe in the aromas which surround us without being consciously aware of their importance to us. It is only when the faculty of smell is impaired for some reason that we begin to realise the essential role the sense of smell plays in our sense of well-being. 嗅觉是强大的。气味在身体、心理和社会层面上影响着我们。然而，在大多数情况下，我们呼吸着我们周围的香气，却没有意识到它们对我们的重要性。只有当嗅觉因某种原因受损时，我们才开始意识到嗅觉在我们的幸福感中起着至关重要的作用。

解析：C 选项直接对应此段最后一句：It is only when the faculty of smell is impaired for some reason that we begin to realise the essential role the sense of smell plays in our sense of well-being. 在原文和题目中，realise 对应 become aware of；faculty 对应 ability；impaired 对应 damaged。此段倒数第二句中出现了 D 选项中的 surround，但与题目无关。其他选项和原文无对应关系。

答案：C

第 2 题

题目：The experiment described in Paragraph B

    A   shows how we make use of smell without realising it.

    B   demonstrates that family members have a similar smell.

    C   proves that a sense of smell is learnt.

    D   compares the sense of smell in males and females.

预判：直接定位 B 段，此题考查细节。A 选项考点为否定词 without 及其后部分，B 选项考点为形容词 similar，C 选项考点为 learnt 对象的判断，D 选项考点为 compares，males 及 females（原文中可能会是 men，women）。注意：要多点精准定位句子。

原文：Odours are also essential cues in social bonding. One respondent to the survey believed that there is no true emotional bonding without touching and smelling a loved one. In fact, infants recognise the odours of their mothers soon after birth and adults can often identify their children or spouses by scent. In one well-known test, women and men were able to distinguish by smell alone clothing worn by their marriage partners from similar clothing worn by other people. Most of the subjects would probably never have given much thought to odour as a cue for identifying family members before being involved in the test, but as the experiment revealed, even when not consciously considered, smells register. 气味也是社交关系中的重要线索。调查中的一位受访者认为，如果不触摸和闻一

闻所爱的人，就没有真正的情感纽带。事实上，婴儿在出生后很快就能识别出母亲的气味，成年人通常可以通过气味识别出他们的孩子或配偶。在一项著名的测试中，女性和男性能够仅通过气味区分婚姻伴侣穿的衣服和其他人穿的类似衣服。在参与测试之前，大多数受试者可能从来没有考虑过气味作为识别家庭成员的线索，但正如实验所揭示的那样，即使没有意识到，气味也是线索。

解析：A 选项对应此段最后一句：...but as the experiment revealed, even when not consciously considered, smells register. 选项中 A 的 without realising it 对应原文中的 when not consciously considered。再来看看如何排除其他选项。B 选项中提及"家人有相似的气味"，但原文中无相关信息。similar 通常对应 the same, identical, not different 等，但原文中并未出现这些表达。C 选项指出"嗅觉是习得的"，这与原文中的 In fact, infants recognise the odours of their mothers soon after birth...（事实上，婴儿在出生后很快就能识别出母亲的气味……）相悖。D 选项认为此段"对比了男性与女性的嗅觉"，而原文中提及"男性与女性"的信息是：...women and men were able to distinguish by smell alone clothing worn by their marriage partners from similar clothing worn by other people.（女性和男性能够仅通过气味区分婚姻伴侣穿的衣服和其他人穿的类似衣服。）此处并不是对比男性与女性的嗅觉。

答案：A

第 3 题

题目：What is the writer doing in Paragraph C?

A supporting other research

B making a proposal

C rejecting a common belief

D describing limitations

预判：直接定位 C 段，此题为主旨概括题。A 选项考点为 support, other，原文中可能会出现同义替换词。B 选项考点为 proposal，原文中可能会出现同义替换词 suggestion 等。C 选项考点为 rejecting，原文中可能会出现 deny 等否定表达。D 选项考点为 limitations，原文中可能会出现 restrict 等消极的同义表达。

原文：In spite of its importance to our emotional and sensory lives, smell is probably the most undervalued sense in many cultures. The reason often given for the low regard in which smell is held is that, in comparison with its importance among animals, the human sense of smell is feeble and undeveloped. While it is true that the olfactory powers of humans are nothing like as fine as those possessed by certain animals, they are still remarkably acute. Our noses are able to recognise thousands of smells, and to perceive odours which are present only in extremely small quantities. 尽管气味对我们的情感和感官生活很重要，但在许多文化中，它可能是最被低估的感觉。人们对嗅觉的重视程度较低的原因是，与它在动物中的重要性相比，人类的嗅觉是微弱的，而且不发达。虽然人类的嗅觉确实不如

某些动物的嗅觉那样精细，但它们仍然非常敏锐。我们的鼻子能够识别成千上万种气味，并能感知仅以极少量存在的气味。

解析：此段第一句话 "In spite of its importance to our emotional and sensory lives, smell is probably the most undervalued sense in many cultures." 非常关键，因为段落的主旨大意通常是段落的开头。In spite of 这个重要的让步考点和后面含有否定前缀的 undervalued 充分表明这是在欲扬先抑，是在驳斥一种观点。解题时一定要对否定让步转折非常敏感。由此可见 C 选项正确。在其他选项中，D 选项为干扰项，但是要注意 "While it is true that the olfactory powers of humans are nothing like as fine as those possessed by certain animals, they are still remarkably acute. Our noses are able to recognise thousands of smells, and to perceive odours." 这里的连词 while 是转折对比，重点是后半句（但它们仍然非常敏锐），因而突出的是人类嗅觉的重要性而非其"局限性"。

答案：C

第 4 题

题目：What does the writer suggest about the study of smell in the atmosphere in Paragraph E?

A The measurement of smell is becoming more accurate.

B Researchers believe smell is a purely physical reaction.

C Most smells are in offensive.

D Smell is yet to be defined.

预判：直接定位 E 段，suggest 表明此题为主旨推断题。A 选项考点为 measurement, more accurate，预判原文中会出现数字或者同义形容词 precise。B 选项考点为 purely physical reaction，预判原文中会出现同义词 totally 等以及 physical reaction 的细节。C 选项考点为含有极端意味的 Most 以及否定形容词 in offensive。D 选项考点为 yet to be defined，预判原文中会出现否定表达。

原文：Most of the research on smell undertaken to date has been of a physical scientific nature. Significant advances have been made in the understanding of the biological and chemical nature of olfaction, but many fundamental questions have yet to be answered. Researchers have still to decide whether smell is one sense or two — one responding to odours proper and the other registering odourless chemicals in the air. Other unanswered questions are whether the nose is the only part of the body affected by odours, and how smells can be measured objectively given the nonphysical components. Questions like these mean that interest in the psychology of smell is inevitably set to play an increasingly important role for researchers. 迄今为止，大多数关于气味的研究都是物理科学性质的。在理解嗅觉的生物和化学性质方面取得了重大进展，但很多基本问题尚未得到解答。研究人员仍需确定气味是一种感觉还是两种感觉——一种是对气味的反应，另一种是记录空气中的无气味化学物质。其他悬而未决的问题是，鼻子是否是身体中唯一受气味影响的部分，

以及如何根据非物理成分客观地测量气味。诸如此类的问题意味着，对嗅觉心理学的兴趣不可避免地将对研究人员发挥越来越重要的作用。

解析：选项 D 对应此段第二句 "Significant advances have been made in the understanding of the biological and chemical nature of olfaction, but many fundamental questions have yet to be answered." 重点依然在转折词 but 后面，yet 也保留了。A 选项中的 measurement 虽然在原文中出现了同义替换词 measured，但没有 accurate 对应的表述。B 选项 Researchers believe smell is a purely physical reaction. 与原文中的 "Researchers have still to decide whether smell is one sense or two—one responding to odours proper and the other registering odourless chemicals in the air." 相悖。C 选项中的 in offensive 在原文中无对应的内容。

答案：D

第 7 章 雅思阅读真题同源文章精读

在备考雅思阅读的过程中，考生不仅要关注各种题型的解题技巧，更要具备对各类型文章的全文解读能力。雅思阅读中 3 篇文章所考查的单句细节理解能力和全文浏览能力及阅读速度都是需要通过大量的阅读练习来提升的。如果没有大量的阅读作为基础，只关注题型的解法是不能整体提升阅读能力的。阅读部分虽然题型众多，但"万变不离其宗"，就是考查考生阅读篇章的能力。

在雅思阅读题型中，有一类要求浏览全文，以段落标题题和段落信息匹配题为代表题型。在近年的考试中，段落标题题和段落信息匹配题的比重日益增加，尤其是在考试中的第 2 篇文章，往往以这种需要浏览全文的题目作为主导题型，以考查考生综合浏览篇章的能力。所以，在备考过程中，练习全文浏览也是不能跳过的一部分。

此外，雅思阅读考试所选取的学术文章学科内容涵盖范围较广，这也给备考造成了很大障碍。所以，我们在本章精心挑选了 20 篇真题同源学术文章作为精读范本。这些文章涵盖了雅思阅读试题中常见的动植物、天文、科技、环境、健康等话题，旨在引导考生通过精读提高对不同学科学术文章的理解。

精读时，考生并不需要逐字逐句翻译文章和查询生词，而是要优先掌握每句话主干部分的意思以及段落中句子之间的逻辑联系。在接下来的精读部分，大家首先可以尽量找出每句话的主干部分，同时将主句的谓语动词作为重点内容标注出来。这么做的目的是训练快速抓住关键信息的能力。其次，大家可以找出句子或分句之间的逻辑关系词，例如举例、解释、因果、转折关系等。如果大家能做到以上这两步，就能大大提升对文章细节及整体框架的把握。最后，大家要标注并整理每篇文章的生词，特别是动词。在理解句意乃至文意时，动词的重要性往往要大于其他词性（如名词、形容词和副词等）。掌握句中动词的意思才能掌握整个句子想要表达的内容。在学术文章中，与学科内容相关的词汇占很大比重，但掌握这些学科词汇并不是重点考查的能力之一。因而，与学科内容最为相关的名词并不那么重要。而形容词和副词通常在句中用作修饰语，其重要性也远不及动词。因而，大家在首次浏览词汇时，可以通过对动词的掌握情况（词义和用法等）来检测自己的词汇量是否达标。

7.1 真题同源文章1

Record Salinity and Low Water Imperil Great Salt Lake
创纪录的盐度和低水位危及大盐湖
Drought spurs efforts to restore shrinking lake's water supplies
干旱促使人们努力恢复萎缩的湖水供应

Utah's Great Salt Lake is smaller and saltier than at any time in recorded history. In July, the U. S. Geological Survey (USGS) reported that the world's third-largest saline lake had dropped to the lowest level ever documented. And this week researchers measured the highest salt concentrations ever seen in the lake's southern arm, a key bird habitat. Salinity has climbed to 18.4%, exceeding a threshold at which essential microorganisms begin to die.

犹他州的大盐湖处于历史上最小、最咸的时期。7月，美国地质调查局（USGS）报告称，这个世界第三大盐湖已经下降到有记录以来的最低水平。本周，研究人员在该湖的南部——一个重要的鸟类栖息地——测量了有史以来最高的盐浓度。盐度已攀升至18.4%，超过了基本微生物开始死亡的阈值。

The trends, driven by drought and water diversion, have scientists warning that a critical feeding ground for millions of migrating birds is at risk of collapse.

这种趋势是由干旱和调水引起的。科学家们警告说，数百万候鸟的重要觅食地正面临崩溃的风险。

"We're into uncharted waters," says biochemist Bonnie Baxter of Westminster College, who has been documenting the lake's alarming changes. "One week the birds are gone from a spot we usually see them. The next week we see dead flies along the shore. And each week we have to walk further to reach the water."

威斯敏斯特学院的生物化学家邦尼·巴克斯特一直在记录湖泊令人震惊的变化。她说："我们进入了未知的水域，前一周，这些鸟从我们通常看到的地方消失了。下一周，我们沿着海岸看到了死苍蝇。每周我们都要走得更远才能到达水域。"

After years of inaction, the prospect of a dying lake, plus the risk of harmful dust blowing from the

在多年的不作为之后，一个湖泊濒临消失的可能性，加上从干涸的湖床

dry lakebed, is galvanising policymakers to find ways to restore water to the shrinking lake.

吹来的有害尘土的风险，正在激励政策制定者寻找方法，为不断缩小的湖泊恢复水源。

The Great Salt Lake is really two lakes, divided in 1959 by a railroad causeway. Over time, the northern arm, which has few sources of fresh water, became saltier than the southern arm, which is fed by three rivers. Historically, salinity in the northern arm has hovered around 32%—too salty to support more than microorganisms—and about 14% in the southern arm.

✎ 大盐湖实际上是两个湖，1959 年被一条铁路堤坝分隔开了。随着时间的推移，淡水来源很少的北部变得比由三条河流供水的南部更咸。从历史上看，北部的盐度一直徘徊在32%左右——盐度过高，无法支持微生物的生存，而南部的盐度约为14%。

Although the southern part is about four times saltier than seawater, it supports a vibrant ecosystem characterised by billions of brine shrimp and brine flies, which feed on photosynthetic cyanobacteria and other microorganisms. Birds, in turn, devour prodigious numbers of flies and shrimp when they arrive at the lake to nest, molt, or rest during migrations. A diving waterbird called the eared grebe, for example, needs 28,000 adult brine shrimp each day to survive.

✎ 虽然南部的盐度大约比海水咸四倍，但它支持着一个充满活力的生态系统，其特征是数十亿只盐水虾和盐水蝇，它们以光合蓝藻和其他微生物为食。反过来，当鸟类来到湖边筑巢、蜕皮或在迁徙过程中休息时，它们会吃掉大量的苍蝇和虾。例如，一种名叫长耳䴙䴘的潜水水鸟，每天需要食用28000只成年盐水虾才能生存。

The low water and rising salinity threaten to destroy the base of this food web, researchers say. The receding shoreline has already dried out many reeflike mats of cyanobacteria, known as microbialites, that dot the lake bottom. Baxter fears the saltier water now threatens even the microbialite communities that remain submerged. "In laboratory tests, when the salinity passes 17% we see the cyanobacteria start to die off," she says. Loss of the mats could also harm brine fly populations, Baxter says. The flies lay eggs on the lake surface, producing larvae that swim down to the microbialites,

✎ 研究人员说，低水位和盐度上升有可能破坏这个食物网的基础。后退的海岸线已经使点缀在湖底的许多蓝藻（称为微生物岩）的礁石状垫层变干。巴克斯特担心，现在更咸的水甚至威胁到了留在水下的微生物群落。她说："在实验室测试中，当盐度超过17%时，我们会看到蓝藻开始死亡。"巴克斯特说，垫层的消失也可能损害盐水蝇的数量。这些苍蝇在湖面上产卵，产生的幼虫游到微生物群落中，在那里化蛹，然后再变成成虫。一些

where they pupate before maturing into adults. Some bird species feed on the larvae or adults, whereas others eat the pupae—which have been showing up dead by the billions during this fall's migration season.

鸟类以幼虫或成虫为食，而其他鸟类则以蛹为食——在今年秋天的迁徙季节，数十亿只蛹已经死亡。

Soon the brine shrimp could dwindle as well. "The fear is that in some future year, [the lake] will become so salty that its populations…will collapse," a pair of state ecologists wrote recently.

很快，盐水虾也会减少。两位州生态学家最近写道："令人担心的是，在未来的某一年，[湖泊]将变得非常咸，以至于其种群……将崩溃。"

In the meantime, researchers are mobilising to track the unfolding crisis. Baxter is bringing in a brine fly expert to assess the situation. Conservation groups are tracking shorebird populations across the intermountain West. And USGS has established a program to monitor hydrology and ecology at other saline lakes in Oregon, California, Nevada, and Utah, which are facing similar stress.

与此同时，研究人员正在动员跟踪正在发生的危机。巴克斯特正在请一位盐水蝇专家来评估情况。保护团体正在跟踪整个西部山地间的岸鸟种群。美国地质调查局已经建立了一个项目，以监测俄勒冈州、加利福尼亚州、内华达州和犹他州的其他盐湖的水文和生态，这些湖泊正面临着类似的压力。

The shrinkage of the lake threatens people as well as wildlife. In a 2019 state-funded report, atmospheric scientist Kevin Perry of the University of Utah estimated that 9% of the exposed lakebed sediments contain problematic levels of arsenic or metals, thought to be derived from industry, wastewater treatment, or agriculture. Winds are likely to erode the crust that holds the sediment in place and carry dust far and wide. With more than 1 million residents living near the lake, in Salt Lake City and its suburbs, the worst-case scenario would be an air pollution disaster—akin to those experienced by communities in Iran near other saline lakes. Even Utah's famed ski slopes are imperiled by the dust; scientists have documented how storms are already dumping lakebed particles onto the snow, darkening it and hastening the melt.

湖泊的萎缩威胁着人们以及野生动物。在2019年国家资助的一份报告中，犹他大学的大气科学家凯文·佩里估计，9%的裸露湖床沉积物含有有问题的砷或金属，这些砷或金属被认为来自工业、废水处理或农业。风可能会侵蚀固定沉积物的地壳，并将尘土带到很远很远的地方。盐湖城及其郊区有超过100万居民居住在湖边，最坏的情况将是一场空气污染灾难——就像伊朗其他盐湖附近的群落所经历的那样。甚至犹他州著名的滑雪场也受到了尘土的威胁；科学家们已经记录了风暴是如何将湖床颗粒倾倒在雪地上，使其变黑并加速融化的。

For years, conservationists have urged policy-makers to reduce the water that farmers and other users divert from streams that flow into the lake. But, "Conventional wisdom has been it's just a salty lake—we should be using the water upstream," says Utah State Representative Tim Hawkes. "For many in Utah the lake's been a little bit out of sight, out of mind."

This year, however, policymakers sprang into action. In April, Utah Governor Spencer Cox signed a landmark series of bills aimed at rescuing the lake and addressing the drought. They include new rules that allow farmers to sell water rights they are not using to groups that will allow the water to flow to the lake. The state earmarked ＄450 million for water infrastructure and conservation projects, including a ＄40 million fund that could acquire water for the lake in the future.

Such policies could take years to have a noticeable impact, especially if the current drought continues. Baxter, for one, wonders: "Is any of this enough?" But Marcelle Shoop, who heads the Saline Lakes Program for the National Audubon Society, says she is "optimistic, because there are so many people trying to develop solutions."

In the meantime, the lake may get temporary relief from a different source: the upcoming winter wet season. If it produces a good snowpack in nearby mountains, the runoff could help refill the region's parched streams.

✎ 多年来，环保主义者一直敦促政策制定者减少农民和其他用户从流入湖泊的溪流中分流的水量。但是，犹他州众议员蒂姆·霍克斯说："传统观点认为，这只是一个咸水湖——我们应该使用上游的水。对犹他州的许多人来说，这个湖已经有点看不见、想不起来了。"

✎ 然而，今年，政策制定者迅速采取了行动。4 月，犹他州州长斯宾塞·考克斯签署了一系列具有里程碑意义的法案，旨在拯救该湖并解决干旱问题。其中包括新的规定，允许农民将他们未使用的水权出售给允许水流入湖泊的团体。该州为水利基础设施和保护项目预留了 4.5 亿美元，其中包括一笔 4000 万美元的基金，用于未来为湖泊取水。

✎ 这些政策可能需要数年时间才能产生显著的影响，尤其是在当前干旱持续的情况下。巴克斯特想知道："这些够了吗？"但国家奥杜邦学会盐湖项目负责人马塞尔·肖普表示，她"很乐观，因为有这么多人在努力制定解决方案"。

✎ 与此同时，该湖可能从另一个源头得到暂时的缓解：即将到来的冬季雨季。如果附近的山区产生良好的积雪，径流可以帮助重新补充该地区干涸的溪流。

核心词汇

saline *adj.*	盐的；含盐的；咸的

例句 Wash the lenses in **saline** solution. 用盐溶液清洗镜片。

concentration *n.*	浓度；含量

例句 High glucose **concentrations** in the blood can indicate diabetes or other metabolic disorders. 血液中的高葡萄糖浓度可指示糖尿病或其他代谢紊乱。

threshold *n.*	阈值

例句 I have a high pain **threshold**. 我的疼痛阈值很高。

diversion *n.*	转向；转移

例句 The government initiated a river **diversion** project to manage water resources effectively and mitigate the impact of drought in the region.
政府启动了一项河流改道工程，以有效管理水资源并减轻该地区干旱的影响。

uncharted *adj.*	人迹罕至的；地图上未绘出（或未标明）的

例句 The ship hit an **uncharted** rock. 这艘船撞上了海图上未标出的岩石。

prospect *n.* 可能性；希望	

例句 There is no immediate **prospect** of peace. 短期内没有和平的可能。

vibrant *adj.*	充满生机的；精力充沛的

例句 Thailand is at its most **vibrant** during the New Year celebrations.
在欢度新年期间，泰国举国欢腾。

submerge *v.*	（使）潜入水中；没入水中；浸没；淹没

例句 The fields had been **submerged** by floodwater. 农田被洪水淹没了。

dwindle *v.*	（逐渐）减少；变小；缩小

例句 Membership of the club has **dwindled** from 70 to 20.
俱乐部会员人数已从 70 人减少到 20 人。

sediment *n.*	沉淀物

例句 Many organisms that die in the sea are soon buried by **sediment**.
许多在海里死亡的生物很快便被沉淀物掩埋了。

7.2 真题同源文章2

Ancient DNA Pioneer Svante Pääbo Wins Nobel
古代 DNA 先驱斯万特·派博获诺贝尔奖

By sequencing ancient hominins' DNA, Pääbo explored
"what makes us uniquely human"
通过对古人类的 DNA 进行测序，派博探索了"是什么让我们成为独特的人类"

The Nobel Prize in Physiology or Medicine was awarded this week to Swedish geneticist Svante Pääbo, honoring work that illuminates both the distant past and the genetic heritage of people living today.

✎ 本周，诺贝尔生理学或医学奖被授予瑞典遗传学家斯万特·派博，以表彰其照亮遥远过去和当今人类遗传遗产的工作。

A director at the Max Planck Institute for Evolutionary Anthropology (EVA) in Leipzig, Germany, since 1997, Pääbo pioneered the now-booming field of ancient DNA research. He was the first to successfully retrieve and sequence bits of ancient DNA from a Neanderthal in 1997. Then, after refining his methods to avoid contamination, his team sequenced a complete Neanderthal genome in 2009 and a Denisovan, another archaic human, the following year. His research has offered insights into the genetic evolution of modern humans, including a better understanding of disease risks.

✎ 派博自 1997 年起担任德国莱比锡马克斯–普朗克进化人类学研究所（EVA）所长，他开创了现在蓬勃发展的古代 DNA 研究领域。1997 年，他是第一个成功地从尼安德特人身上提取古代 DNA 片段并进行测序的人。然后，在完善了他的方法以避免污染之后，他的团队在 2009 年对尼安德特人的完整基因组进行了测序，并在第二年对另一种古人类——丹尼索瓦人进行了测序。他的研究为现代人类的遗传进化提供了见解，包括更好地了解疾病风险。

The ancient genomes "allow us to understand what makes humans humans," says Johannes Krause, who did his Ph. D. in Pääbo's lab and now is also a director at EVA. Comparing modern and

✎ 约翰内斯·克劳斯在派博的实验室里获得了博士学位，现在也是 EVA 的主任，他说，古代基因组"使我们了解是什么使人类成为人类"。他指出，

extinct human lineages has given scientists new insights into brain development, autism, and the immune system's response and other diseases, he notes. "It will probably take us a few more years to figure them all out," Krause says. "But it will enable us to understand what makes us so special."

Pääbo "will be the first to say it's not just his work. It's a team of people," says paleoanthropologist Chris Stringer of the Natural History Museum in London, a Neanderthal specialist. "But he's built a great team."

Says evolutionary biologist Beth Shapiro of the University of California, Santa Cruz: "Svante's insights …inspired a generation of scientists and established paleogenomics as a rigorous field of research … [The field] has since allowed unexpected insights into human evolution, paleontology, ecology, and so many other disciplines."

When Pääbo first heard the news, he thought it was "an elaborate prank by my research group," he told a press conference last week. His interest in ancient DNA originated in a childhood fascination with ancient Egypt. In a 1985 *Nature* paper, he reported finding small amounts of DNA in the cells of Egyptian mummies. That early work was questioned because the smallest speck of human tissue can introduce modern DNA. Pääbo then pushed to develop techniques to minimise contamination during sampling and to differentiate ancient molecules from modern ones.

"His Ph.D. work was on recovering DNA from mummies and it was pretty much a failure. He got nothing," Stringer says. "Another kind of person might

通过比较现代和灭绝的人类谱系，科学家们对大脑发育、自闭症、免疫系统反应和其他疾病有了新的见解。克劳斯说："我们可能还需要几年的时间才能把它们全部弄清楚。但这将使我们了解是什么让我们如此特别。"

✎ 伦敦自然历史博物馆的古人类学家、尼安德特人专家克里斯·斯金格说，派博"将会第一个说这不仅仅是他一个人的工作。这是一个团队，但他建立了一个伟大的团队"。

✎ 加州大学圣克鲁兹分校的进化生物学家贝丝·夏皮罗说："斯万特·派博的见解……激励了一代科学家，并将古基因组学确立为一个严格的研究领域……［该领域］从此对人类进化、古生物学、生态学以及许多其他学科产生了意想不到的见解。"

✎ 当派博第一次听到这个消息时，他认为这是"我的研究小组精心策划的恶作剧"，他在上周的新闻发布会上说。他对古代DNA的兴趣源于童年时对古埃及的迷恋。在1985年《自然》杂志的一篇论文中，他报告了在埃及木乃伊的细胞中发现了少量的DNA。这项早期工作受到了质疑，因为最小的一点点人类组织也能引入现代DNA。派博随后推动了技术的发展，以尽量减少采样过程中的污染，并将古代分子与现代分子区分开来。

✎ 斯金格说："他的博士工作是从木乃伊中恢复DNA，但几乎失败了。他一无所获。另一种人可能会说，'好

have said, 'Well, I'm giving up; this is useless. ' But he didn't. He kept going. " In the late 1980s, Pääbo's work got a boost from the polymerase chain reaction technology, which made it possible to replicate small fragments of DNA many times over. He reached out to museums in Germany for Neanderthal bone samples, grinding small amounts into powder and sequencing the DNA contained inside.

吧，我放弃了，这行不通。'但他没有。他一直在努力。"20 世纪 80 年代末，派博的工作得到了聚合酶链式反应技术的推动，这使得多次复制 DNA 的小片段成为可能。他向德国的博物馆索取尼安德特人的骨骼样本，将少量的骨骼研磨成粉末，并对其中的 DNA 进行测序。

Published in *Cell* in 1997, the results were a watershed moment, showing significant amounts of DNA could be recovered from bones 50, 000 years old or more. The initial work relied on mitochondrial DNA, which is more plentiful in cells than DNA from the nucleus. The results were enough to show humans and Neanderthals were two separate groups that diverged about 500, 000 years ago.

1997 年发表在《细胞》杂志上的结果是一个分水岭，该结果显示大量的 DNA 可以从 5 万年或更久远的骨骼中恢复出来。最初的工作依赖于线粒体 DNA，它在细胞中比来自细胞核的 DNA 更丰富。研究结果足以表明人类和尼安德特人是两个独立的群体，在大约 50 万年前出现了分化。

Fast-moving advances in sequencing technology, along with new samples, eventually allowed his team to successfully sequence more than 4 billion base pairs. They published a draft Neanderthal genome in *Science* in 2010. Comparing the Neanderthal and modern human genomes showed individuals in Europe and Asia today derive between 1% and 4% of their ancestry from Neanderthals.

测序技术的快速发展，加上新的样本，最终使他的团队成功地测出了超过 40 亿个碱基对。他们于 2010 年在《科学》杂志上发表了尼安德特人基因组草案。对尼安德特人和现代人的基因组对比显示，今天欧洲和亚洲的个体有 1% 到 4% 的血统来自尼安德特人。

"Svante…showed pretty convincingly that we had interbred with the Neanderthals, and that DNA is still active in our genomes, " Stringer says. "So it does have medical importance. "

斯金格说："斯万特·派博……非常令人信服地表明，我们已经与尼安德特人杂交，而且 DNA 在我们的基因组中仍然活跃，所以它确实具有医学意义。"

In 2008, Pääbo and his team recovered DNA from a finger bone fragment in a Siberian cave that revealed a previously unknown ancient human population, now known as Denisovans. Here, too, the

2008 年，派博和他的团队从西伯利亚山洞的一块指骨碎片中找到了 DNA，发现了一个以前不为人知的古人类群体，该群体现在被称为丹尼索

genetic results offered insights into modern human populations, revealing that adaptations to living at high altitude found in modern Tibetan populations may be derived from Denisovan ancestors.

瓦人。在这里，基因结果也为现代人类种群提供了见解，揭示了在现代西藏人口中发现的对高海拔地区生活的适应性可能来自丹尼索瓦人的祖先。

The Nobel Prize in Physiology or Medicine isn't often awarded to a single scientist. But, Krause says, "Who else would you give it to?" Many groups are using Pääbo's tools, he adds, "but they are largely his scientific progeny...Clearly there's no one else who deserves it the way he does."

✎ 诺贝尔生理学或医学奖通常不会颁发给单独的一位科学家。但是，克劳斯说："你还会把它颁给谁？"他补充说，许多团体都在使用派博的工具，"但他们基本上都是他的科学后代……显然，没有其他人像他一样值得获得这个奖项。"

The award is "also a great honor for the field in general," says paleoanthropologist Katerina Harvati of the University of Tübingen. It underlines "how our past can affect our lives, our biology, and health to-day."

✎ 图宾根大学的古人类学家卡捷琳娜·哈瓦蒂说，该奖项"对整个领域来说也是一大荣誉"。它强调了"我们的过去如何影响我们今天的生活、生物学和健康"。

核心词汇

illuminate *v.*	照亮；阐明
例句 This text **illuminates** the philosopher's early thinking. 这篇课文阐述了这位哲学家的早期思想。	

heritage *n.*	遗产
例句 The building is part of our national **heritage**. 这座建筑是我们民族遗产的一部分。	

retrieve *v.*	检索
例句 The program allows you to **retrieve** items quickly by searching under a keyword. 这个程序通过关键词进行搜索，能让你迅速获取数据项。	

contamination *n.*	污染
例句 Some people are still suffering ill effects from the **contamination** of their water. 一些人仍在遭受其水质污染的恶果。	

genome *n.*	基因组
例句 The human **genome** has now been sequenced. 人类基因组的序列现已测定。	

autism *n.* 自闭症

例句 **Autism** does not allow learning or thinking in the same ways as in children who are developing normally.
自闭症儿童的学习和思考方式与正常发育的儿童不同。

rigorous *adj.* 谨慎的；严格的

例句 The work failed to meet their **rigorous** standards. 这项工作没有达到他们的严格标准。

elaborate *adj.* 复杂的；详尽的；精心制作的

例句 All these have been demonstrated in **elaborate** experiments.
所有这些都在精心设计的实验中得到了证明。

molecule *n.* 分子

例句 A **molecule** of water consists of two atoms of hydrogen and one atom of oxygen.
水分子由两个氢原子和一个氧原子构成。

replicate *v.* 复制；（精确地）仿制

例句 Subsequent experiments failed to **replicate** these findings.
后来的实验没有得出同样的结果。

7.3 真题同源文章 3

Ambitious Bill Leads to 40% Cut in Emissions, Models Show
模型显示，雄心勃勃的法案带来了 40% 的减排量
But more action is needed to reach Biden's pledge to halve greenhouse gas emissions by 2030
但要实现拜登关于到 2030 年将温室气体排放减半的承诺，还需要采取更多行动

For climate advocates in the United States, the past month felt like a roller coaster. In early July, negotiations in Congress on clean energy legislation of historic proportions collapsed, and the effort seemed doomed. But backroom talks continued

对于美国的气候倡导者来说，过去的一个月就像过山车一样。7 月初，国会关于清洁能源立法的历史性谈判破裂，这一努力似乎注定要失败。但幕后谈判仍在继续，上周，关键参议

and last week key senators suddenly announced an agreement on a $369 billion bill that would provide the most climate funding ever seen in the United States. "It was the best kept secret, potentially, in Washington history," says Leah Stokes, a political scientist at the University of California (UC), Santa Barbara.

员突然宣布就一项 3690 亿美元的法案达成协议，该法案将提供美国有史以来最多的气候资金。加州大学圣巴巴拉分校的政治学家利亚·斯托克斯说："这可能是华盛顿历史上保守得最好的秘密。"

The backers—Senate Majority Leader Chuck Schumer (D–NY) and Senator Joe Manchin (D–WV)—who had initially balked at the cost—announced that the draft bill would ensure U. S. carbondioxide (CO_2) emissions would fall by 40% by 2030, compared with 2005.

✎ 支持者——参议院多数党领袖查克·舒默和参议员乔·曼钦（他最初对成本犹豫不决）——宣布该法案草案将确保美国二氧化碳排放量到 2030 年比 2005 年下降 40%。

Sponsors of the bill, which must still pass the full Senate and the House of Representatives, might be expected to oversell its impact. But energy and climate modelers have now scrutinised its 725 pages and concluded the 40% claim is about on target. They plugged major provisions, including subsidies for renewable energy and tax cuts for electric vehicles, as well as controversial incentives for the fossil fuel industry, into their models. Three models now agree that if the bill's provisions are carried out, U. S. green house gas emissions would fall by perhaps 40% by 2030, although only part of that stems from the bill alone. One model also finds that the renewable energy subsidies will likely create 1. 5 million jobs and prevent thousands of premature deaths from air pollution, especially in disadvantaged communities.

✎ 该法案仍必须在参议院和众议院全体通过，预计提案人可能会夸大其影响。但是，能源和气候模型专家现在已经仔细研究了该法案的 725 页，并得出结论：40% 的说法是有针对性的。他们在模型中加入了主要条款，包括可再生能源补贴和电动汽车减税，以及有争议的化石燃料行业激励措施。三个模型现在一致认为，如果该法案的条款得以实施，到 2030 年，美国的温室气体排放量可能会下降 40%，尽管其中只有一部分来自该法案。一个模型还发现，可再生能源补贴可能会创造 150 万个就业机会，并防止数千人过早死于空气污染，尤其是在弱势社区。

"It's a historic step, no doubt about it," says Marshall Shepherd, an atmospheric scientist at the University of Georgia and former head of the

✎ 佐治亚大学大气科学家、美国气象学会前负责人马歇尔·谢波德说："毫无疑问，这是历史性的一步。它

American Meteorological Society. "It really does a lot to enhance the transition to a renewable energy economy."

U.S. emissions have been falling by about 1% per year since 2005, when they peaked, largely because of replacing coal power with wind and solar, as well as natural gas, and rising fuel economy in light cars. But this pace is nowhere near fast enough to meet President Joe Biden's goal of a 50% to 52% cut in emissions by 2030 relative to 2005. Officials pledged that dramatic reduction as the U.S. contribution to the Paris accord's goal of holding global temperature rise to 1.5℃.

Biden's major effort had been *The Build Back Better Act*, which would have invested $560 billion in cutting greenhouse gases but died in the Senate after Manchin objected. The smaller new bill, called *The Inflation Reduction Act of 2022*, preserves much of the bang for clean energy, says energy system expert Jesse Jenkins of Princeton University's Rapid Energy Policy Evaluation and Analysis Toolkit Project, which runs one of the models. "I think [Senate staff] did a miraculous job," he says. In particular, the bill provides subsidies to expand renewable energy and lure consumers to buy electric vehicles, solar panels, and climate-friendly home heat pumps.

To evaluate the climate impacts of the legislation, Jenkins and other modelers simulate the entire U.S. energy system, from the smallest electric vehicles to nuclear plants, and add the proposed policies to see how they impact CO_2 emissions. Scientists also fold in results from other models that

确实对促进向可再生能源经济的过渡起到了很大作用。"

✎ 自 2005 年美国的排放量达到峰值以来，每年下降约 1%，这主要是因为使用风能、太阳能和天然气取代了煤电，以及轻型汽车燃油经济性的提高。但这一速度远不足以实现乔·拜登总统到 2030 年将排放量比 2005 年减少 50% 至 52% 的目标。官员们承诺，随着美国对《巴黎协定》将全球气温上升控制在 1.5℃ 这一目标的贡献，气温将大幅下降。

✎ 拜登的主要努力是《重建更好法案》，该法案本应投资 5600 亿美元用于减少温室气体排放，但由于曼钦的反对而在参议院中夭折。普林斯顿大学快速能源政策评估和分析工具包项目的能源系统专家杰西·詹金斯表示，这项规模较小的新法案，即《2022 年减少通货膨胀法》，保留了清洁能源的大部分收益，该项目负责其中一个模型。他说："我认为［参议院工作人员］做了一项奇迹般的工作。"特别是，该法案提供补贴，以扩大可再生能源，吸引消费者购买电动汽车、太阳能电池板和气候友好型家用热泵。

✎ 为了评估立法对气候的影响，詹金斯和其他建模人员模拟了从最小的电动汽车到核电站的整个美国能源系统，并添加了拟议的政策，以了解它们如何影响二氧化碳排放。科学家们还综合了其他模型的结果，这些模型

focus on factors such as the impact of agricultural policies on two other causes of greenhouse warming: methane emissions from livestock and nitrous oxide released from fertilised fields. Modelers put everything together to forecast emission trends, says modeler Ben King of the Rhodium Group, an independent research firm.

Just a day after the bill was released, Rhodium posted preliminary estimates on its website. The top-line result: a 31% to 44% reduction in greenhouse gas emissions from 2005. Compared with current policies, that's an additional drop of 7 to 9 percentage points. Variables such as the price of natural gas account for much of the uncertainty: If gas prices drop, utilities might favour gas over renewable power, slowing the decline in carbon emissions.

Other provisions of the proposed bill could eventually lead to further CO_2 reductions, such as investment in technologies that directly remove carbon from the atmosphere and capture it from fossil fuel plants.

The bill also includes some climate-unfriendly provisions, apparently added at Manchin's request. It requires the federal government to offer several lease sales of offshore oil and gas resources, with more on the table if public lands are opened to renewable energy efforts like wind farms. The leases could boost oil and gas production from federal lands by an extra 50 million tons per year in 2030, according to Energy Innovation. Overall, however, climate wins out, analysts say: For each additional ton of CO_2 from fossil fuels, other provisions of the bill would reduce emissions by 24 tons.

关注的因素包括农业政策对温室变暖的另外两个原因的影响：牲畜的甲烷排放和施肥田释放的一氧化二氮。独立研究公司荣鼎集团的建模师本·金说，建模人员把所有东西放在一起预测排放趋势。

就在法案发布的第二天，荣鼎在其网站上发布了初步估计。最重要的结果是：从2005年起，温室气体排放量减少了31%至44%。与目前的政策相比，这又下降了7到9个百分点。天然气价格等变量解释了大部分不确定性：如果天然气价格下跌，公用事业公司可能会青睐天然气而非可再生能源，从而减缓碳排放的下降。

拟议法案的其他条款最终可能导致二氧化碳排放的进一步减少，例如投资于直接从大气中去除碳并从化石燃料厂捕获碳的技术。

该法案还包括一些对气候不友好的条款，显然是应曼钦的要求增加的。它要求联邦政府提供一些近海石油和天然气资源的租赁销售，如果公共土地向风电场等可再生能源开放，则会有更多的租赁。据能源创新公司称，到2030年，这些租约可能会使联邦土地上的石油和天然气产量每年增加5000万吨。然而，分析人士表示，总体而言，气候是赢家。化石燃料每增加一吨二氧化碳，法案的其他条款将减少24吨的排放。

The bill must still pass the Senate, where Democrats need every possible vote in their party, and then it will go back to the House. Stokes, who advised Democrats on the bill, says she's hopeful the measure will be on Biden's desk by mid-August. "The United States is really going to be a climate leader globally if we can get this bill over the finish line."

✎ 该法案仍必须在参议院获得通过，民主党人需要在其党内获得所有可能的投票，然后才能返回众议院。为民主党人提供该法案建议的斯托克斯表示，她希望该措施能在 8 月中旬之前提交给拜登。"如果我们能让这项法案通过，美国将真正成为全球气候的领导者。"

The measure won't be enough, however, for the United States to reach its Paris goal of a 50% greenhouse emission reduction by 2030. For that, more federal regulation and state action will be necessary, King and others say. "It's all hands on deck," says energy and climate modeler John Bistline of the Electric Power Research Institute.

✎ 然而，该措施还不足以让美国实现到 2030 年减少 50% 温室气体排放的巴黎目标。金和其他人说，为此，更多的联邦监管和州政府行动将是必要的。电力研究所的能源和气候建模师约翰·比斯特林说："这需要所有人的努力。"

The ultimate—and necessary—goal is cutting U.S. emissions to zero, says Emily Grubert, a civil engineer and environmental sociologist at the University of Notre Dame. "People keep talking about this as the biggest climate investment in a generation. I can only say—I hope not."

✎ 圣母大学土木工程师和环境社会学家艾米丽·格鲁伯特表示，最终也是必要的目标是将美国的排放量降至零。"人们一直在谈论这是一代人以来最大的气候投资。我只能说——我希望不是。"

核心词汇

pledge *n.*	保证；诺言

例句 Management has given a **pledge** that there will be no job losses this year.
资方保证今年不会削减工作职位。

advocate *n.*	拥护者；支持者

例句 He is a strident **advocate** of nuclear power. 他是发展核能的坚定拥护者。

collapse *v.* （突然）倒塌；坍塌

例句 The building **collapsed** as an indirect result of the heavy rain.

暴雨间接导致了那座楼房的倒塌。

balk *v.* 畏缩；回避

例句 Many parents may **balk** at the idea of paying $100 for a pair of shoes.

许多父母可能不愿出100美元买一双鞋。

scrutinise *v.* 仔细查看；认真检查

例句 The statement was carefully **scrutinised** before publication.

这项声明在发表前经过了仔细的审查。

incentive *n.* 激励；刺激；鼓励

例句 There is no **incentive** for people to save fuel. 没有使人们节约燃料的鼓励办法。

enhance *v.* 提高；增强；增进

例句 This is an opportunity to **enhance** the reputation of the company.

这是提高公司声誉的机会。

preliminary *adj.* 预备性的；初步的；开始的

例句 The doctors have successfully concluded **preliminary** tests.

医生们已经成功地完成了初步的化验。

ultimate *adj.* 最后的；最终的

例句 The **ultimate** decision lies with the parents. 最后的决定权掌握在父母手中。

federal *adj.* 联邦的

例句 The new environmental regulations were implemented as part of a **federal** initiative to standardise pollution control measures across the country.

新的环境法规是作为联邦倡议的一部分而实施的，旨在统一全国范围内的污染控制措施。

7.4　真题同源文章 4

Scientists Scramble to Set up Monkeypox Vaccine Trials
科学家们争相开展猴痘疫苗试验
Logistical and ethical challenges are complicating the design of efficacy studies
组织和伦理方面的挑战使疗效研究的设计变得复杂化

When monkeypox suddenly started spreading globally in May, the world was fortunate in one respect: a vaccine was available. MVA, originally developed by Bavarian Nordic as a smallpox vaccine, was already licensed for monkeypox in Canada and the United States. EU regulators have since followed suit. By now clinics have delivered thousands of doses to people in high-risk groups.

There's little doubt the vaccine can help, but that's about all that's certain. Exactly how well MVA protects against monkeypox and for how long is not known. Nor is it clear how much protection is lost by giving just a single dose rather than the recommended two doses, as some countries are doing to stretch supply, or how much protection a vaccine given after exposure can offer.

But the ethical and logistical complexities of the monkeypox crisis, which is overwhelmingly affecting men who have sex with men (MSM), are making these questions hard to answer. Placebo-controlled clinical trials are fraught because MVA is already licensed and people are clamoring to get it. And vaccine clinics are often set up at short notice as doses become available, making it harder to

✎ 当猴痘于 5 月突然开始在全球蔓延时，有一件事情是幸运的：有可用的疫苗。MVA 最初是由巴伐利亚北欧公司作为天花疫苗开发的，在加拿大和美国已经获得了猴痘许可。此后，欧盟监管机构纷纷效仿。到目前为止，诊所已经向高危人群提供了数千剂疫苗。

✎ 毋庸置疑，该疫苗可以提供帮助，但这也是唯一可以确定的事情。MVA 对猴痘的保护究竟有多好、能持续多长时间，目前还不清楚。只接种一剂而不是推荐的两剂，会失去多少保护作用（一些国家正在这么做以扩大供应），或者暴露后接种疫苗能提供多少保护，这些也不清楚。

✎ 但猴痘危机在伦理和组织方面的复杂性使得这些问题难以回答，因为猴痘危机绝大多数情况下影响着男男性行为者（MSM）。安慰剂对照的临床试验很令人担忧，因为 MVA 已经获得许可，而且人们都在争相获取它。疫苗诊所往往是在短时间内建立起来的，因为剂量已经到位，这使得组织试验

organise a trial and enroll subjects. Researchers are responding with a plethora of inventive trial designs.

The first evidence that smallpox vaccines also protect against monkeypox came from a study in the 1980s in the Democratic Republic of the Congo (then called Zaire), where the virus occasionally jumps from animals to people, who then infect others in their household. A study among patients' contacts suggested smallpox vaccination was 86% effective at preventing monkeypox as well. But the study looked at a small number of cases, the virus was genetically quite different than the one now spreading, and the smallpox vaccine was an older one with more side effects; MVA was developed as a safer alternative.

MVA was licensed for monkeypox based on data from animal experiments and the immune response it triggers in humans. But its efficacy has barely been tested in people, and not at all for preventing sexual transmission, which results in "very significant mucosal exposure, which is not the same thing as just brushing up against somebody," says Anne Rimoin, an epidemiologist at the University of California, Los Angeles.

So far, there's scant data on how well the vaccine is working in the current outbreak. Among 276 individuals who received a shot at a Paris hospital as post-exposure prophylaxis (PEP) after reporting a high-risk contact, 12 developed a monkeypox infection, French scientists reported in a recent preprint. But there was no control group, making it impossible to tell how many people would

和招募受试者变得更加困难。研究人员正在用大量富有创造性的试验设计来应对。

✎ 天花疫苗也能预防猴痘的第一个证据来自20世纪80年代在刚果民主共和国（当时叫扎伊尔）进行的一项研究，在那里，病毒偶尔会从动物传播到人身上，然后人们又感染家中的其他人。一项针对患者接触者的研究表明，接种天花疫苗对预防猴痘也有86%的有效性。但这项研究只着眼于少量病例，该病毒在基因上与现在传播的病毒完全不同，而且天花疫苗是一种较老的疫苗，有较多的副作用；MVA是作为一种更安全的替代品开发的。

✎ 基于动物实验的数据和它在人类中引发的免疫反应，MVA被授权用于猴痘。加利福尼亚大学洛杉矶分校的流行病学家安妮·里莫恩说，但是它的疗效几乎没有在人身上进行过测试，也根本没有在预防性传播方面进行过测试，因为性传播会导致"非常显著的黏膜暴露，这与仅仅是跟某人擦身而过是两回事"。

✎ 到目前为止，关于该疫苗在当前的疫情中效果如何，还缺乏数据。法国科学家在最近的一份预印本中报告称，在报告高风险接触后在巴黎一家医院接受注射作为暴露后预防（PEP）的276人中，有12人感染了猴痘。但是没有对照组，因此无法判断如果没有人接种疫苗，会有多少人患上猴

have developed monkeypox if no one had been vaccinated. And people eager to be vaccinated may have lied about having had a high-risk contact. "That makes results from these studies on PEP really hard to evaluate," says immunologist Leif Erik Sander of the Charité clinic in Berlin, who's setting up a vaccine study in Germany.

痘。而且急于接种疫苗的人有可能谎称有过高风险接触。柏林查理特诊所的免疫学家雷夫·埃里克·桑德正在德国进行一项疫苗研究，他说："这使得这些关于 PEP 的研究结果真的很难评估。"

A randomised trial—in which one group receives the vaccine and the other does not—would avoid such problems. Without a randomised study, "you can end up in this evidence limbo and find that if you had just done the trial, you would have been in a much better situation," says virologist Natalie Dean of the University of Florida.

✎ 一项随机试验——一组接种疫苗，另一组不接种——可以避免这些问题。佛罗里达大学病毒学家娜塔莉·迪恩指出，如果没有随机研究，"你可能最终会陷入这种证据困境，并发现如果你刚刚做了试验，你的情况会好很多。"

Giving a control group a placebo instead of a presumably effective vaccine is ethically dicey, many researchers say. But University of Oxford epidemiologist Richard Peto sees another way. Because demand for the vaccine is so much higher than supply, "Why not randomise the order in which people in the highest risk group are called in?" Peto asks. So far, however, no one seems to have taken up that idea.

✎ 许多研究人员表示，给对照组服用安慰剂而不是可能有效的疫苗，这在伦理上是很危险的。但牛津大学的流行病学家理查德·佩托看到了另一种方法。因为对疫苗的需求远高于供应，佩托问道："为什么不随机安排最高风险组人群的接种顺序呢？"然而，到目前为止，似乎还没有人采纳这个想法。

Sander considered a randomised design but decided against it. "There was a lot of pushback," he says. Instead, he has started a so-called cohort study in which he hopes to enroll 5,000 vaccinated and 10,000 unvaccinated people at risk of monkeypox and follow them for 12 months. (Over time, some of the unvaccinated people will receive the shot so the groups may become more similar in size.) So far, about 800 people have been enrolled.

✎ 桑德考虑了一个随机化的设计，但决定不这样做。他说："有很多阻力。"相反，他已经开始了一项所谓的队列研究，希望招募 5000 名接种疫苗和 10000 名未接种疫苗的猴痘高危人群，并对他们进行 12 个月的追踪。（随着时间的推移，一些未接种疫苗的人将接种疫苗，因此这两组人的规模可能会变得更加相近）。到目前为止，已有约 800 人报名。

The groups may differ in ways other than their vaccine status—people with lots of sexual contacts may try harder to get vaccinated, for example—but there is still an element of randomisation, Sander says: Many doctors are using lottery-type procedures to decide who gets the vaccine first.

Another option is a "test-negative" design, in which researchers look at people who seek testing for monkeypox and compare the percentages of people who were vaccinated among those who test positive and negative. This is "probably the strongest nonrandomised approach to measuring vaccine efficacy," says Michael Marks, an epidemiologist at the London School of Hygiene & Tropical Medicine who is planning a vaccine trial soon with colleagues in Spain.

The test-negative setup requires good linkage between vaccination and testing data. "If we can solve that issue we may use such a design in our study," Marks says. The Canadian province of Ontario is going ahead with a similar design, says Jeff Kwong of the University of Toronto. The drawback is that testing and vaccination data alone can't answer many other questions, such as how immunity develops over time or whether disease severity is different among the vaccinated and the unvaccinated; that requires additional studies.

The U. S. National Institute of Allergy and In-fectious Diseases (NIAID) does plan a randomised trial, aimed at finding out if the vaccine supply can be stretched by giving people much smaller doses. Participants will either get two full doses or two one-fifth doses 4 weeks apart; a third arm may be

桑德说，这些群体可能在疫苗状态之外的其他方面有所不同——例如，有很多性接触的人可能会更努力地接种疫苗——但是仍然有随机化的因素：许多医生正在使用抽签式程序来决定谁先接种疫苗。

另一种选择是"检测阴性"设计，研究人员观察寻求猴痘检测的人，并比较接种疫苗的人与检测阳性和阴性的人的百分比。伦敦卫生与热带医学院的流行病学家迈克尔·马克斯说，这"可能是衡量疫苗效力的最有力的非随机方法"，他正计划很快与西班牙的同事一起进行疫苗试验。

检测阴性设置要求在疫苗接种和测试数据之间建立良好的联系。马克斯说："如果我们能解决这个问题，那么我们可以在研究中使用这样的设计。"多伦多大学的邝杰夫表示，加拿大安大略省也在进行类似的设计。缺点是，仅凭检测和疫苗接种数据无法回答许多其他的问题，例如免疫力如何随着时间的推移而发展，或者接种疫苗和未接种疫苗人群的疾病严重程度是否不同；这需要更多的研究。

美国国家过敏和传染病研究所（NIAID）确实计划进行一项随机试验，旨在找出是否可以通过给人们提供更小的剂量来扩大疫苗供应。NIAID的约翰·贝格尔参与了这项研究的设计，他说，参与者将获得两次

added to test one-tenth of the normal dose, says NIAID's John Beigel, who is involved in designing the study. The lower doses will be injected into the skin, which is known to cause a more vigorous immune response than the standard subcuteanous shot. But the study, expected to start in September, will only test whether fractional doses trigger a similar reaction as the full dose; it won't measure vaccine efficacy directly.

One strategy not tested in the trial, even though it is being used, is giving just one full dose. Available data suggest that regimen is inferior to two full doses, Beigel says: "We don't think it's scientifically supported." With so many unanswered questions it's hard to provide good vaccine information to those at risk, says Will Nutland, a U.K community organiser who runs an organisation for MSM sexual health. That should not deter people from seeking the shots, he says: "I think most people understand...that it is better to receive some level of protection than no protection at all."

完整剂量或两次五分之一剂量，间隔 4 周；可能会增加第三次来测试正常剂量的十分之一。较低的剂量将被注射到皮肤中，众所周知，这会比标准的皮下注射引起更强烈的免疫反应。但这项预计将于 9 月开始的研究将只测试部分剂量是否会引发与全剂量类似的反应；它不会直接衡量疫苗的功效。

✎一种未在试验中测试的策略（尽管它正在使用中）是只提供一剂全剂量。贝格尔说，现有数据表明，该方案不如两剂全剂量方案："我们认为它没有得到科学的支持。"英国社区组织者威尔·纳特兰德经营着一个 MSM 性健康组织，他说，由于有这么多未解答的问题，很难为那些有风险的人提供良好的疫苗信息。这不应该阻止人们寻求注射，他说："我想大多数人都明白……接受一定程度的保护总比完全没有保护要好。"

核心词汇

vaccine *n.*	疫苗
例句 There is no **vaccine** against HIV infection. 现在还没有防止艾滋病病毒感染的疫苗。	
stretch *v.*	延伸
例句 Fields and hills **stretched** out as far as we could see. 放眼望去，田野山丘绵延不绝。	
trial *n.*	试验；试用
例句 The new drug is undergoing clinical **trials**. 这种新药正在进行临床试验。	
infect *v.*	传染；使感染
例句 A single mosquito can **infect** a large number of people. 一只蚊子就能传染很多人。	

| **virus** *n.* | 病毒 |

例句 There's a **virus** going around the office. 办公室里流行着一种病毒性疾病。

| **trigger** *v.* | 发动；引起；触发 |

例句 Nuts can **trigger** off a violent allergic reaction. 坚果可以引起严重的过敏反应。

| **outbreak** *n.* | （暴力、疾病等坏事的）爆发；突然发生 |

例句 Vaccine supplies started to run dry as the flu **outbreak** reached epidemic proportions.
由于流感爆发已大肆流行，疫苗供应开始消耗殆尽。

| **drawback** *n.* | 缺点；不利条件 |

例句 The main **drawback** to it is the cost. 它的主要缺点是成本高。

| **fractional** *adj.* | 很小的；很少的；微不足道的 |

例句 The worker was very unsatisfied with a **fractional** decline in earnings.
由于收入有了小幅的下降，这名工人非常不满。

| **regimen** *n.* | 生活规则；养生之道；养生法 |

例句 Few mortals could stick to that harsh **regimen**, especially for years onend.
很少有人能坚持这么苛刻的养生法，尤其是坚持这么多年。

7.5 真题同源文章5

Star's Midlife Crisis Illuminates Our Sun's History—And Future
恒星的中年危机照亮了我们太阳的历史和未来

Soon after European astronomers developed the first telescopes at the start of the 17th century, they observed dark spots speckling the Sun's surface. They also handed their modern successors a mystery. From about 1645 to 1715, the spots, now known to be indicators of solar activity, all but disappeared. Gathering sunspot counts and other

在欧洲天文学家于 17 世纪初开发出最早的望远镜后不久，他们就观察到了太阳表面的黑点。他们也把一个谜题交给了他们的现代继承人。从大约 1645 年到 1715 年，这些现在被认为是太阳活动指标的黑点几乎消失了。天文学家约翰·艾迪收集了太阳

historical observations, astronomer John Eddy concluded nearly 50 years ago that the Sun had essentially taken a 70-year nap, which he called the Maunder Minimum after an astronomer couple who had previously studied it (*Science*, 18 June 1976, p. 1189).

Now, it appears the Sun is not the only star that takes long naps. By building a decades-long record of observations of a few dozen stars at specific wavelengths that trace stellar activity, a team of astronomers has identified another star going through its own Maunder Minimum period. "I am more convinced this is a Maunder Minimum star than anything else I've seen," says Jennifer van Saders, an astronomer at the University of Hawaii, Manoa, who was not involved in the discovery.

The finding, reported in a preprint last month on arXiv, could help explain what triggered the Sun's strange behaviour 400 years ago and suggests more such episodes are likely. "This is the way to study the past and future of the Sun," van Saders says. She adds the discovery supports a theory she and colleagues have advanced: that such events are an occasional symptom of a critical transition in the magnetic field of Sun-like stars about halfway through their lifetime—a midlife crisis of sorts. Some astronomers speculate that the Sun's transition helped favour the emergence of life on Earth, and that searching for stars in a similar stage could help identify other solar systems conducive to complex life.

Scientists have known for decades that our Sun's activity surges and ebbs on a roughly 11-year cycle, which corresponds to how often its magnetic

黑子计数和其他历史观测结果，在近 50 年前得出结论，太阳基本上已经小睡了 70 年，他以一对之前研究过此现象的天文学家夫妇的名字称之为"蒙德极小期"（《科学》，1976 年 6 月 18 日，第 1189 页）。

✒ 现在看来，太阳并不是唯一长时间小睡的恒星。通过创建数十年来对几十颗恒星在特定波长下的观测记录、追踪恒星活动，一个天文学家小组已经发现了另一颗正在经历蒙德极小期的恒星。夏威夷大学马诺阿分校的天文学家詹妮弗·凡·萨德斯没有参与这一发现，她说："比起我见过的其他任何恒星，我更确定这是一颗蒙德极小期恒星。"

✒ 上个月在 arXiv 网站的预印本中报告的这一发现，有助于解释 400 年前是什么触发了太阳的奇怪行为，并表明可能会有更多这样的事件发生。凡·萨德斯说："这是研究太阳的过去和未来的方法。"她补充说，这一发现支持了她和同事们提出的一个理论：这类事件是类太阳恒星寿命过半时磁场发生关键转变的一个偶然症状——某种中年危机。一些天文学家推测，太阳的转变有助于地球上生命的出现，而寻找处于类似阶段的恒星有助于识别其他有利于复杂生命的太阳系。

✒ 几十年来，科学家们一直知道，我们的太阳活动以大约 11 年的周期起伏，这与其磁极翻转方向的频率一

poles flip their orientation. During a solar maximum, sunspots proliferate, marking weak points in the magnetic field, where plasma from the Sun's atmosphere can lash out in violent loops. Astronomers have spotted young Sun-like stars with similar cycles, and older ones that have totally stable activity. But no one had spotted a cycling star suddenly turning flat.

In 2018, as part of undergraduate research at Pennsylvania State University, University Park, Anna Baum set out to combine observations of the telltale wavelengths from 59 stars taken by the Mount Wilson Observatory and the W. M. Keck Observatory to produce a 50-year chronology of star evolution. During a 7-year gap in data while Keck was upgrading a detector, one star appeared to show a drastic shift. Its activity went from cycling over a 17-year period to being virtually flat, and it's stayed that way for the past 18 years.

Baum thought at first she'd made an error; perhaps the observatories were even looking at two different stars. But earlier this year, her colleagues came across additional observations that filled in the data gap, capturing the star's emissions as it switched from active to quiet. The recovered data set "hit the jackpot," says Jacob Luhn, an astronomer at the University of California, Irvine, and lead author on the preprint.

The discovery reinforces one popular theory about why these extended quiescent periods happen. Stars spin more slowly with age because their solar winds act as "magnetic brakes," like a child sticking out their arms while revolving in a

致。在太阳活动高峰期，太阳黑子激增，标志着磁场的薄弱点，来自太阳大气层的等离子体会在那里形成猛烈的环流。天文学家已经发现了周期相似的年轻类太阳恒星，以及活动完全稳定的年长恒星。但是没有人发现一个循环的恒星突然变得平缓。

2018年，作为宾夕法尼亚州立大学帕克分校本科生研究的一部分，安娜·鲍姆着手将威尔逊山天文台和W. M.凯克天文台对59颗恒星的波长观测结果相结合，生成了一份50年的恒星演化年表。在凯克升级探测器的7年数据空白期，一颗恒星似乎出现了剧烈的变化。它的活动从17年的循环变成了几乎持平，并且在过去的18年里一直保持这种状态。

鲍姆起初以为她犯了一个错误；也许这两个天文台甚至在观察两颗不同的恒星。但是今年早些时候，她的同事们发现了其他的观测数据，填补了数据空白，捕捉到了这颗恒星从活跃到安静时的放射。加州大学欧文分校的天文学家、预印本的主要作者雅各布·卢恩说，恢复的数据集"中了大奖"。

这一发现强化了一种流行的理论，即为什么会出现这些延长的静止期。恒星随着年龄的增长旋转得越来越慢，因为它们的太阳风起到了"磁刹车"的作用，就像一个孩子在椅子上

chair. In 2016, van Saders and her colleague Travis Metcalfe of the White Dwarf Research Corporation noticed that at some point, stars stop hitting the brakes and their velocity stabilises—a shift, they proposed, that stems from a change in the stars' magnetic field. Then, last year, Dibyendu Nandi and colleagues at the Centre of Excellence in Space Sciences India pinned down the idea with computer simulations that linked the stabilising of the spin rate to a weakening magnetic field. During this transition, as the star heads toward a "lazy" state in which its activity is flat rather than cycling, random perturbations in its magnetic field can result in temporary cycle shutoffs like the Maunder Minimum, Nandi says.

The theory predicts that this transition state will emerge in middle-aged stars—just like our Sun and this newly identified napping star. "Everything about this discovery has actually corroborated what we've been talking about for the last 5 years," Metcalfe says. "We definitely knew about stars that were not cycling, but we didn't know how they got there—this is like the missing link in that evolutionary picture."

Our Sun's magnetic transition probably began around the same time life on Earth first crawled out of the sea, and that may be no coincidence, Metcalfe suggests. The incoming particles and radiation from active stars damage DNA and promote mutations, speeding evolution. They "may be part of the necessary ingredients to get life started," he says. But at some point, energetic space weather poses a threat to complex life— "like a giant cosmic reset button that's always going off," he adds.

旋转时伸出手臂一样。2016 年，凡·萨德斯和她在白矮星研究公司的同事特拉维斯·梅特卡夫注意到，在某个时刻，恒星停止刹车，速度稳定下来——他们提出，这一转变源于恒星磁场的变化。然后，去年，印度空间科学卓越中心的迪拜恩度·南迪和同事们通过计算机模拟将自旋率的稳定与磁场的减弱联系起来，确定了这一想法。南迪说，在这一转变过程中，当恒星转向一种"惰性"状态，即其活动是平缓的，而不是循环的，其磁场中的随机扰动可能会导致像蒙德极小期这样的临时循环中止。

✎ 该理论预测，这种过渡状态将在中年恒星中出现——就像我们的太阳和这颗新发现的"打盹"恒星一样。梅特卡夫说："关于这一发现的一切实际上都证实了我们在过去 5 年中一直在谈论的事情。我们确定那些恒星没有循环，但我们不知道它们是如何达到这种状态的——这就像进化图中缺失的一环。"

✎ 梅特卡夫认为，我们太阳的磁性转变可能与地球上的生命首次从海洋中爬出来的时间差不多，这可能不是巧合。来自活跃恒星的入射粒子和辐射会破坏 DNA 并促进突变，从而加速进化。他说，它们"可能是生命开始所必需的成分之一"。但在某种程度上，高能空间天气对复杂的生命构成了威胁——"就像一个巨大的宇宙重置按钮总是在响，"他补充道。

Stars undergoing a transition from cycling to stable could provide the ideal balance of spark and protection to nurture life. "If we're looking for technological civilisations," Metcalfe says, "maybe the best place to look is around stars that are in the second half of [their] lifetimes—in other words, just entering a midlife crisis."

✎ 正在经历从循环到稳定过渡的恒星可以提供火花与保护的理想平衡，以孕育生命。梅特卡夫说："如果我们要寻找技术文明，也许最好的地方是在那些处于其生命后半期的恒星周围寻找——换句话说，也就是那些刚刚进入中年危机的恒星。"

核心词汇

astronomer *n.*   天文学家

例句 She was an **astronomer** to help work on the project.
她是来协助帮助完成这个项目的天文学家。

telescope *n.*   望远镜

例句 The **telescope** was pointing in the wrong direction. 这台望远镜对错了方向。

indicator *n.*   指示信号；标志；迹象

例句 Body weight is not always the best **indicator** of health and a thin person still needs to eat well and exercise regularly.
体重并不总是健康的最佳指标，瘦人仍然需要健康饮食，有规律地锻炼。

episode *n.*   一段经历；(小说的) 片段，插曲

例句 The final **episode** will be shown next Sunday. 最后一集将于下周日播放。

occasional *adj.*   偶尔的；偶然的；临时的

例句 He spent five years in Paris, with **occasional** visits to Italy.
他在巴黎度过了五年，偶尔去意大利看看。

speculate *v.*   推测；猜测；推断

例句 It is useless to **speculate** why he did it. 对他为什么这么做妄加猜测毫无用处。

conducive *adj.*   使容易 (或有可能) 发生的

例句 In short, team spirit and effective communication are **conducive** to employee and business performance alike. 总之，团队精神和有效的沟通有利于员工和企业的绩效。

orientation *n.*　　　　　　　　　　　　　　　　　　　　　　方向；目标；定向

例句　Companies have been forced into a greater **orientation** to the market.

各公司不得不转变，更加面向市场。

proliferate *v.*　　　　　　　　　　　　　　　　　　迅速繁殖（或增殖）；猛增

例句　Books and articles on the subject have **proliferated** over the last year.

过去一年以来，论及这一问题的图书和文章大量涌现。

chronology *n.*　　　　　　　　　　　　　　　　按事件发生的年代排列的顺序；年表

例句　Historians seem to have confused the **chronology** of these events.

历史学家好像把这些事件发生的年代顺序搞混了。

transition *n.*　　　　　　　　　　　　　　　　　　　　过渡；转变；变革；变迁

例句　We need to ensure a smooth **transition** between the old system and the new one.

我们得确保新旧制度间的平稳过渡。

7.6 真题同源文章 6

Ancient DNA from the Near East probes a cradle of civilisation
来自近东的古代 DNA 探究文明的摇篮
Studies seek clues to origins of farming, early languages
研究寻求农耕和早期语言起源的线索

Few places have shaped Eurasian history as much as the ancient Near East. Agriculture and some of the world's first civilisations were born there, and the region was home to ancient Greeks, Troy, and large swaths of the Roman Empire. "It's absolutely central, and a lot of us work on it for precisely that reason," says German Archaeological Institute archaeologist Svend Hansen. "It's always been a bridge of cultures and a key driver of innovation and change."

很少有地方像古代近东那样塑造欧亚历史。农业和世界上最早的一些文明在那里诞生，该地区是古希腊人、特洛伊和罗马帝国大片领土的所在地。德国考古研究所考古学家司文德·汉森说："它是绝对的中心，我们很多人正是出于这个原因才研究它的。它一直是文化的桥梁，是创新和变革的关键驱动力。"

But one of the most powerful tools for unraveling the past, ancient DNA, has had little to say about this crucible of history and culture, in part because DNA degrades quickly in hot climates.

✎ 但是，揭开过去的最有力工具之一——古代 DNA，对这个历史和文化的熔炉却没有什么可说的，部分原因是 DNA 在炎热的气候中会迅速降解。

Now, in three papers in this issue, researchers present DNA from more than 700 individuals who lived and died in the region over more than 10,000 years. Taken together, the studies survey the history of the Near East through a genetic lens, exploring the ancestry of the people who first domesticated plants and animals, settled down into villages, spread the precursors of modern languages, and peopled Homer's epics.

✎ 现在，在本期的三篇论文中，研究人员展示了来自超过 1 万年来在该地区生活和死亡的 700 多人的 DNA。总的来说，这些研究通过遗传学视角调查了近东的历史，探索了最早驯化动植物、定居村庄、传播现代语言的先驱以及荷马史诗中人物的祖先。

That narrative is no simple tale. The geneticists, led by David Reich and Iosif Lazaridis of Harvard University, worked with archaeologists and linguists, gathering thousands of skeletal samples and extracting and analyzing DNA, mostly from the dense petrous bone of the ear, over nearly 4 years. They applied better extraction methods and compared new samples with existing data, allowing them to identify even short bits of DNA.

✎ 这种叙述不是简单的故事。由哈佛大学的戴维·莱克和约瑟夫·拉扎里迪斯领导的遗传学家与考古学家和语言学家合作，在近 4 年的时间里收集了数以千计的骨骼样本，并提取和分析了 DNA，这些 DNA 主要是从耳朵的密集岩质骨中提取的。他们应用了更好的提取方法，并将新样本与现有数据进行比较，从而能够识别甚至是短小的 DNA 片段。

Their genetic story starts with the early days of farming, a period known as the Neolithic. Farming began in Anatolia in what is present-day Turkey. But the DNA shows that the people who experimented with planting wheat and domesticating sheep and goats starting about 10,000 years ago weren't simply descendants of earlier hunter-gatherers living in the area. Dozens of newly sequenced genomes suggest Anatolia absorbed at least two separate migrations from about 10,000 to 6500 years ago. One

✎ 他们的遗传故事始于早期的农耕时代，这个时期被称为新石器时代。农业始于安纳托利亚，也就是今天的土耳其。但 DNA 显示，从大约 1 万年前开始尝试种植小麦和驯化绵羊及山羊的人并不只是生活在该地区的早期狩猎采集者的后代。数十个新测序的基因组表明，安纳托利亚在大约 1 万年至 6500 年前至少吸收了两个独立的移民群体。一个来自今天的伊拉克和叙

came from today's Iraq and Syria and the other from the Eastern Mediterranean coast. In Anatolia they mixed with each other and with the descendants of earlier hunter-gatherers. By about 6500 years ago, the populations had coalesced into a distinct genetic signature.

Another genetic contribution came from the east about 6500 years ago, as hunter-gatherers from the Caucasus entered the region. Then about 5000 years ago, a fourth group—nomads from the steppes north of the Black Sea, known as the Yamnaya—arrived, adding to the genetic picture but not fundamentally redrawing it. "The people of the Southern Arc are mostly coming from Levantine, Anatolian, and Caucasus components," Lazaridis says. "The Yamnaya are like a layer of sauce, added after 3000 B. C. E. "

But other scholars question the team's conclusion about the origins of a different cultural shift, the spread of Indo-European languages. Nearly every language spoken in Europe today stems from a common root, shared with Indian languages. Researchers have for years traced it to the Bronze Age Yamnaya, who rode both east and west from the steppes. But the authors of the new papers argue the Black Sea steppe wasn't the birthplace of Indo-European, but rather a stop along a journey that began earlier and farther to the south, perhaps around modern-day Armenia.

Because of similarities between Indo-European and Anatolian languages such as ancient Hittite, linguists had guessed the Yamnaya had left both genes and language in Anatolia, as well as Europe.

利亚，另一个来自东地中海沿岸。在安纳托利亚，他们相互混合，并与早期狩猎采集者的后代混合。到大约6500 年前，这些人群已经融合成一个独特的基因特征。

✎ 另一个基因贡献来自大约 6500 年前的东部，因为来自高加索的狩猎采集者进入了这个地区。然后在大约 5000 年前，第四个群体——来自黑海以北大草原的游牧民族，被称为亚姆纳亚人——来到了这里，这增加了基因图谱，但并没有从根本上重新绘制它。拉扎里迪斯说："南弧的人主要来自黎凡特、安纳托利亚和高加索地区。亚姆纳亚人就像一层酱汁，是在公元前 3000 年后加入的。"

✎ 但其他学者质疑该团队关于另一种文化转变——印欧语言传播——起源的结论。今天，欧洲几乎每一种语言都源于一个共同的词根，与印度语言共享。多年来，研究人员一直将其追溯到青铜时代从大草原向东和向西骑行的亚姆纳亚人。但新论文的作者认为，黑海大草原并不是印欧语系的发源地，而是在更早和更远的南方——也许是在现代的亚美尼亚附近开始的旅程中的一个站点。

✎ 由于印欧语和安纳托利亚语言（如古赫梯语）之间的相似性，语言学家曾猜测亚姆纳亚人在安纳托利亚和欧洲都留下了基因和语言。但是新的分

But the new analysis finds no Yamnaya ancestry among ancient Anatolians. The team suggests they and the Yamnaya instead share common ancestors in a hunter-gatherer population in the highlands east of Anatolia, including the Caucasus Mountains. That area, they argue, is the most likely place for people to have spoken an Anatolian-IndoEuropeanroot language, perhaps between 5000 and 7000 years ago. "That Caucasus component is a unifying type of ancestry we find in all places where ancient Indo-European languages are spoken," says Lazaridis, who is first author on all three papers.

However, Guus Kroonen, a linguist at Leiden University, says this contradicts linguistic data. The early people of the Caucasus would have been familiar with farming, he says, but the deepest layers of Indo-European have just one word for grain and no words for legumes or the plow. Those speakers "weren't very familiar with agriculture," he says. "The linguistic evidence and the genetic evidence don't seem to match."

Throughout, the papers address some critiques of previous ancient DNA work. Some archaeologists have complained that earlier research attributed almost everything—status, identity, power shifts—to pulses of migration recorded in DNA. But the new papers acknowledge, for example, that some migrations into Anatolia may not have been relevant or even perceptible to those living at the time. "That's a response to criticisms coming from the archaeological literature," says Hartwick College archaeologist emeritus David Anthony, who is not a co-author but has worked with the team.

析发现在古代安纳托利亚人中没有亚姆纳亚人的祖先。研究小组认为，他们和亚姆纳亚人的共同祖先是安纳托利亚东部高地（包括高加索山脉）的一个狩猎采集者群体。他们认为，该地区是最有可能使用安纳托利亚—印欧语根语言的地方，也许是在 5000 至 7000 年前。这三篇论文的第一作者拉扎里迪斯说：“高加索的成分是我们在所有使用古代印欧语的地方发现的统一类型的祖先。”

✎ 然而，莱顿大学的语言学家古斯·克隆斯表示，这与语言学数据相矛盾。他说，高加索地区的早期居民应该熟悉农业，但是印欧语的最深层只有一个单词表示谷物，而没有单词表示豆类或犁。他说，这些演讲者“对农业不是很熟悉”“语言证据和基因证据似乎不匹配”。

✎ 自始至终，这些论文都对以前的古代 DNA 工作提出了一些批评。一些考古学家抱怨说，早期的研究几乎将一切——地位、身份、权力的转变——都归因于 DNA 中记录的迁徙脉冲。但新的论文承认，例如，一些迁移到安纳托利亚的人可能与当时的生活者无关，甚至未被察觉。“这是对考古文献批评的回应，”哈特威克学院名誉考古学家大卫·安东尼说，他不是合著者，但曾与该团队合作。

In another example, Yamnaya were buried in elite tombs after they moved into the region north of Greece, suggesting a link between ancestry and social status. But during the later Mycenaean period in Greece—the time Homer mythologised—the new data suggest Yamnaya descendants had little impact on Greek social structure.

Evidence comes in part from the spectacular Mycenaean burial of the Griffin Warrior, a man who died in 1450 B.C.E. near Pylos, Greece. He carried no traces of steppe ancestry, though dozens of both elite and humbler graves in Greece did. University of Cincinnati archaeologist Shari Stocker, who helped excavate the tomb in 2015 and collaborated on the new studies, says the lack of correlation between social status and steppe ancestry is no surprise—and a welcome dose of nuance from geneticists.

The papers also acknowledge the nuances of identity in later periods, for example in Imperial Rome. Previous genetic studies had shown that as the empire coalesced, the ancestry of people in and around the city of Rome shifted, with most having roots not in Europe, but farther east.

✎ 在另一个例子中，亚姆纳亚人迁移到希腊北部地区后，被埋葬在精英墓中，这表明祖先和社会地位之间存在联系。但在希腊迈锡尼后期，也就是荷马神话化时期，新的数据表明，亚姆纳亚的后代对希腊的社会结构几乎没有影响。

✎ 部分证据来自壮观的迈锡尼狮鹫战士的墓葬，此人于公元前1450年死于希腊皮洛斯附近。他身上没有草原血统的痕迹，尽管在希腊的几十座精英和普通人的坟墓中都有这种痕迹。辛辛那提大学考古学家莎莉·斯托克在2015年帮助挖掘了这座坟墓并参与了新的研究。她说社会地位和草原血统之间缺乏关联并不奇怪，而且遗传学家提供的细微差别是受欢迎的。

✎ 这些论文也承认了后期身份的细微差别，例如在罗马帝国时期。先前的遗传学研究表明，随着帝国的合并，罗马城及其周围地区人们的祖先发生了变化，大多数人的祖先不在欧洲，而是在更远的东方。

核心词汇

civilization *n.*	文明

例句 Environmental damage threatens the whole of **civilisation**.
环境的破坏威胁着整个文明世界。

precisely *adv.*	准确地；恰好地；精确地

例句 She pronounced the word slowly and **precisely**. 她缓慢而准确地读出了这个词。

unravel *v.*   解开；拆散；揭开

例句 The discovery will help scientists **unravel** the mystery of the Ice Age.
这一发现将有助于科学家揭开冰川时代的奥秘。

degrade *v.*   （使）退化；降解；分解

例句 Certain irrigation practices **degrade** soil quality and reduce agricultural productivity.
某些灌溉措施会使土壤质量退化，并且降低农业生产力。

narrative *n.*   描述；叙述

例句 The novel contains too much dialogue and not enough **narrative**.
这部小说对话过多，而叙述不足。

extract *v.*   提取；提炼

例句 The team's attempts to **extract** DNA from the 1947 bones all failed.
该小组从1947根骨头中提取DNA的尝试都失败了。

domesticate *v.*   驯养；驯化（动物）

例句 If you **domesticate** this raccoon, it will have trouble living in the wild.
如果你驯养这只浣熊，它在野外生活将会有困难。

descendant *n.*   后裔；后代；子孙

例句 Many of them are **descendants** of the original settlers.
他们中许多人都是早期移民的后裔。

unify *v.*   统一；使成一体

例句 The new leader hopes to **unify** the company. 新领导希望把公司统一起来。

contradict *v.*   反驳；驳斥；批驳

例句 The two stories **contradict** each other. 这两种说法相互抵触。

7.7 真题同源文章7

Researchers Watch How Arctic Storms Chew up Sea Ice
研究人员观察北极风暴如何吞噬海冰
Airborne campaign to study summer cyclones could reveal air-ice interactions
研究夏季气旋的空中活动可揭示空气与冰的相互作用

The storm began somewhere between Iceland and Greenland, as disturbances high and low in the atmosphere united into a full-fledged cyclone. One day later, the vast spiral of winds had grown nearly as big as Mongolia. It was on a beeline for Svalbard, the archipelago between Norway and the North Pole, and heading for the thin floes girding the Arctic's vulnerable pack of summer sea ice. And that made John Methven very, very happy.

这场风暴开始于冰岛和格陵兰岛之间的某处，大气层中高低起伏的扰动结合成一个完整的旋风。一天后，这个巨大的风旋已经变得几乎和蒙古一样大。它正在向挪威和北极之间的斯瓦尔巴群岛进发，驶向北极地区脆弱的夏季海冰群周围的薄浮冰。这让约翰·梅斯文非常高兴。

Last week, Methven, an atmospheric dynamicist at the University of Reading, flew through the storm as part of an airborne campaign based out of Svalbard's Longyearbyen, the world's northern most town. As his Twin Otter plane shuddered through tropical storm-force winds of 100 kilometers per hour, flying just 15 to 30 meters above the sea surface, Methven and the crew took measurements of the ice, water, and air before returning to a bumpy landing on Svalbard. It was the third, and strongest, cyclone that U.K., U.S., and French teams had captured in a monthlong effort.

上周，雷丁大学的大气动力学家梅斯文在世界最北端的斯瓦尔巴群岛朗伊尔城进行了一次空中行动，作为行动的一部分，他飞越了这场风暴。当他的"双水獭"号飞机在每小时100公里的热带风暴中颤抖、飞行高度距离海面仅15至30米时，梅斯文和机组人员对冰、水和空气进行了测量，然后返回斯瓦尔巴群岛颠簸着陆。这是英国、美国和法国团队在长达一个月的努力中捕捉到的第三个也是最强的气旋。

"It's really exciting to get this sequence [of cyclones]," says Methven, leader of the U.K. component of the Thin Ice campaign, the first

"获得这一系列（气旋）真的很令人兴奋，""薄冰运动"英国方面的领导人梅斯文说，这是第一个研究这些

airborne project to study how these summertime storms affect sea ice. "People are going to be pretty pleased."

夏季风暴如何影响海冰的空中项目。"人们会非常高兴的。"

With data from the ice-skimming plane, a second aircraft flying through the tops of the storms, and dozens of weather balloons, the Thin Ice teams hope to learn how these common but poorly understood storms form, function, and chew up sea ice. They also plan to gauge how the properties of the sea ice—smooth, rough, or missing—feed back into the storms themselves. The data should help improve Arctic weather models and sharpen the picture of how summer cyclones may be accelerating the retreat of Arctic sea ice, already on the run because of global warming.

✎ 根据掠冰飞机、第二架飞越风暴顶部的飞机和数十个气象气球的数据，"薄冰"团队希望了解这些常见但鲜为人知的风暴是如何形成、运行和吞噬海冰的。他们还计划测量海冰的性质——光滑、粗糙或缺失——是如何反馈到风暴本身的。这些数据应该有助于改进北极天气模型，并进一步了解夏季气旋如何加速北极海冰的消退。因为全球变暖，北极海冰已经在流失了。

The storms whip up waves that menace Arctic fishing vessels and send storm surges into coastal villages. "A lot of these communities are having to move," says Julienne Stroeve, a polar scientist at the University of Manitoba (U of M). "They're falling into the ocean." The cyclones also threaten the cargo and cruise ships rushing to take advantage of newly ice-free passages in the summer. Better models will "make it safer" to travel the region, says Alex Crawford, an Arctic climate scientist at U of M. "You'll have a better clue to stay in port or go on."

✎ 风暴掀起的巨浪威胁着北极的渔船，并将风暴潮吹向沿海村庄。曼尼托巴大学极地科学家朱利安·斯特罗夫说："很多这样的社区不得不搬迁。它们正在坠入大海。"气旋还威胁到夏季急于利用新无冰通道的货船和游轮。曼尼托巴大学北极气候科学家亚历克斯·克劳福德说，更好的模型将"使该地区的旅行更安全""你将更清楚是留在港口或是继续前行。"

Summertime Arctic cyclones are very different beasts from tropical cyclones: not as powerful but sometimes larger. The aptly named Great Arctic Cyclone of 2012 stretched 5000 kilometers across, spanning the entire Arctic Ocean. With little topographic relief to disrupt them, the storms can wander around the Arctic Ocean for weeks on end. "There's nothing to get rid of them," Methven says.

✎ 夏季的北极气旋与热带气旋截然不同：没有那么强劲，但有时更大。被恰当命名的"2012大北极气旋"，直径达5000公里，横跨整个北冰洋。由于地形起伏干扰很小，风暴可以在北冰洋上连续徘徊数周。"没有什么可以摆脱它们，"梅斯文说。

Hurricanes are fueled by the energy in water vapor rising from a warm ocean, but Arctic cyclones get their spark from horizontal temperature differences. At high altitude, kinks in the polar vortex, a collar of winds 5 to 8 kilometers up that keeps warm midlatitude air separated from cold Arctic air, can start air spinning. Near the surface, temperature differences between the ocean and the ice front, or between land and the ocean, can do the same. When a low-level spin-up meets up with one at the top, they intensify into a cyclone. Other Arctic cyclones are imports—storms from lower latitudes that wind up in the "garbage bin" of the Arctic, Crawford says.

Unlike hurricanes, Arctic cyclones blow across an ocean partly covered by sea ice—with complex consequences for both winds and ice. Early in the summer, the storms' cloud cover can inhibit melting. But by August, as ice thins near the edge of the pack, cyclones can speed melting by pushing floes to warmer waters, breaking up ice into smaller floes that melt more easily, and creating waves that stir up warmer waters. Meanwhile, the rough surface of the ice can act as a brake on the winds. Yet the friction can also help a storm persist by keeping its core stable, Methven says.

Weather and climate models struggle to forecast both the storms and their interactions with sea ice. In early August, two leading models differed by a full day in when they predicted a major storm would arrive, says Jim Doyle, an atmospheric scientist at the Naval Research Laboratory and the leader of the U.S. component of Thin Ice. Methven

✎ 飓风是由温暖海洋中上升的水蒸气能量推动的，但北极气旋是由水平温差引发的。在高海拔地区，极地涡旋中的扭结可以启动空气旋转。极地涡旋是一个 5 千米到 8 千米高的风圈，它能使温暖的中纬度空气与寒冷的北极空气分离。在地表附近，海洋和冰锋之间，或者陆地和海洋之间的温度差异，也可以起到同样的作用。当低处的旋转气流与顶部的旋转气流相遇时，它们就会增强为气旋。克劳福德说，其他北极气旋都是进口的——来自低纬度地区的风暴最终会被扔进北极的"垃圾桶"。

✎ 与飓风不同，北极气旋吹过部分被海冰覆盖的海洋时，对风和冰都有复杂的影响。初夏时，风暴的云层会抑制融化。但到了 8 月，随着冰层边缘附近的冰层变薄，气旋可以通过将浮冰推向更温暖的水域来加速融化，将冰层分解成更容易融化的更小浮冰，并产生激起更温暖水域的波浪。同时，粗糙的冰表面可以起到制动风的作用。然而，梅斯文说，摩擦力也可以通过保持风暴核心的稳定来帮助风暴持续下去。

✎ 天气和气候模型很难预测风暴及其与海冰的相互作用。海军研究实验室的大气科学家、美国"薄冰"研究小组的负责人吉姆·多伊尔说，8 月初，两个主要的模型在预测一场大风暴到来的时间上相差了整整一天。梅斯文说，英国气象局的模型产生的风暴往往会使夏季的冰融化得太快，而欧洲

says the U. K. Met Office's model creates storms that tend to melt summer ice too fast, whereas the model at the European Centre for Medium-Range Weather Forecasts leaves too much ice lingering.

中期天气预报中心的模型则会留下太多的冰。

The models perform poorly in part because data on Arctic conditions are relatively scant, with few weather stations. The models also struggle with the physics of Arctic clouds, which often contain a mix of frozen and liquid droplets. "Getting the balance between the liquid and ice phase is really, really hard," says Ian Renfrew, a meteorologist at the University of East Anglia. Thin Ice's high-flying aircraft will help tune models by gathering detailed cloud data from within the storm.

这些模型表现不佳，部分原因是关于北极条件的数据相对不足，气象站也很少。这些模型在处理北极云层的物理问题上也很吃力，这些云层通常包含冰冻和液态水滴的混合物。东安格利亚大学的气象学家伊恩·伦弗鲁说：“在液态和冰态之间取得平衡真的非常困难。”“薄冰”的高空飞行器将借助从风暴中收集的详细云层数据来帮助调整模型。

The storms are a major driver of sea-ice retreat. The 2012 Great Arctic Cyclone destroyed 500,000 square kilometers of ice—an area the size of Spain, says Steven Cavallo, an atmospheric scientist at the University of Oklahoma, Norman. Cyclones routinely destroy a couple hundred thousand square kilometers of ice and could ultimately be responsible for up to 40% of annual ice losses, he says. "We think it's pretty significant. And it's growing."

风暴是海冰消退的主要驱动力。俄克拉荷马大学诺曼分校的大气科学家史蒂文·卡瓦洛说，“2012北极大气旋”摧毁了50万平方公里的冰层，面积相当于西班牙。他说，旋风通常会摧毁几十万平方公里的冰面，最终可能会造成每年冰面损失的40%。“我们认为这是相当重要的。而且数据还在增加。”

Doyle doesn't see any sign that climate change is creating stronger or more frequent summertime storms, in recent decades at least. But he says warming makes the ice more vulnerable to the regular parade of cyclones. "The ice is thinning, and so the Arctic cyclones are having a much bigger impact."

至少在最近几十年里，多伊尔没有看到任何迹象表明气候变化正在造成更强大或更频繁的夏季风暴。但是他说，气候变暖使冰层更容易受到定期飓风的影响。“冰层正在变薄，因此北极旋风的影响要大得多。”

Models suggest the Arctic will lose all its summer sea ice by 2050, if not sooner. How that will affect the summer storms is "the million-dollar

模型显示，到2050年或者更早，北极将失去所有的夏季海冰。科罗拉多州立大学的大气科学家伊琳娜·沃科

question," says Elina Valkonen, an atmospheric scientist at Colorado State University. Competing forces are at work. The open, warmer ocean is expected to provide more moisture and fuel for storms, but it would also reduce the low-level spin-ups that spark them, by eliminating temperature gradients at what was once the ice front and between ocean and land.

宁说，这将如何影响夏季风暴是"价值数百万美元的问题"。相互竞争的力量正在发挥作用。开阔、温暖的海洋预计将为风暴提供更多的水分和燃料，但它也将减少引发风暴的低水平旋转，因为它消除了曾经的冰锋和海洋与陆地之间的温度梯度。

核心词汇

cyclone *n.*	气旋；旋风

例句 The race was called off as a **cyclone** struck. 由于旋风袭击，比赛被取消了。

airborne *adj.*	空气传播的

例句 Birds in outside cages develop immunity to **airborne** bacteria.
养在户外笼子里的鸟对空气传播的病毒有免疫力。

tropical *adj.*	热带的；来自热带的

例句 The swimming pool is framed by **tropical** gardens. 游泳池四周是热带花园。

crew *n.*	全体工作人员

例句 Rescuers made heroic efforts to save the **crew**. 救援人员不畏艰险，努力营救全体船员。

bumpy *adj.*	不平的；多凸块的；颠簸的

例句 A machine is designed for remote areas with **bumpy** roads and a host of other calamities.
这台机器是为偏远地区崎岖不平的道路和许多其他灾难而设计的。

property *n.*	所有物；财产；性质；特性

例句 Compare the physical **properties** of the two substances.
比较一下这两种物质的物理特性。

accelerate *v.*	（使）加速；加快

例句 Inflation continues to **accelerate**. 通货膨胀不断加速。

retreat *v.*	离开；离去；退去；后退
例句 The flood waters slowly **retreated**. 洪水慢慢地退去了。	
cargo *n.*	（船或飞机装载的）货物
例句 The **cargo** was hoisted aboard by crane. 货物由起重机吊上了船。	
altitude *n.*	海拔；海拔高度
例句 The plane made a dive to a lower **altitude**. 飞机俯冲到了较低的高度。	

7.8 真题同源文章8

Radio Bursts from "Zombie" Black Holes Excite Astronomers
来自"僵尸"黑洞的射电爆发令天文学家兴奋不已
Delayed emissions from black holes that fed on stars earlier
could help explain the formation of powerful jets
早期以恒星为食的黑洞的延迟爆发有助于解释强大喷流的形成

When a hapless star ventures too close to one of the supermassive black holes that lurk at the centre of galaxies, it's torn to shreds and stretched like spaghetti. In this so-called tidal disruption event (TDE), the black hole dines on the stellar remnants, which wrap around the black hole's belly in an accretion disk. During the feast, the black hole can glow brighter than a supernova for months, before returning to a quiet state of hibernation. Or so the story usually goes.

Continued monitoring by patient astronomers has now revealed a few cases in which black holes wake up and belch matter and energy, sending bursts of radio waves toward Earth months or even years after the initial TDE. "What's incredibly

当一颗不幸的恒星过于接近潜伏在星系中心的超大质量黑洞之一时，它就会被撕成碎片，像意大利细面条一样被拉长。在这种所谓的潮汐破坏事件中，黑洞以恒星残骸为食，这些残骸以吸积盘的形式缠绕在黑洞的腹部。在这场盛宴中，黑洞可以在几个月内发出比超新星更亮的光芒，然后再返回到安静的冬眠状态。或者说，故事通常是这样的。

耐心的天文学家们持续监测了现在已经发现的几个例子，在这些例子中，黑洞醒来并喷出物质和能量，在最初的潮汐破坏事件发生数月甚至数年后向地球发出阵阵无线电波。加州

unusual about ［these events］is that the objects came back to life, like a zombie," says Enrico Ramirez-Ruiz, a theoretical astrophysicist at the University of California, Santa Cruz. "This is really challenging the paradigm."

Astronomers aren't sure what's triggering the delayed outbursts, but they think the emissions could help explain the mysterious mechanisms by which black holes convert in falling stellar material into powerful jets that rocket out from their poles. "It's telling us something about the physics of the central engine that's otherwise hidden from us," says Sasha Tchekhovskoy, a computational astrophysicist at Northwestern University. "These jets can explode entire galaxies, so it's a really important process in the evolution of galaxies."

Most of the few dozen known TDEs have been detected from the optical light or X-rays emitted in the initial feast. But, "Radio is now playing a very important role in understanding TDEs," says astronomer Igor Andreoni of the Joint Space-Science Institute. Black holes generate radio waves by expelling plasma—pumping it out in polar jets or belching out material that crashes into surrounding gas. But these outflows normally take place during a TDE, shortly after the black hole rips apart its meal.

In February 2021, however, Assaf Horesh, an astrophysicist at the Hebrew University of Jerusalem, discovered a radio burst that came 6 months after the initial TDE. Then, on 30 June, Yvette Cendes, an astronomer at the Harvard &

大学圣克鲁兹分校的理论天体物理学家恩里克·拉米雷斯·鲁伊兹说："［这些事件］令人难以置信的是，这些天体复活了，就像僵尸一样。这确实是对范式的挑战。"

🖋 天文学家不确定是什么触发了延迟爆发，但是他们认为这些排放可以帮助解释神秘的机制，即黑洞将坠落的恒星物质转化为强大的喷流，从它们的两极发射出去。西北大学计算天体物理学家萨沙·特拉霍夫斯基说："它在告诉我们一些关于中央引擎的物理学知识，否则我们是无法知道的。这些喷流可以引爆整个星系，所以这是星系演化中的一个非常重要的过程。"

🖋 在已知的几十次潮汐破坏事件中，大多数都是从最初的盛宴中发出的光学光或 X 射线中检测出来的。但是，联合空间科学研究所的天文学家伊戈尔·安德里尼说："无线电现在在理解潮汐破坏事件方面发挥着非常重要的作用。"黑洞通过排出等离子体产生无线电波——在极地喷流中把它喷出来，或者把撞向周围气体的材料喷出来。但是这些外流通常发生在潮汐破坏事件期间，即黑洞撕开它的食物后不久。

🖋 然而，在 2021 年 2 月，耶路撒冷希伯来大学天体物理学家阿萨夫·霍雷什发现了一次射电爆发，它出现在最初潮汐破坏事件的 6 个月之后。然后，在 6 月 30 日，哈佛大学和史密森

Smithsonian Centre for Astrophysics, reported finding another delayed flare in a preprint posted to arXiv. Using multiple observatories, she and her colleagues documented a rapid spike in radio activity that launched more than 2 years after the black hole's initial snack. "It's a pretty exceptional case," Cendes says.

Horesh's graduate student Itai Sfaradi may have caught a third example. Reanalyzing a previously spotted TDE, Sfaradi claims in the 10 July issue of *The Astrophysical Journal* that he found delayed radio emissions in combination with an X-ray flare. These tandem emissions are sometimes seen in so-called X-ray binaries—in which star-size black holes suck gas away from a paired star— hinting that the mechanisms may be related, Horesh says.

Shifts in the black hole's accretion disk power the flare-ups from X-ray binaries, and Ramirez-Ruiz thinks the same thing may be happening with the supermassive black holes, months after a TDE. In this scenario, a star's spaghettified gas piles up more slowly over time, causing the accretion disk to grow colder and thinner. Eventually, the disk weakens enough to open an escape path that allows the black hole's magnetic field lines to launch material from the disk into space, where it crashes into surrounding gas and produces radio bursts.

Tchekhovskoy agrees—and he's got models that demonstrate the behaviour. He and colleagues ran computer simulations of accretion disk evolution

尼天体物理中心的天文学家伊维特·山德斯在发布到 arXiv 网站的预印本中报告发现了另一个延迟的耀斑。利用多个观测站，她和她的同事们记录了一个快速的无线电活动尖峰，该活动在黑洞的"最初小吃"发生后两年多才启动。"这是一个相当特殊的例子，"山德斯说。

霍雷什的研究生伊泰·思法拉迪可能捕获了第三个例子。斯法拉迪在 7 月 10 日的《天体物理学杂志》上声称，他对以前发现的一次潮汐破坏事件进行了重新分析，发现了延迟的无线电发射与一个 X 射线耀斑结合在一起。霍雷什说，这些串联发射有时会出现在所谓的 X 射线双星中——恒星大小的黑洞从成对的恒星中吸走气体——这暗示这些机制可能有关联。

黑洞吸积盘的移动为 X 射线双星的爆发提供了动力。拉米雷斯·鲁伊斯认为，在潮汐破坏事件的几个月之后，同样的事情可能发生在超大质量的黑洞上。在这种情况下，一颗恒星的碎片化气体随着时间的推移堆积得越来越慢，导致吸积盘变得越来越冷、越来越薄。最终，吸积盘削弱到足以打开一条逃逸通道，使黑洞的磁场线将物质从吸积盘中发射到太空中，在那里它撞上周围的气体并产生射电暴。

特拉霍夫斯基对此表示赞同——他有一些模型可以证明这种行为。他和同事们对吸积盘的演化进行了计算机

and found they can reach a Goldilocks state in which jets can form efficiently. The key moment comes when the accretion disk is still dense enough to fuel jets, but not so dense as to reabsorb the generated radio waves.

模拟，发现它们可以达到一种黄金分割状态，在这种状态下喷流可以有效形成。关键时刻到来时，吸积盘的密度仍然足以为喷流提供燃料，但密度还不足以重新吸收产生的无线电波。

Perhaps that's why we're seeing these delayed bursts, he says— "We're just waiting for the gas to have the right density. "

✎ 也许这就是我们看到这些延迟爆发的原因，他说："我们只是在等待气体具备合适的密度。"

More clues could come if wide-field radio surveys can capture other zombie awakenings. The Very Large Array, a complex of telescopes in New Mexico, is set to scan the skies for the third time next year, and the Australian Square Kilometre Array Pathfinder will launch a full-sky survey later this year. Both Cendes and Horesh plan to conduct followup radio surveys of TDEs using these observatories, among others. In unpublished works, Cendes has already found what she thinks are several more candidates.

✎ 如果广域射电调查能够捕捉其他黑洞的觉醒，就会有更多线索。位于新墨西哥州的"超大型阵列"望远镜群将在明年第三次扫描天空，而澳大利亚的"平方公里阵列探路者"将在今年晚些时候发起一次天空全域调查。山德斯和霍雷什都计划利用这些天文台对潮汐破坏事件进行后续的无线电调查以及其他调查。在未发表的作品中，山德斯已经发现了她认定的几个候选者。

Discovering a larger population of these TDEs with delayed outbursts would unlock a natural laboratory, enabling theorists to investigate black hole behaviour under a wide range of conditions, Ramirez-Ruiz says. For physicists, he says, "Black hole gastronomy really provides a new playground. "

✎ 拉米雷斯·鲁伊斯说，发现更大的这些具有延迟爆发的潮汐破坏事件将开启一个天然的实验室，使理论家能够在各种条件下研究黑洞的行为。他说，对于物理学家来说，"黑洞美食真的提供了一个新的游乐场"。

核心词汇

formation *n.*	组成；形成

例句 My profession had an important influence in the **formation** of my character and temperament.
我的职业对我的性格和性情的形成有重要的影响。

lurk *v.* 埋伏；潜伏

例句 At night, danger **lurks** in these streets. 夜晚，这些街上隐藏着危险。

shred *n.* （撕或切的）细条，碎片

例句 His jacket had been torn to **shreds** by the barbed wire.
他的夹克衫被铁丝网挂得稀烂。

hibernation *n.* 冬眠

例句 Animals which save energy by **hibernation** or lethargy (e. g. bats or hedgehogs) live much longer than those which are always active.
通过冬眠或昏睡来节省能量的动物（例如蝙蝠或刺猬）比那些一直很活跃的动物活得更久。

burst *n.* 突发；猝发；迸发；爆破

例句 I tend to work in **bursts**. 我的工作劲头往往是一阵一阵的。

initial *adj.* 最初的；开始的

例句 My **initial** reaction was to decline the offer. 我最初的反应是婉言谢绝这项提议。

paradigm *n.* 范式；典范；范例；样式

例句 The war was a **paradigm** of the destructive side of human nature.
那场战争尽显人性中具有破坏性的一面。

mechanism *n.* 方法；机制

例句 Pain acts as a natural defence **mechanism**. 疼痛算是一种自然防护机制的作用。

convert *v.* （使）转变；转换；转化

例句 We've **converted** from oil to gas central heating.
我们已经把中央供暖系统由燃油改成了燃气。

dense *adj.* 密集的；稠密的

例句 The area was covered in **dense** jungle. 这个地区丛林密布。

7.9 真题同源文章 9

The Most Unusual Birds Are also the Most at Risk

最不寻常的鸟类也是最濒危的鸟类

Two studies predict homogenisation of the avian world as climate change and other human impacts continue

两项研究预测，随着气候变化和其他人类影响的持续，鸟类世界将出现同质化现象

It's bad enough that Earth could be losing thousands of species each year. Now, two independent studies of birds have concluded the ones most likely to disappear are those that serve unique—and possibly irreplaceable—functions in their ecosystems. Consider the toucan: Its iconic beaklets can eat and disperse seeds and fruit too large for other birds in South American rainforests. Yet these striking creatures, as well as vultures, ibises, and others with distinctive physical traits, are likely to be the first to go extinct, homogenising the avian world, according to one study. A second predicts communities will grow more alike as the climate changes and species flock to cooler regions.

"That's alarming because we know that diversity of sizes and shapes and behaviours is a signature of a healthy community," says Scott Edwards, an evolutionary biologist at Harvard University. "This is laying out the grim world we are going to be facing."

🖎 地球每年可能失去数以千计的物种，这已经很糟糕了。现在，两项独立的鸟类研究得出结论，最有可能消失的是那些在其生态系统中具有独特的——可能是不可替代的——功能的鸟类。例如巨嘴鸟，其标志性的小喙可以吃和散播种子和水果——这些水果对南美热带雨林中的其他鸟类来说太大了。然而，根据一项研究，这些引人注目的生物，以及秃鹰、朱鹭和其他具有独特身体特征的鸟类，很可能会成为最早灭绝的鸟类，这将使鸟类世界变得单一化。另一项研究预测，随着气候的变化和物种涌向更凉爽的地区，鸟类群体将变得更加相似。

🖎 哈佛大学进化生物学家斯科特·爱德华兹说："这是令人震惊的，因为我们知道大小、形状和行为的多样性是一个健康群落的标志。这是我们将要面临的严峻的世界。"

He and others hope the studies will spur conservationists to think more broadly about what biodiversity means. "The impacts of human actions can actually be worse than what we might think just based on species tallies alone," says Jedediah Brodie, an ecologist at the University of Montana, Missoula. "We haven't focused on what kinds of functions we might be losing," adds macroecologist Marta Jarzyna of Ohio State University.

他和其他人希望这些研究将促使保护主义者更广泛地思考生物多样性的含义。蒙大拿大学米苏拉分校的生态学家杰迪迪亚·布罗迪说："人类行为的影响实际上可能比我们仅仅根据物种统计所认为的更糟糕。"俄亥俄州立大学宏观生态学家马尔塔·贾兹纳补充说："我们还没有关注我们可能会失去什么样的功能。"。

Every ecosystem depends on diverse organisms to fill a variety of roles. Among birds, some eat and disperse seeds whereas others eat carrion, helping recycle remains. Special traits aid these tasks: Pointed beaks help vultures tear into flesh whereas long legs keep wading birds' bodies dry. "When communities are homogenised, they lose a lot of those ecological functions," Brodie says.

每个生态系统都依赖不同的生物体来充当各种角色。在鸟类中，有的吃种子和传播种子；有的吃腐肉，帮助回收残骸。特殊的特征有助于完成这些任务：尖喙帮助秃鹰撕咬肉食，而长腿则使涉水鸟的身体保持干燥。布罗迪说："当群落被同质化时，它们会失去这些生态功能中的很大部分。"

To assess whether birds with certain sets of traits are disappearing, Emma Hughes, a newly minted Ph. D. at the University of Sheffield, spent several years measuring the beak size and shape, lower limb and wing length, and body size of museum specimens of almost 8500 birds from around the world. Working with conservation biologist David Edwards and macroecologist Gavin Thomas, both also at Sheffield, she used statistical techniques to chart similarities and differences among the species based on these traits. Many birds, such as songbirds, clustered together in shape. Outliers included big albatrosses and tiny hummingbirds.

为了评估具有某些特征的鸟类是否正在消失，谢菲尔德大学新近获得博士学位的艾玛·休斯花了几年时间测量世界各地近8500种鸟的博物馆标本的喙部大小和形状、下肢和翅膀长度以及身体尺寸。她与同在谢菲尔德大学的保护生物学家大卫·爱德华兹以及宏观生态学家加文·托马斯合作，根据这些特征使用统计技术描绘物种之间的相似性和差异。许多鸟，如鸣禽，是因为体型归为一类的。体型异常的包括大信天翁和小蜂鸟。

Next, the researchers began to pare down this chart by removing the birds most likely to go extinct, using the International Union for Conservation of Nature's Red List of Threatened Species, which ranks species according to their probability of disappearing. The most threatened species also turned out to be the most distinctive in body shape and ecosystem function, the group reported last week in *Current Biology*. As the researchers sequentially removed species from most to least threatened, toucans, ibises, and other distinctive species dropped out; similar birds—think finches and starlings—remained.

To identify regions where the trend might hit hardest, the Sheffield team analyzed birds in 14 major habitats, such as tropical grasslands. They found that species homogenisation will affect 12 of the 14 and will be most extreme in flooded grasslands and tropical forests. The "most imperiled" regions included southern Vietnam, Cambodia, and the Himalayan foothills, as well as islands such as Hawaii, which has already lost all its distinctive honeycreepers, Hughes notes. "In some cases, there are no other organisms that can replace the unique ecological roles that these species play," Brodie says.

A separate study led by Alke Voskamp, a macroecologist at the Senckenberg Biodiversity and Climate Research Centre, identified another homogenising force: climate-driven shifts in birds' ranges. Her European team mapped the current ranges of 9882 bird species compiled by BirdLife International. Then they applied projections from

🖊 接下来，研究人员开始缩小这个图表的范围，利用国际自然保护联盟的"濒危物种红色名录"删除最有可能灭绝的鸟，该名录根据物种消失的概率进行排名。该小组上周在《当代生物学》上报告说，最受威胁的物种在身体形状和生态系统功能方面也是最独特的。当研究人员按顺序将物种从最受威胁到最不受威胁名录中删除时，巨嘴鸟、朱鹮和其他独特的物种被剔除了；而相似的鸟类——如雀鸟和椋鸟——则保留下来了。

🖊 为了确定受这一趋势影响最大的地区，谢菲尔德团队分析了14个栖息地主要栖息地的鸟类，如热带草原。他们发现，物种同质化将影响14个中的12个，并且在被淹没的草原和热带森林中最为极端。休斯指出，"最濒危"地区包括越南南部、柬埔寨和喜马拉雅山麓，以及夏威夷等岛屿（那里已经失去了所有独特的蜜鸟）。布罗迪说："在某些情况下，没有其他生物可以取代这些物种所发挥的独特生态作用。"

🖊 森肯贝格生物多样性和气候研究中心的宏观生态学家阿尔克·沃斯坎普领导的另一项研究发现了另一种同质化的力量：气候导致的鸟类活动范围的转变。她的欧洲团队绘制了由国际鸟类协会汇编的9882种鸟当前栖息地的范围。然后，他们应用全球气候模

global climate models to predict where those species could find hospitable habitat through 2080, and analyzed how the altered distributions would change the makeup of bird communities. "［Moving］reshuffles the communities," Voskamp says.

As expected, tropical and subtropical regions will likely lose the most species as they either go extinct or shift ranges. A few species will move in, but most are expected to be closely related to one another and to have similar traits, Voskamp and colleagues reported on 19 July in *the Proceedings of the Royal Society B*.

Northern North America and Eurasia will gain species as birds migrate away from warmer regions. But there, too, many of the newcomers will be closely related to species already present, the data showed. For example, the collared flycatcher（Ficedula albicollis）will move farther into northeastern Europe, joining its similar-size cousin, the pied flycatcher（F. hypoleuca）.

Taken together, the papers forecast a more uniform avian world, a sad prospect for birdwatchers as well as a blow to ecosystems. Some evidence suggests homogenisation is happening in amphibians and mammals, too. In the future, "It's the more unique species that will be at a disadvantage," Jarzyna says.

型的预测来预测这些物种到 2080 年可以在哪里找到适宜的栖息地，并分析了改变后的分布将如何改变鸟类群落的构成。沃斯坎普说："［迁移］会重组群落。"

✎ 正如预期的那样，热带和亚热带地区将可能失去最多的物种，因为它们要么灭绝，要么转移范围。少数物种将迁入，但预计大多数物种将彼此密切相关并具有类似的特征。沃斯坎普及其同事于 7 月 19 日在《英国皇家学会会刊 B》上做了以上报告。

✎ 随着鸟类从温暖地区迁走，北美洲北部和欧亚大陆的物种将增加。但数据显示，在这些地区，许多新来者也将与现有物种密切相关。例如，白领姬鹟将进一步向欧洲东北部迁移，加入其体型相似的表亲斑姬鹟的行列。

✎ 总的来说，这些论文预测了一个更加统一的鸟类世界，这对观鸟者来说是一个可悲的前景，也是对生态系统的一个打击。一些证据表明，两栖动物和哺乳动物也正在发生同质化。贾兹纳说，在未来，"更独特的物种将处于不利的地位。"

核心词汇

disperse *v.*	（使）分散；散开；疏散；驱散

例句 The crowd **dispersed** quickly. 人群很快便散开了。

trait *n.*	特征；特性；特点

例句 We call this **trait** sensation-seeking. 我们把这种特质称为寻求刺激。

grim *adj.*	严肃的；坚定的；阴冷的

例句 She looked quite **grim**. 她的表情很严肃。

conservationist *n.*	自然环境保护主义者

例句 Today's explorer must also be a **conservationist**.
今天的探险者还必须是一位自然环境保护主义者。

specimen *n.*	样品；样本；标本

例句 Astronauts have brought back **specimens** of rock from the moon.
宇航员从月球带回了岩石标本。

cluster *v.*	群聚；聚集

例句 The children **clustered** together in the corner of the room. 孩子们聚集在房间的角落里。

compile *v.*	编写；编纂

例句 We are trying to **compile** a list of suitable people for the job.
我们在努力编制一份适合做这项工作的人员的名单。

hospitable *adj.*	好客的；热情友好的；殷勤的

例句 The local people are very **hospitable** to strangers. 当地人对外来客人十分友好热情。

distribution *n.*	分配；分布

例句 They studied the geographical **distribution** of the disease.
他们研究了这种疾病的地域分布情况。

avian *adj.*	鸟（类）的；关于鸟（类）的

例句 Hypotheses regarding dinosaurian and **avian** evolution are unusually diverse—and often at odds with one another.
关于恐龙和鸟类进化的假说有不同寻常的分歧，而且常常互相矛盾。

7.10 真题同源文章10

U.S. to Require Free Access to Papers on All Research It Funds

美国要求对其资助的所有研究论文开放免费查阅

The plan, to start at the end of 2025, is a blow to journal paywalls, but its impact on publishing is unclear

该计划将于2025年底开始实施，这是对期刊付费墙的一个打击，但其对出版业的影响尚不清楚

A decades-long battle over how best to provide public access to the fruits of research funded by the U.S. government has taken a major turn.

关于如何最好地让公众获得美国政府资助的研究成果，一场长达数十年的斗争发生了重大转折。

Last week, President Joe Biden's administration announced that, by the end of 2025, federal agencies must make papers that describe taxpayer-funded work freely available to the public as soon as the final peer-reviewed manuscript is published by a journal. Data underlying those papers should also be made freely available "without delay."

上周，乔·拜登总统的政府宣布，到2025年底，一旦期刊发表了经过同行评审的最终手稿，联邦机构必须向公众免费提供描述纳税人资助工作的论文。这些论文所依据的数据也应"毫不拖延"地免费提供。

Officials are still working out details of the new policy, including how to pay for publishing costs. But it significantly reshapes and expands fiercely contested rules on free access that have been in place since 2013. Most notably, the White House substantially weakened, but did not end, the ability of journals to keep final versions of federally funded papers behind a subscription paywall for up to 1 year.

官员们仍在制定新政策的细节，包括如何支付出版费用。但是，它极大地重塑并扩大了自2013年以来一直存在的关于自由访问的激烈争议的规则。最值得注意的是，白宫大大削弱了但并没有终止期刊将联邦资助论文的最终版本保留在订阅付费墙后长达一年的能力。

Many commercial publishers and nonprofit scientific societies have long fought to maintain that 1-year embargo, saying it protects subscription

许多商业出版商和非营利科学协会长期以来一直在努力维持这一为期一年的禁令，称其保护了为编辑、制作

revenues that fund editing, production, and society activities. But critics of paywalls argue they slow the flow of information, have enabled price gouging by publishers, and force U.S. taxpayers to "pay twice" —once to fund research and again to see the results. Since the late 1990s, the critics have urged policymakers to require immediate "open access" to U.S.-funded research.

The Biden administration heeded those pleas, although the new policy does not expressly embrace the term open access— it uses "public access." But it is "de facto an open-access mandate," says Stefano Bertuzzi, CEO of the American Society for Microbiology (ASM), which publishes 16 journals. And many open-access advocates are applauding it.

"This is an enormous leap forward," says Heather Joseph, executive director of the Scholarly Publishing and Academic Resources Coalition, which promotes open access. "Getting rid of that embargo is huge."

The embargo and related policies "were pure sellouts of the public interest," tweeted biologist Michael Eisen of the University of California, Berkeley, a co-founder of the PLOS journals, which helped pioneer an open-access business model in which authors pay a fee to make their papers free. "The best thing I can say about this new policy is that publishers will hate it."

Many publishers say they support a transition to immediate public access but criticise the policy.

和社会活动提供资金的订阅收入。但付费墙的批评者认为，付费墙减缓了信息的流动，导致出版商哄抬价格，并迫使美国纳税人"支付两次"——一次是资助研究，另一次是看结果。自 20 世纪 90 年代末以来，批评者一直敦促政策制定者，要求立即"开放访问"美国资助的研究。

✎ 拜登政府听取了这些呼吁，尽管新政策没有明确包含"开放访问"一词，而是使用了"公共访问"。但出版 16 种期刊的美国微生物学会首席执行官斯蒂法诺·贝图齐表示，这是"事实上的开放访问授权"。许多开放访问倡导者对此表示赞赏。

✎ "这是一个巨大的飞跃，"促进开放访问的学术出版和学术资源联盟的执行主任希瑟·约瑟夫说。"摆脱这种封锁有着巨大的意义。"

✎ 加州大学伯克利分校的生物学家迈克尔·艾森在推特（注：2023 年 7 月更名为 X）上说，"封锁和相关政策"纯粹是对公众利益的出卖，他是 PLOS 期刊的创始人之一，PLOS 期刊帮助开创了一种开放访问的商业模式，即作者支付费用使其论文免费。"关于这项新政策，我可以说的最好的一点是，出版商会讨厌它。"

✎ 许多出版商说，他们支持向立即公开访问过渡，但批评了这项政策。贝

"We would have preferred to chart our own course to open access without a government mandate," Bertuzzi says.

The Association of American Publishers, a leading trade group, complained in a statement that the policy arrived "without formal, meaningful consultation or public input...on a decision that will have sweeping ramifications, including serious economic impact."

The impact of the new policy could vary depending on which of the more than 20 U.S. funding agencies underwrites the research. Each agency is expected to finalise its policy by the end of 2024 and implement it by the end of 2025.

The policy is not intended to mandate any particular business model for publishing, says Alondra Nelson, acting director of the White House Office of Science and Technology Policy (OSTP). For example, it will not require federally funded researchers to publish only in pay-to-publish open-access journals. Researchers who publish in subscription journals might be able to satisfy the policy by depositing the near-final, peer-reviewed, and accepted version into a public repository, leaving journals free to keep their final version of a paper behind a paywall. (Some researchers say only that published version is adequate for scholarly purposes. The not-quite-final, "author accepted" versions often lack some editing, type setting, and formatted data tables.)

Nelson says OSTP is acutely aware of concerns about who will pay the costs associated with the

图齐说："我们更愿意在没有政府授权的情况下制定我们自己的开放访问路线。"

✍ 美国出版商协会是一个主要的贸易团体，它在一份声明中抱怨说，该政策"在没有正式的、有意义的咨询或公众意见的情况下……就做出了一个将产生广泛影响的决定，包括严重的经济影响。"

✍ 新政策的影响可能会有所不同，这取决于美国20多个资助机构中的哪一个承担了研究。每个机构预计将在2024年底前确定其政策，并在2025年底前实施。

✍ 白宫科技政策办公室（OSTP）代理主任阿朗德拉·纳尔逊说，该政策无意强制要求任何特定的出版商业模式。例如，它将不要求联邦资助的研究人员只以付费方式出版开放访问期刊。在订阅期刊上发表论文的研究人员可能能够满足这一政策，将经过同行评审并被接受的、接近最终版本的论文存入公共存储库，而让期刊可以自由地将论文的最终版本放在付费墙后面。（一些研究人员表示，只有出版的版本才足以用于学术目的。"作者认可"的非最终版本往往缺乏一些编辑、排版和格式化的数据表。）

✍ 纳尔逊说，科技政策办公案敏锐地意识到人们对谁将支付与该政策

policy, especially if publishing in pay-to-publish open-access journals becomes a widespread practice. Some fear the U. S. policy—combined with similar policies adopted in Europe and elsewhere—could accelerate the rise of such journals. That could make publishing more difficult for authors with modest or no grant funding, especially ones who work in underresourced institutions and in developing countries.

有关的费用的担忧, 特别是当在付费出版的开放访问期刊上发表文章成为一种普遍的做法时。一些人担心, 美国的政策——加上欧洲和其他地方采取的类似政策——可能会加速这种期刊的兴起。这可能会使那些只有少量资金或者没有资金的作者, 特别是那些在资源不足的机构和发展中国家工作的作者更难出版。

OSTP wants "to ensure that public access policies are accompanied by support for more vulnerable members of the research ecosystem," it wrote in a blog post. Agencies could, for example, allow researchers to use grant funds to cover publishing costs—as some do already—or fund the expansion of public repositories. "We're not naïve about the challenges we face," Nelson says. "Implementation on any new policy is key. "

科技政策办公室在一篇博客文章中写道, 它希望"确保公共访问政策同时支持研究生态系统中更脆弱的成员"。例如, 机构可以允许研究人员使用拨款来支付出版成本——就像一些机构已经做的那样——或者资助公共知识库的扩展。纳尔逊说:"对于我们面临的挑战, 我们并不天真。任何新政策的实施都是关键。"

The policy reflects the profound changes that began rocking academic publishing 3 decades ago. Then, subscription-based print journals were the primary means of disseminating research results, and publishers fiercely resisted any policy that threatened an often highly profitable business model. But pressure from university libraries upset by rising subscription fees and patient groups angry about having to pay to read taxpayer-funded biomedical studies helped catalyze efforts to change policy. At the same time, the rise of the Internet led to publishing experiments, such as free online journals and the posting of free "preprints" that have not been peer reviewed.

这项政策反映了30年前开始动摇学术出版的深刻变化。当时, 基于订阅的印刷期刊是传播研究成果的主要手段, 出版商强烈抵制任何威胁常规高利润商业模式的政策。但来自大学图书馆的压力 (因订阅费上涨而感到不安) 以及患者团体对必须付费阅读纳税人资助的生物医学研究感到愤怒, 这些促使人们努力改变政策。与此同时, 互联网的兴起导致了出版实验, 如免费在线期刊和发布未经同行评审的免费"预印本"。

In recent years, pressure for change grew. In 2018, a group of European science funders called Coalition Sun veiled a similar open-access policy, which takes full effect in 2025. (Coalition S requires publishers to give up copyright; the U. S. policy does not.) In 2019, the U. S. National Cancer Institute's "Cancer Moonshot" program, which Biden helped create, required grantees to make papers it funded open access. And in 2020, publishers made all papers related to COVID-19 free to read, at least temporarily.

近年来，要求变革的压力越来越大。2018年，一个名为"阳光联盟"的欧洲科学资助者团体宣布了一项类似的开放访问政策，该政策将于2025年全面生效。（该联盟要求出版商放弃版权；美国政策则不需要。）2019年，拜登帮助创建的美国国家癌症研究所的"癌症登月"计划要求受资助者将其资助的论文开放访问。2020年，出版商让所有与新冠肺炎相关的论文免费阅读，至少暂时免费。

The U.S. policy will affect a substantial share of the world's academic literature. In 2020, OSTP estimates federal funding produced 195,000 to 263,000 articles, or some 7% to 9% of the 2.9 million papers published worldwide that year. Bertuzzi says the policy is likely to have a global impact that will be hard to ignore.

美国的政策将影响世界学术文献的很大一部分。科技政策办公室估计，2020年，联邦资金产生了19.5万至26.3万篇文章，约占当年全球发表的290万篇论文的7%至9%。贝图齐表示，这项政策可能会产生难以忽视的全球影响。

核心词汇

manuscript *n.*	手稿；原稿
例句 The original **manuscript** has been lost. 原稿已经遗失。	
contest *v.*	争辩；就……提出异议
例句 The divorce was not **contested**. 这桩离婚案没有人提出异议。	
version *n.*	版本，改编形式，改写本
例句 The English **version** of the novel is due for publication next year. 这部小说的英文译本预定明年出版。	
revenue *n.*	财政收入；税收收入；收益
例句 The company's annual **revenues** rose by 30%. 这家公司的年收入增加了30%。	

| heed *v.* | 留心；注意；听从（劝告或警告） |

例句 I regret that I didn't **heed** his advice.
我很后悔当初没有听他的建议。

| embrace *v.* | 欣然接受；乐意采纳（思想、建议等） |

例句 In response, local manufacturers have been quick to **embrace** automation.
作为回应，当地制造商欣然采纳了自动化进程。

| mandate *n.* | 授权；委托书 |

例句 The election victory gave the party a clear **mandate** to continue its programme of reform.
选举获胜使得这个政党拥有了明确的继续推行改革的权力。

| applaud *v.* | 称赞；赞许；赞赏 |

例句 I **applaud** her for having the courage to refuse. 我赞赏她敢于拒绝。

| implement *v.* | 使生效；贯彻；执行；实施 |

例句 Leadership is about the ability to **implement** change. 领导才能是一种实行变革的能力。

| disseminate *v.* | 散布；传播（信息、知识等） |

例句 Their findings have been widely **disseminated**. 他们的研究成果已经广为传播。

7.11 真题同源文章 11

The FDA and Scientific Priorities
美国食品药品监督管理局和科学优先事项

Earlier this year, when I was confirmed as the new commissioner of the US Food and Drug Administration (FDA), the world faced ongoing public health issues related to the pandemic and war in Ukraine, among other challenges. Most notably,

✎ 今年早些时候，当我被确认为美国食品药品监督管理局（FDA）新任局长时，世界面临着与疫情和乌克兰战争相关的持续公共卫生问题以及其他挑战。最值得注意的是，与其他高收

the US is experiencing a flattening or decline in life expectancy compared with other high-income countries. As part of a wider effort to reverse this decline, relationships between FDA and the biomedical ecosystem should be reimagined to facilitate more effective translation of science into successful health interventions.

The biomedical community's response to COVID-19 has provided multiple tools—vaccines, antiviral medications and other therapeutics; diagnostic testing—that can help prevent infection and transmission and treat patients. FDA's flexibility and guidance regarding compressed time frames for research, development, testing, and regulatory approval were crucial in responding to this ever-changing public health threat. Equally important was the ability to streamline dithecal trials to efficiently produce data that enabled a dear understanding of the risks and benefits for new or purposed therapeutics. FDA will apply these lessons, where relevant, to other areas of biomedical product development. A reciprocal emphasis on reinventing research translation across bionomical sectors is needed to meet the moment.

Despite progress in treating cancer and rare diseases, declines in US life expectancy are driven by common, chronic diseases (CCDs), including cardiometabolic, lung, and kidney disease, along with mental health conditions. Use of tobacco products and increases in deaths due to opioid overdose are also driving negative national statistics. Existing approaches to develop and assess pharmacologic therapies, medical devices,

入国家相比，美国人的预期寿命正在趋于平缓或下降。作为扭转这种下降趋势的更广泛努力的一部分，FDA 和生物医学生态系统之间的关系应该重新构想，以促进科学更有效地转化为成功的健康干预措施。

✎ 生物医学界为 COVID-19 的应对措施提供了多种工具——疫苗、抗病毒药物和其他治疗方法，以及可以帮助预防感染和传播并治疗患者的诊断测试。FDA 在压缩研究、开发、测试和监管审批时间框架方面的灵活性和指导对于应对这一不断变化的公共卫生威胁至关重要。同样重要的是，能够简化双硫醚类药物试验，有效地产生数据，使人们能够深入了解新的或有目的的治疗方法的风险和益处。FDA 将把这些经验教训应用到生物医学产品开发的其他领域。为了应对这一时刻，需要相互强调重新发明跨生物学领域的研究翻译。

✎ 尽管在治疗癌症和罕见病方面取得了进展，但美国人预期寿命的下降是由常见的慢性疾病导致的，包括心脏代谢、肺部和肾脏疾病，以及心理健康状况。烟草制品的使用和阿片类药物过量导致的死亡人数增加也导致国家统计数据出现负值。生物医学界应该重新审查现有的开发和评估慢性疾病和成瘾药物疗法、医疗设备以及干

and interventions for CCDs and addiction, including behavioural techniques, should be reexamined by the biomedical community. While the FDA revitalises its approaches, the biomedical community should also review its priorities so that it can deliver more new therapies in these areas, particularly for those suffering most: racial and ethnic minorities, people with less education and wealth, and those living in rural areas. Consortia comprising patients, researchers, regulators, and the medical product industries are needed, as exemplified by substantial progress in therapies for cystic fibrosis, type I diabetes and multiple myeloma. FDA will focus on translating new science into treatments and diagnostics, working closely with the National Institutes of Health and its grantees, the recently formed Advanced Research Projects Agency for Health, and patient advocacy groups.

Integrating research and clinical care with access to digital information presents enormous potential to benefit the research enterprise and health outcomes. However, societal norms for research participation and data sharing should be revamped, including attention to cyber-attack vulnerability. It is hoped that modernising FDA's digital infrastructure will prompt complementary efforts by the biomedical community to evolve a national digital infrastructure that enables swift, systematic gathering of patient data, collectively yielding detailed understanding of "real world" benefits and risks of medical products. This network should also support faster, more comprehensive approaches to risk-benefit issues for food, where considerations of nutritional value, supply-chain data, presence of toxic substances,

预措施（包括行为技术）的方法。在FDA 重振其方法的同时，生物医学界也应该审查其优先事项，以便能够在这些领域提供更多新疗法，特别是针对那些受苦最深的人：种族和少数民族、教育程度和财富较少的人以及生活在农村地区的人。需要由患者、研究人员、监管机构和医疗产品行业组成的联盟，囊性纤维化、I 型糖尿病和多发性骨髓瘤治疗方面取得的重大进展就是例证。FDA 将专注于将新科学转化为治疗和诊断，与美国国立卫生研究院及其受赠方、最近成立的卫生高级研究计划署，以及患者倡导团体密切合作。

🖉 将研究和临床护理与数字信息的获取相结合，为研究企业和健康结果带来了巨大的潜力。然而，应该修改研究参与和数据共享的社会规范，包括对网络攻击脆弱性的关注。希望 FDA 数字基础设施的现代化将促使生物医学界共同努力，发展国家数字基础设施，从而能够快速、系统地收集患者数据，共同详细了解医疗产品的"现实世界"效益和风险。该网络还应支持更快、更全面地解决食品的风险效益问题，将营养价值、供应链数据、有毒物质的存在、全基因组病原体测序和意向性基因修饰的影响等因素与健康结果相结合。面对全球气候变

whole genorne pathogen sequencing, and impact of intentional gene modification can be integrated with health outcomes. In the face of global climate change, a safe, resilient, and effective food system is a priority. Involving consumers and patients directly in the process of FDA's technology development represents a major opportunity to harness social science and human behavioural research and engage with the public more meaningfully.

化，建立安全、有弹性和有效的粮食系统是当务之急。让消费者和患者直接参与 FDA 的技术开发过程，是利用社会科学和人类行为研究并更有意义地与公众接触的重要机会。

Misinformation has undermined the credibility of science and evidence-based processes that improve societal well-being. The FDA is working to restore public confidence by prioritising clear, direct, and transparent communication as a priority. However, broader efforts spanning the biomedical ecosystem are needed to create an effective consortium that ensures access to truthful information about biomedical science and health.

✎ 虚假信息破坏了科学和循证程序的可信度，这些程序可以改善社会福祉。FDA 正致力于通过优先考虑清晰、直接和透明的沟通来恢复公众信心。然而，需要在生物医学生态系统中做出更广泛的努力，以建立一个有效的联盟，从而确保获得有关生物医学科学和健康的真实信息。

Although FDA's primary mission is to safeguard the well-being of Americans, it operates in a global environment. FDA will continue to work with scientific, public health, and regulatory communities around the world to establish robust information systems for monitoring viral and biological environments, disease transmission, and the safety of medicines and food produced outside the US.

✎ 尽管 FDA 的首要任务是保障美国人的福祉，但它是在全球环境中运作的。FDA 将继续与世界各地的科学、公共卫生和监管机构合作，建立健全的信息系统，用于监测病毒和生物环境、疾病传播以及美国以外生产的药品和食品的安全性。

核心词汇

commissioner *n.*   委员；专员

例句 The mayor appointed a new **commissioner** for the transportation committee.
市长任命了一位新的交通委员会委员。

life expectancy   预期寿命

例句 In recent years, the average **life expectancy** has increased.

近年来，平均预期寿命有所增加。

ecosystem *n.*   生态系统

例句 Researchers are working hard to protect the coral reef **ecosystem**.

研究人员正在努力保护珊瑚礁生态系统。

reimagine *v.*   重新构想；重新设想

例句 The historic district of the city is being **reimagined** as a modern cultural centre.

该市的历史街区正在被重新构想为现代文化中心。

vaccine *n.*   疫苗

例句 **Vaccines** play a crucial role in public health.

疫苗在公共卫生中发挥着至关重要的作用。

revitalise *v.*   使恢复活力；使复兴

例句 The project aims to **revitalise** the economy of the region.

该项目旨在振兴该地区的经济。

infrastructure *n.*   基础设施

例句 The government plans to invest billions of dollars to improve the country's **infrastructure**.

政府计划投资数十亿美元改善国家基础设施。

comprehensive *adj.*   全面的；综合的

例句 The report provides a **comprehensive** analysis. 这份报告提供了全面的分析。

pathogen *n.*   病原体

例句 Scientists are studying a newly discovered **pathogen**.

科学家们正在研究一种新发现的病原体。

resilient *adj.*   有弹性的；适应力强的

例句 Small amounts of trauma can make us more **resilient**, a new study has found.

新的研究表明，少量的创伤能够增强我们的心理复原能力。

credibility *n.*   可信度；信誉

例句 His performance earned him high **credibility** among his colleagues.

他的表现使他在同事中赢得了很高的信誉。

7.12 真题同源文章12

Plant to Mine Metals and Remediate Land
开采金属和修复土地的工厂
Engineered plants can clean up pollution and recover technology-critical metals
工程工厂可以清除污染并回收技术关键金属

Human activities have released significant amounts of metals, metalloids, and persistent organic pollutants (POPs) into the environment. This has resulted in severe consequences for human health, while the reserves of valuable metals essential for technology are depleting. One potential solution to address these issues is the use of specially engineered plants for phytoremediation, which involves the cleanup of polluted environments, and phytomining, a method to recover valuable metals.

人类活动已向环境中释放了大量的金属、类金属和持久性有机污染物。这对人类健康造成了严重后果，而对技术至关重要的贵重金属储量正在耗尽。这些问题的一个潜在解决方案是使用专门设计的植物进行植物修复，其中包括清理受污染的环境和植物采矿，这是一种回收贵重金属的方法。

POPs, such as polychlorinated biphenyls and dioxins, are highly toxic carcinogens that are primarily produced by industrial processes and chemical manufacturing. These pollutants are resistant to degradation in the environment and pose a challenge for remediation. Plant root networks can play a crucial role in addressing these challenges. Additionally, planting in polluted areas can restore biodiversity, improve soil health, reduce pollution exposure, and have aesthetic benefits that are widely accepted by the public. While plants themselves lack the ability to degrade most POPs, they follow a detoxification pathway that leads to the sequestration or incorporation of pollutants into structures such as lignin. This renders the original pollutant

持久性有机污染物，如多氯联苯和二噁英，是剧毒致癌物，主要由工业过程和化学品制造产生。这些污染物难以在环境中降解，对修复提出了挑战。植物根系网络在应对这些挑战方面可以发挥至关重要的作用。此外，在污染地区种植可以恢复生物多样性，改善土壤健康，减少污染暴露，并且具有被公众广泛接受的美学效益。虽然植物本身缺乏降解大多数持久性有机污染物的能力，但它们遵循解毒途径，将污染物隔离或纳入木质素等结构中。这使得原始污染物在生物上无法利用，直到植物生命结束时发生微生物分解。

biologically unavailable until microbial decomposition occurs at the end of the plant's life.

The plant kingdom offers a diverse range of biochemical mechanisms to detoxify xenobiotics. However, in cases where plants lack sufficient enzymatic activities, microbial enzymes can be employed. Genetically modified (GM) plants can be engineered to express microbial xenobiotic-degrading enzymes, expanding their ability to degrade and detoxify organic pollutants. For instance, rice engineered with a specific enzyme has shown effectiveness in degrading pollutants from industrial mine wastes. Similarly, the expression of a bacterial enzyme in switchgrass has been successful in mineralising the military explosive and toxic pollutant RDX. These technologies have been tested on military ranges with positive outcomes.

植物界提供了多种生化机制来解毒外源物质。然而，在植物缺乏足够酶活性的情况下，可以使用微生物酶。转基因植物可以被设计为表达微生物外源降解酶，从而扩大其降解和解毒有机污染物的能力。例如，用特定酶改造的水稻在降解工业矿山废物中的污染物方面表现出了有效性。同样，柳枝稷中细菌酶的表达已成功地矿化了军用爆炸物和有毒污染物 RDX。这些技术已经在军事靶场进行了测试，并且取得了积极的成果。

Critical metals used in various industries, including platinum group metals (PGMs), noble metals like gold and silver, and rare earth elements (REEs), are often geopolitically controlled. These metals are crucial for developing technologies and currently have no viable substitutes, making their supply chains vulnerable to disruptions. Moreover, traditional mining processes have a significant carbon footprint and cause substantial environmental damage. Metal pollution arises from commercial mining, metal smelting and processing, catalytic exhaust emissions along roadside verges, and wastes from artisanal gold mining. While these wastes contain valuable metals, the levels are often too low for conventional mining practices to be economically viable. Additionally, there has been an increase in catastrophic dam failures from mine

各行业使用的关键金属，包括铂族金属、金和银等贵金属以及稀土元素，通常受到地缘政治控制。这些金属对于技术发展至关重要，目前没有可行的替代品，使其供应链容易受到干扰。此外，传统采矿过程会产生大量碳足迹，并对环境造成严重的破坏。金属污染来自商业采矿、金属冶炼和加工、路边催化废气排放以及手工金矿开采产生的废物。虽然这些废物含有有价值的金属，但其含量往往太低，传统采矿方法在经济上不可行。此外，全球范围内因尾矿而造成的灾难性大坝溃坝事件有所增加。植物修复与植物采矿相结合可以帮助恢复裸露的环境、减少大坝溃决并回收贵重金属。这一过程可以由金属含量

tailings worldwide. Phytoremediation combined with phyto-mining can help restore denuded environments, reduce dam breaches, and recover valuable metals. This process can be implemented by small holders in high-metal sites, including challenging-to-access locations, and the recovered "ecometal" can command a premium price.

高地点的小农户实施，包括难以进入的地点，并且回收的"生态金属"可以卖个好价钱。

The process of plant metal uptake begins in the rhizosphere, where plant roots and associated microbes release compounds that solubilise metals in the soil. These metal cations then enter the plant through various transporters. However, uncontrolled concentrations of metals can be toxic, interfering with electron transport activities and generating reactive oxygen species (ROS) that damage cellular components. Metals can also disrupt critical cellular enzyme activities by interacting with sulfhydryl, carboxyl, amino, and phosphoryl groups in proteins. As a result, cellular metal levels need to be tightly regulated. The regulation of influx transporters reduces metal uptake, while efflux transporters pump metals out of plant roots. This mechanism allows certain species known as "excluders" to successfully inhabit metalliferous environments. Once metals are taken up, they undergo detoxification by complexing with chelators. Metals are then transported through the xylem and compartmentalised into the vacuole or cell wall.

✎ 植物吸收金属的过程始于根际，植物根系和相关微生物释放出溶解土壤中金属的化合物。然后这些金属阳离子通过各种转运蛋白进入植物。然而，不受控制的金属浓度可能有毒，会干扰电子传输活动并产生活性氧，从而损害细胞成分。金属还可以通过与蛋白质中的巯基、羧基、氨基和磷酰基相互作用来破坏关键的细胞酶活性。因此，需要严格调节细胞金属水平。流入转运蛋白的调节减少了金属的吸收，而流出转运蛋白则将金属从植物根部泵出。这种机制使得某些被称为"排斥者"的物种能够成功地栖息在含金属环境中。一旦金属被吸收，它们就会通过与螯合剂络合来进行解毒。然后金属通过木质部运输并分隔到液泡或细胞壁中。

While phytoremediation and phyto-mining show promise, there are still challenges and considerations to address. The scale of these processes is an important factor, as it may take several years or even decades for plants to accumulate metals to economically viable levels. Additionally, the choice of suitable plant species for a specific contaminated

✎ 虽然植物修复和植物采矿显示出了前景，但仍然存在挑战和需要解决的考虑因素。这些过程的规模是一个重要的因素，因为工厂可能需要几年甚至几十年的时间才能将金属积累到经济上可行的水平。此外，为特定污染场地选择合适的植物品种对于实现有

site is crucial for achieving efficient remediation or phyto-mining. The genetic engineering of plants to enhance metal uptake and tolerance is an active area of research and development.

Another consideration is the potential for the release of pollutants or metals from the harvested biomass during processing. Proper containment and disposal methods must be in place to prevent secondary pollution. Additionally, the economic viability of phytoremediation and phyto-mining projects needs to be carefully evaluated, considering factors such as the market value of the targeted metals, the cost of plant cultivation and harvesting, and the overall efficiency of metal recovery.

In conclusion, phytoremediation and phyto-mining hold promise as sustainable and environmentally friendly approaches to address pollution and recover valuable metals. Through the use of specially engineered plants or naturally occurring hyperaccumulators, these methods can help restore contaminated environments, reduce the reliance on traditional mining practices, and recover valuable resources. Continued research and development in this field will further improve the efficiency and feasibility of phytoremediation and phyto-mining technologies.

效修复或植物开采至关重要。增强金属吸收和耐受性的植物基因工程是一个活跃的研究和开发领域。

✎另一个考虑因素是加工过程中收获的生物质可能释放污染物或金属。必须采取适当的遏制和处置方法，防止二次污染。此外，需要仔细评估植物修复和植物采矿项目的经济可行性，考虑目标金属的市场价值、植物种植和收获的成本以及金属回收的整体效率等因素。

✎总之，植物修复和植物采矿有望成为解决污染和回收贵重金属的可持续且环保的方法。通过使用专门设计的植物或天然存在的超富集植物，这些方法可以帮助恢复受污染的环境，减少对传统采矿实践的依赖，并回收宝贵的资源。该领域的持续研究和开发将进一步提高植物修复和植物采矿技术的效率和可行性。

核心词汇

remediate *v.*	治理；修复
例句 Efforts are being made to **remediate** the environmental damage caused by the industrial spill. 正在努力治理工业泄漏造成的环境破坏。	
metal *n.*	金属
例句 The mining industry is responsible for extracting various **metals** from the earth. 采矿业负责从地球中提取各种金属。	

pollutant *n.* 污染物

例句 Air pollution is mainly caused by the emission of **pollutants** from vehicles and factories.
空气污染主要是由车辆和工厂排放的污染物引起的。

deplete *v.* 耗尽；减少

例句 Most native mammal species have been severely **depleted**.
大多数本地哺乳动物的数量都已经大大减少了。

biodiversity *n.* 生物多样性

例句 The preservation of **biodiversity** is crucial for the long-term health of ecosystems.
保护生物多样性对生态系统的长期健康至关重要。

pathway *n.* 路径；途径

例句 Education can be a **pathway** to social and economic mobility.
教育可以成为社会和经济流动的途径。

military *adj.* 军事的；军用的

例句 The country has a strong **military** presence in the region.
这个国家在该地区拥有强大的军事力量。

contaminate *v.* 污染

例句 The water supply was **contaminated** with harmful bacteria. 饮用水被有害细菌污染了。

disposal *n.* 处置；处理

例句 Proper **disposal** of hazardous waste is essential to the environment.
妥善处理危险废物对环境至关重要。

cultivation *n.* 种植；培养

例句 The **cultivation** of crops requires fertile soil and favourable weather conditions.
农作物的种植需要肥沃的土壤和有利的气候条件。

toxic *adj.* 有毒的；有害的

例句 Exposure to **toxic** chemicals can have severe health consequences.
暴露在有毒化学物质中可能会造成严重的健康后果。

compound *n.* 化合物

例句 Chemical **compounds** are formed when two or more elements combine chemically.
化学化合物是由两个或更多元素化学结合而成的。

7.13 真题同源文章13

The New Storytellers
新的故事讲述者
Computer-crafted tales offer insight into human creativity
计算机创作的故事让人了解人类的创造力

Storytelling is an essential feature of the human condition, propose Mike Sharples and Rafael Pérez in *Story Machines*. It allows us to make meaning in the world and in our lives, to communicate with one another, to teach, to learn, and to explore. The book, which provides a readable, engaging, and instructive introduction to the mechanisms according to which computers have been made to produce "stories", also confronts more fundamental questions: What constitutes our own creativity? Can stories do their cultural work without connecting a reader to a human writer? If computers cannot understand, appreciate, or intend the meaning of their compositions, does that limit their creative potential and the work they might do?

The landscape of artificial intelligence (AI) literature so often tends toward over-confidence, even hubris, but Sharples and Pérez, refreshingly, do not claim to answer these questions in the book, although they remain at the heart of the project, nor do the pair pronounce what the future will or should be for computerised writing. The authors are as interested in what can be learned about people as storytellers and meaning-makers as they are in the automation of literary composition.

迈克·沙普勒斯和拉斐尔·佩雷兹在《故事机器》一书中提出，讲故事是人类生活的一个基本特征。它使我们能够在世界和生活中创造意义，相互交流、教学、学习和探索。这本书以可读性、吸引力和指导性的方式介绍了计算机制造"故事"的机制，同时也提出了一些更基本的问题：什么是我们自己的创造力？如果不将读者与人类作家联系起来，故事能发挥其文化作用吗？如果计算机无法理解、欣赏其作品或了解其意图，这是否会限制它们的创造潜力和它们可能完成的工作？

人工智能（AI）文学作品往往过于自信，甚至妄自尊大，但令人耳目一新的是，沙普勒斯和佩雷兹并没有声称要在书中回答这些问题，尽管它们仍然是项目的核心，两人也没有宣布计算机化写作的未来将会或者应该是怎样的。作者们既对文学创作的自动化感兴趣，也对作为故事讲述者和意义创造者的人的知识感兴趣。

The book begins with an engaging survey of historical, cognitive, and cultural perspectives on human storytelling and a discussion of the long tradition of attempts to automate the production of compelling stories. Readers are then taken through a detailed exploration of the main approaches to AI-driven story production, which doubles as an accessible introduction to different approaches to AI in general.

✎ 本书首先对人类讲故事的历史、认知和文化视角进行了有趣的梳理，并讨论了将引人入胜的故事创作自动化的悠久传统。然后，作者带领读者详细探讨了人工智能驱动创作故事的主要方法，并对人工智能的不同方法进行了通俗易懂的介绍。

We meet researchers who have sought to identify a set of rules, or grammars, informed by both linguistics and the formal study of myths, fairy tales, and novels, that could be translated into computer programs. As with most other domains of AI research that seek to convincingly simulate complex human behaviour according to a set of rules in this fashion, the stories produced by rule-bound generators tend to be disappointing.

✎ 我们遇到过一些研究人员，他们试图找出一套可以转化为计算机程序的规则或语法，而这些规则或语法既有语言学方面的知识，也有对神话、童话和小说的正规研究。与人工智能研究的其他大多数领域一样，这些领域试图以这种方式令人信服地根据一系列规则模拟复杂的人类行为，但规则约束生成的故事往往令人失望。

The authors then introduce more advanced strategies, such as neural networks, which are trained on massive data sets（in this case, of existing stories and prose）. Such approaches—which empower algorithms to generate their own protocols on the basis of patterns and correlations they identify in the data, allowing for predictions about how to construct effective sentences, plots, characters, and structures—can produce far more compelling stories, but they often come at the cost of our access and understanding.

✎ 随后，作者介绍了更先进的策略，例如基于海量数据集（这里指已有的故事和散文）训练的神经网络系统。这些方法能让算法根据它们在数据中识别出的模式和相关性生成自己的协议，从而预测如何构建有效的句子、情节、人物和结构，这样能产生更引人入胜的故事，但它们往往以我们的访问和理解为代价。

For Sharples and Pérez, the goal of automation is not just to find any means to produce compelling computer story generation; they seek automated tools that can report on themselves, thereby

✎ 对沙普勒斯和佩雷兹来说，自动化的目标不仅仅是找到方法来生成引人入胜的计算机故事。他们寻求的是能够自我报告的自动化工具，从而促进

facilitating a refined understanding of human creativity. This, they believe, could allow for new forms of storytelling, creative collaboration, and readership. The authors praise methods of story automation that are based on both active models of human creativity and the construction of what they call "story worlds", which consist of places, characters, and constraints that a computer might explore and tell stories within and about.

One of the most valuable features of the book is its rich presentation of examples. Readers come away having read nearly 100 instances of mechanically and computationally generated stories, which provide a clear sense of the variety of approaches and the kind of story they produce. Readers are even invited at several moments to experiment with these methods themselves. The authors also integrate computer-generated prose into the book's text, which serves as a frequent reminder that the act of reading may shift and transform as automation and authorship converge in different ways.

The book largely frames auto-mated storytelling as a benign, creative, intellectual, and exciting field. However, it also hints at darker and deeply concerning possibilities. The authors mention believable computer generation of fake news stories, targeted custom narrative production that could infiltrate our Internet browsing, fabricated texts made to convincingly read like those written by specific people, and many other potentially exploitative and extractive applications. Indeed, the most powerful tools for automated story production described in the book have been developed by entities such as Microsoft's Open AI and Facebook,

对人类创造力的深入理解。他们认为，这将带来新形式的故事创作、创意合作和读者群。作者推崇的故事自动化方法既基于人类创造力的主动模型，也基于他们所称的"故事世界"的构建。"故事世界"由地点、人物和约束条件组成，计算机可以在其中探索并讲述故事。

✎ 本书最有价值的特点之一就是列举了丰富的实例。读者在阅读了近100个机械和计算生成的故事后，可以清楚地感受到各种方法及其产生的故事类型。读者甚至数次被邀请亲自尝试这些方法。作者还将计算机生成的散文融入书中的文字，这经常提醒人们，随着自动化和作者身份以不同的方式融合，阅读行为可能会发生转变。

✎ 本书在很大程度上将自动匹配的叙事方式描绘成一个良性的、富有创造力的、智慧的和令人兴奋的领域。然而，它也暗示了更灰暗、更令人深感忧虑的潜在可能。作者提到了由可信计算机生成的假新闻故事、有针对性的定制化叙事制作（可以渗透到我们的互联网浏览中）、以令人信服的方式编造读起来像是特定的人写出的文本，以及许多其他潜在的剥削和榨取性应用。事实上，本书中描述的最强大的自动故事制作工具是由微软的 Open AI 和 Facebook 等实体开发的，

which have a reputation for prioritising power, control, and profit over all else. The main drawback of the book is that it attends only in passing, and almost hesitantly, to these realities.

这些实体以优先考虑权力、控制和利益而著称。本书的主要缺点是，它只是顺便地、几乎是犹豫地关注了这些现实问题。

核心词汇

insight *n.*	洞察力；领悟

例句 The project would give scientists new **insights** into what is happening to the earth's atmosphere.
该项目将使科学家对地球大气层的状况有更新的深入了解。

cognitive *adj.*	认知的

例句 As children grow older, their **cognitive** processes become sharper.
孩子们越长越大，他们的认知过程变得更为敏锐。

accessible *adj.*	易到达的；易进入的；易够到的

例句 The centre is easily **accessible** to the general public. 普通大众可随意进入该中心。

collaboration *n.*	合作；协作

例句 She wrote the book in **collaboration** with one of her students.
她和她的一个学生合写了这本书。

integrate *v.*	（使）加入；（使）融入

例句 He didn't **integrate** successfully into the Italian way of life.
他没有顺利地融入意大利的生活方式中。

infiltrate *v.*	渗透；潜入

例句 Rebel forces were **infiltrated** into this area. 反叛力量潜入了这个地区。

drawback *n.*	缺点；缺陷

例句 He felt the apartment's only **drawback** was that it was too small.
他觉得这间公寓唯一的缺点就是太小了。

| linguistics *n.* | 语言学 |

例句 Modern **linguistics** emerged as a distinct field in the nineteenth century.
现代语言学是在 19 世纪作为一个独立的领域出现的。

| artificial *adj.* | 人工的；人造的 |

例句 The juice contains no **artificial** preservatives. 这种果汁不含人工防腐剂。

| automation *n.* | 自动化 |

例句 **Automation** meant the loss of many factory jobs. 自动化意味着许多工厂的工人失业。

7.14 真题同源文章14

Sparkling Waters
波光粼粼的水域

In the 18th century, the French naturalist Godeheu de Riville was sailing across the Indian Ocean when he came upon a remarkable sight. The sea "was covered over with small stars; every wave which broke about us dispersed a most vivid light, in complexion like that of a silver tissue electrified in the dark," he recounted in his journal. When de Riville examined the sparkling water with his microscope, he discovered that the "small stars" were tiny crustaceans now known as ostracods.

18 世纪，法国博物学家戈德霍·德·里维尔在印度洋上航行时，发现了一个奇特的景象。他在日记中记述道："海面上布满了小星星；我们周围的每一朵浪花都散射出极其耀眼的光芒，其颜色就像在黑暗中通电的银色组织。"当德里维尔用显微镜观察波光粼粼的海水时，他发现这些"小星星"是现在被称为介形虫的微小甲壳类动物。

Centuries later, in 1980, marine biologist James Morin was scuba diving just after sunset in the Virgin Islands when he noticed bright blue dots blinking on and off several meters away. When he shone his flashlight through the water, he saw scores of ostracods flitting across its beam. After multiple

几个世纪后的 1980 年，海洋生物学家詹姆斯·莫林在维尔京群岛日落后潜水时，注意到几米外有明亮的蓝点一闪一闪。当他用手电筒照向水面时，他看到数十只介形虫在光束中飞舞。多次潜水后，他发现这些闪光并

dives, he discerned that the flashes weren't random. The ostracods lit up in specific patterns in space and time, much like the courtship flashes of fireflies that light up summertime meadows. The realisation changed the course of Morin's career.

不是随机的。介形虫在空间和时间上以特定的模式发光，很像萤火虫求偶时照亮夏日草地的闪烁光芒。这一发现改变了莫林的职业生涯。

Now a professor emeritus at Cornell University, Morin has spent the past 4 decades working with a small, dedicated group of colleagues to unravel the mysteries of what they describe as the most spectacular natural wonder that most people will never see. Male ostracods only display for about an hour, shortly after sunset on moonless nights in warm Caribbean seas. Most recreational divers don't dive at night, and those who do tend to use lights, which prompt the creatures to switch off for the evening.

✎ 莫林现在是康奈尔大学的名誉教授，在过去的 40 年里，他和一小群敬业的同事一起，努力揭开这个被他们称为"多数人不会见到的最壮观自然奇观"的神秘面纱。雄性介形虫只在加勒比海温暖的无月之夜日落后不久出现大约一个小时。大多数休闲潜水者都不在夜间潜水，而那些潜水的人往往会使用灯光，这就促使这些生物在晚上"熄灯"。

No bigger than a grain of sand, ostracods abound in fresh and saltwater. "They are very cute but also sort of bizarre—like a cross between a crab and a tiny spaceship," says Timothy Fallon, an evolutionary biochemist at the University of California (UC), San Diego.

✎ 介形虫比一粒沙子大不了多少，在淡水和海水中比比皆是。加州大学圣地亚哥分校的进化生物化学家蒂莫西·法伦说："它们非常可爱，但也有点儿怪异，就像螃蟹和小飞船的杂交体。"

Only seagoing ostracods are bioluminescent, and it's not their bodies that glow. Rather they spew out glowing mucus. In most of the world's oceans, ostracods do this for defense—to startle and distract would-be predators. But in the Caribbean, and only in the Caribbean, as Morin and colleagues discovered, those bright blue dots can double as mating calls. Today, thousands of dives later, they believe those signals have driven Caribbean ostracods to diversify into more than 100 species.

✎ 只有海生介形虫才会发出生物荧光，而且发光的不是它们的身体。相反，它们会喷出发光的黏液。在世界上大多数海洋中，介形虫这么做是为了防御——惊吓和分散潜在捕食者的注意力。但在加勒比海，也只有在加勒比海，莫林及其同事发现，这些明亮的蓝点同时可以作为求偶之舞。如今，在数千次潜水之后，他们相信这些信号已经促使加勒比海的介形虫多样化，形成了 100 多个物种。

With modern genetic tools, they've been using these creatures to investigate the factors that wedge species apart, including sexual selection, driven by female preferences; geographic isolation; and genetic drift—the accumulation of random genetic changes. In just the past 2 years, researchers have figured out how to grow ostracods in the lab, a development that will allow them to dissect the molecular mechanisms of evolution in a way once possible only in more conventional lab animals such as nematodes and fruit flies.

"The ability to ask interesting questions about evolutionary patterns across multiple species is a powerful tool," says Christopher Cratsley, a behavioural ecologist at Fitchburg State University who works on fireflies. Ostracods are an "elegant system" for doing so, he says. The mechanics and biochemistry of their light flashes are relatively simple, and many species of ostracods overlap in small areas. Compared with other animals with complex mating rituals—songbirds, say—they may more readily yield clues about the forces that generate biological diversity.

In Japan, dried ostracods are popular as curiosities because they glow when rehydrated. They're called umi-hotaru— "sea fireflies" —and in the first half of the 20th century, they caught the eye of Princeton University biochemist E. Newton Harvey. He used dried ostracods to work out the basic biochemistry of bioluminescence, which has evolved independently about 100 times. Organisms as disparate as bacteria, fungi, fish, and insects use it to evade predators, attract prey, or communicate with their own kind. For several, such as fireflies, it's a means

借助现代基因工具，他们一直在利用这些生物研究导致物种分化的因素，包括由雌性偏好驱动的性选择、地理隔离和遗传漂移——随机遗传变化的累积。仅在过去的两年里，研究人员就弄清了如何在实验室里培育介形虫，这一进展将使他们能够以一种曾经只能在线虫和果蝇等更传统的实验动物身上才能实现的方式来剖析进化的分子机制。

菲奇堡州立大学研究萤火虫的行为生态学家克里斯托弗·克拉兹利说："能够就多个物种的进化模式提出有趣的问题是一种强大的工具。"他说，介形虫是一个"优雅的系统"。它们闪光的机制和生物化学原理相对简单，而且许多种类的介形虫会在小范围内重叠。与其他具有复杂交配仪式的动物——比如鸣禽——相比，它们可能更容易提供关于产生生物多样性力量的线索。

在日本，干介形虫作为奇特生物很受欢迎，因为它们在重新水合后会发光。它们被称为"海萤火虫"。在20世纪上半叶，它们引起了普林斯顿大学生物化学家 E. 牛顿·哈维的注意。他利用干介形虫研究出了生物发光的基本生物化学原理，这种生物发光已经独立进化了大约 100 次。细菌、真菌、鱼类和昆虫等截然不同的生物都利用生物发光来躲避捕食者、吸引猎物或与同类交流。对萤火虫等生物来

of courtship.

In the Caribbean, the light show takes place underwater. When male ostracods sense the water is dark enough, they take off from the reef or seagrass bed where they spend most of their time and begin their display. Females swim toward the flashes, as do nonflashing males racing to intercept them.

To watch the spectacle, sea firefly researchers in scuba gear position themselves on the sea floor just after dark, using red lights to find their way. It's an eerie experience. At night, shallow reefs resound with snapping shrimp and the crunch of parrot fish chomping on coral. Deeper waters are spookily quiet.

In the early days, biologists used a night vision monocular attached to a VHS camera to capture the displays. The images were grainy and had a limited field of view. "It was very hard to see a whole display," says Gretchen Gerrish, one of Morin's first sea firefly graduate students and now an evolutionary ecologist at the University of Wisconsin, Madison. The video equipment has improved, but even now researchers often take waterproof notes by writing on pieces of PVC pipe with a mechanical pencil. A rubber band, rolled down a finger's width after each line, helps them keep their place. After documenting a display, they swim to the flashes and scoop up the creatures with a net.

Back in the lab—often a makeshift setup in a hotel room—they sort through their catch and examine their collected ostracods under a microscope to identify the species. Sometimes a subtle difference in the shape and size of the

说，这是求偶的一种手段。

✎ 在加勒比海，灯光秀在水下进行。当雄性介形虫感觉水足够暗时，它们就会从珊瑚礁或海草床（它们大部分时间都待在这些地方）起飞，并开始表演。雌性介形虫游向闪光处时，不闪光的雄性介形虫会竞相拦截。

✎ 为了观看这一奇观，海萤火虫研究人员在夜幕降临后穿着潜水装备，在海底用红灯指引方向。这是一种奇异的体验。夜晚，浅礁上回荡着虾的鸣叫声和鹦鹉鱼啃咬珊瑚的嘎吱声。深海则安静得令人毛骨悚然。

✎ 早期，生物学家使用夜视单筒望远镜连接 VHS 摄像机来捕捉这些景象。这些图像模糊不清，而且视野有限。莫林的第一批海萤火虫研究生之一、现为威斯康星大学麦迪逊分校进化生态学家的格雷琴·格里什说："很难看到整个表演过程。"虽然视频设备已经有所改进，但即使是现在，研究人员也经常用机械铅笔在 PVC 管上写下防水笔记。每写完一行，就用橡皮筋卷起一指宽，帮助他们保持自己的位置。记录完表演后，他们游到闪光处，用网捞起这些生物。

✎回到实验室（通常是在酒店房间里临时搭建的）后，他们将捕获的介形虫分类，并在显微镜下检查收集到的介形类，以确定物种。有时，生殖器官的形状和大小或身体各部分相对比

reproductive organs or in the relative proportions of body parts is all that distinguishes one species from another. So far, they've named more than 20 species; about 100 more await formal description.

例的细微差别就是区分一个物种和另一个物种的唯一标准。到目前为止，他们已经命名了 20 多个物种，还有大约 100 个物种等待正式的描述。

核心词汇

disperse *v.*	分散；散布；疏散

例句　Police used tear gas to **disperse** the crowds. 警察使用催泪瓦斯驱散人群。

unravel *v.*	（使）解开；（使）松开

例句　He could **unravel** a knot that others wouldn't even attempt.
他可以解开他人甚至不敢尝试的绳结。

recreational *adj.*	娱乐的；消遣的

例句　These areas are set aside for public **recreational** use.
这些区域已经划出来用于公共娱乐。

bizarre *adj.*	奇异的；古怪的

例句　He tends to write **bizarre** and highly experimental pieces of music.
他倾向于创作具有高度试验性且风格奇异的音乐作品。

conventional *adj.*	依照惯例的，遵循习俗的

例句　It has taken me a long time to break out of my own **conventional** training.
我花了很长时间才摆脱掉自身所受的传统训练的羁绊。

disparate *adj.*	迥然不同的；多元的

例句　Scientists are trying to pull together **disparate** ideas in astronomy.
科学家正试图把天文学界各种迥然不同的观点汇集起来。

chomp *v.*	大声地吃

例句　On the diet I would **chomp** my way through breakfast, even though I'm never hungry in the morning. 我的饮食习惯是大口地吃早餐，尽管我早上从来不饿。

spectacle *n.*	精彩的表演，壮观的场面

例句　The sunset was a stunning **spectacle**. 夕阳西斜，异常壮观。

evade *v.*	规避，逃避

例句 She is trying to **evade** all responsibility for her behaviour.
她在试图逃避应为自己行为承担的所有责任。

distinguish *v.*	使有别于；看清；认出；区别；分清

例句 It is very important to **distinguish** fact from fiction.
区别真实和虚构是很重要的。

7.15 真题同源文章15

Carbon Dioxide Is Detected Around Alien World for First Time
首次在外星世界探测到二氧化碳

Astronomers have found carbondioxide (CO_2) in the atmosphere of a Saturn-size planet 700 light-years away—the first unambiguous detection of the gas in a planet beyond the Solar System. The discovery, made by the James Webb Space Telescope, provides clues to how the planet formed. The result also shows just how quickly Webb may identify a spate of other gases, such as methane and ammonia, which could hint at a planet's potential habitability for life.

Webb is "ushering in this new era of the atmospheric science of exoplanets", says Nikku Madhusudhan of the University of Cambridge, who was not involved in the study.

The Webb telescope is sensitive to infrared wavelengths of light that are mostly blocked by Earth's atmosphere. It has already dazzled

✎ 天文学家在700光年外一颗土星大小的行星大气层中发现了二氧化碳（CO_2），这是首次在太阳系外的行星中明确探测到了这种气体。这一发现是由詹姆斯·韦伯太空望远镜完成的，为了解这颗行星是如何形成的提供了线索。这一结果还表明，韦伯可能以多快的速度发现一系列其他气体，如甲烷和氨气，这些气体可能暗示行星是否具有潜在的生命宜居性。

✎ 没有参与这项研究的剑桥大学的尼库·马德胡苏丹说："韦伯正在开创系外行星大气科学的新时代。"

✎ 韦伯望远镜对大部分被地球大气层遮挡的红外波段的光非常敏感。它能够将宇宙中最遥远的恒星和星系呈

astronomers with its ability to bring the universe's most distant stars and galaxies into view.

现在天文学家眼前，这已经让他们眼花缭乱了。

But the infrared sensitivity is also critical for researchers studying worlds much closer to home, in the Milky Way. When an exoplanet's orbit takes it in front of its star, some of the starlight passes through the planet's atmosphere and carries fingerprints of its composition. The atmospheric gases absorb specific wavelengths of light, which show up as dips in brightness when the starlight is spread out into a spectrum.

✎ 但是，红外敏感度对于研究银河系中离家更近的世界的研究人员来说也是至关重要的。当系外行星的轨道运行到恒星前方时，部分星光会穿过行星的大气层，并携带有行星成分的指纹。大气中的气体会吸收特定波长的光，当星光散射成光谱时，这些气体就会显示出亮度的下降。

For most gases of interest, the dips occur at infrared wavelengths. The Hubble Space Telescope and its infrared sibling, the Spitzer Space Telescope, have detected water vapor, methane, and carbon monoxide around a few hot, giant exoplanets, but little more.

✎ 对于大多数相关气体来说，亮度衰减发生在红外线波长处。哈勃太空望远镜和它的红外同胞兄弟斯皮策太空望远镜已经在几颗炙热的巨型系外行星周围探测到了水蒸气、甲烷和一氧化碳，但几乎没有探测到更多物质。

Webb promises to reveal many more gases in smaller Neptune-size planets and potentially even rocky planets similar in size to Earth, although it is unlikely to be able to confirm the existence of life.

✎ 韦伯有望揭示更多海王星大小的小行星中的气体，甚至有可能揭示与地球大小相似的岩石行星，尽管它不太可能证实生命的存在。

For its first exoplanet observations, astronomers targeted the hot gas giant WASP-39b, which orbits its star every 4 days in an orbit much tighter than Mercury's. The first data were taken on 10 July and the team started work on them a few days later. Even in raw data based on a single transit across the star, the spectral dip of CO_2 "sticks out like a sore thumb," says Webb team member Jacob Bean of the University of Chicago. There have been some tentative detections of the gas before, he says, but none of them held up under scrutiny. Webb's spectrum was "the right size, the right

✎ 在首次系外行星观测中，天文学家将目标锁定在热气巨行星 WASP-39b 上，该行星每 4 天绕其恒星运行一次，其轨道比水星的轨道紧密得多。第一批数据是在 7 月 10 日采集的，研究小组几天后就开始对这些数据进行了处理。韦伯研究小组成员、芝加哥大学的雅各布·比恩说，即使是基于该恒星单次凌日的原始数据，二氧化碳的光谱凹陷也"非常突出"。他说，以前曾有过一些对这种气体的初

shape, and in the right position," Bean says. "CO_2 just popped out."

Bean and his colleagues reported the results yesterday on the preprint server arXiv and they will appear in *Nature* in the near future.

Hubble and Spitzer have previously found water vapor, sodium, and potassium in WASP-39b's atmosphere. Webb has now added CO_2, as well as another gas whose spectral signature was initially a mystery. Later observations revealed what it is, but Bean would not say anything about it until the result is peer reviewed.

In the coming months the team will publish the planet's full spectrum from optical to midinfrared, and "make a complete chemical inventory of its atmosphere," says team member Laura Kreidberg of the Max Planck Institute for Astronomy.

Finding CO_2 is valuable because it is a clue to a planet's "metallicity" —the proportion of elements heavier than helium in its makeup. Hydrogen and helium produced in the big bang are the starting materials for all the visible matter in the universe, but anything heavier was forged later in stars. Researchers believe a good supply of heavy elements is crucial for creating giant planets. When planets form out of a disk of material around a new star, heavier elements form solid grains and pebbles that glom together into a solid core that eventually is massive enough to pull in gases with its own gravity and grow into a gas giant.

步探测，但没有一次探测经得起仔细检查。比恩说，韦伯的光谱"大小合适，形状合适，位置也合适"。"二氧化碳突然冒了出来。"

✎ 比恩和他的同事昨天在预印本服务器 arXiv 上报告了这一结果，这些结果不久将发表在《自然》杂志上。

✎ 哈勃和斯皮策之前在 WASP-39b 的大气层中发现了水蒸气、钠和钾。韦伯现在又发现了二氧化碳以及另一种气体，这种气体的光谱特征最初是个谜。后来的观测揭示了这是什么气体，但在结果通过同行评审之前，比恩不会透露任何信息。

✎ 团队成员、马克斯-普朗克天文学研究所的劳拉·克赖德伯格说，在未来几个月里，团队将公布这颗行星从光学到中红外的全部光谱，并"对其大气层进行完整的化学盘点"。

✎ 找到二氧化碳是非常有价值的，因为它是行星"金属性"的线索——比氦更重的元素在行星构成中所占的比例。大爆炸中产生的氢和氦是宇宙中所有可见物质的起始材料，但任何更重的物质都是后来在恒星中形成的。研究人员认为，充足的重元素供应是形成巨行星的关键。当行星从新恒星周围的物质盘中形成时，较重的元素会形成固体颗粒和鹅卵石，这些颗粒和鹅卵石会凝结成一个固体内核，最终形成足够大的质量，以自身的引力吸入气体，成长为一颗气态巨行星。

From the CO_2 signal of WASP-39b, the team estimates the planet's metallicity roughly matches Saturn's. Curiously, WASP-39b is roughly the same mass as Saturn. The planets share some commonalities even though they have wildly different orbits, Bean says. "Can we find a common story for these two objects?" he says. "I don't know yet."

With Webb, finding "important chemicals will be the norm rather than the exception," Madhusudhan says. He predicts that when Webb starts to study cooler planets closer in size to Earth, there will be some real surprises—perhaps some gases that could indicate whether the planets are amenable to life. "It's anyone's guess," he says. "A whole zoo of chemicals is possible."

✎ 根据 WASP-39b 的二氧化碳信号，研究小组估计这颗行星的金属性与土星大致相当。奇怪的是，WASP-39b 的质量与土星大致相同。比恩说，尽管这两颗行星的轨道大相径庭，但它们有一些共同点。他说："我们能找到这两个天体的共同点吗？我还不知道。"

✎ 马德胡苏丹说，有了韦伯，发现"重要的化学物质将成为常态，而不是例外"。他预测，当韦伯开始研究体积更接近地球的较冷行星时，将会有一些真正的惊喜——也许一些气体可以表明这些行星是否适合生命存在。他说："这谁也说不准，整个化学物质动物园都是有可能的。"

核心词汇

habitability *n.*	可居住性；适于居住

例句 The **habitability** of Earth depends on a lot more than just orbit location and its mass.
地球的可居住性不仅仅取决于其轨道位置和质量。

unambiguous *adj.*	不含糊的；明白的；清楚的

例句 The programming is concise and **unambiguous**. 这种编程简洁而清晰。

spate *n.*	一连串

例句 A **spate** of strikes has thrown a spanner into the workshop of the world.
一连串的罢工已经给这个世界工厂带来了麻烦。

hint *n.*	暗示；提示

例句 She gave us a further heavy **hint**. 她给了我们一个明显的提示。

infrared *adj.*	红外线的

例句 It lies in the **infrared** range of the spectrum. 它位于光谱的红外线区域。

| **exoplanet** *n.* | 太阳系外行星 |

例句 The first habitable **exoplanet** already has a checkered history.
第一颗可居住的太阳系外行星的发现史可谓是一波三折。

| **tentative** *adj.* | 试探性的；暂定的；踌躇的；犹豫不定的 |

例句 I'm taking the first **tentative** step towards fitness. 我试探性地开始实施健身计划。

| **massive** *adj.* | 大量的；结实的；大规模的 |

例句 This could mean a **massive** furlough of government workers.
这会意味着政府工作人员的一次大规模停职。

| **commonality** *n.* | 公共；共性 |

例句 We don't have the same **commonality** of interest. 我们没有利益共同点。

| **amenable** *adj.* | 服从的 |

例句 This doesn't mean that all programs are **amenable** to sequential solutions.
这不意味着所有程序都遵循有序的解决方案。

7.16 真题同源文章 16

The Mozart Effect
莫扎特效应

Music has been used for centuries to heal the body. In the *Ebers Papyrs* (one of the earliest medical documents, circa 1500 B. C.), it was recorded that physicians chanted to heal the sick (Castleman, 1994). In various cultures, we have observed singing as part of healing rituals. In the world of Western medicine, however, using music in medicine lost popularity until the introduction of the radio. Researchers then started to notice that

几个世纪以来，音乐一直被用来疗愈身体。在《埃伯斯纸草文稿》（最早的医学文献之一，约公元前1500年）中，记载了医生们为治愈病人而吟唱（卡斯特曼，1994）。在各种文化中，我们观察到歌唱是疗愈仪式的一部分。然而，在西方医学界，音乐在医学中的应用直到无线电的出现才不再流行。研究人员随后开始注意

listening to music could have significant physical effects. Therapists noticed music could help calm anxiety and researchers saw that listening to music could cause a drop in blood pressure. In addition to these two areas, music has been used with cancer chemotherapy to reduce nausea, during surgery to reduce stress hormone production, during childbirth, and in stroke recovery (Castleman, 1994 and Westley, 1998). It has been shown to decrease pain as well as enhance the effectiveness of the immune system. In Japan, compilations of music are used as medication, of sorts. For example, if you want to cure a headache or migraine, the album suggested Mendelssohn's *Spring Song*, Dvorak's *Humoresque*, or part of George Gershwin's *An Americanin Paris* (Campbell, 1998). Music is also being used to assist in learning, in a phenomenon called the Mozart Effect.

Frances H. Rauscher, Ph. D., first demonstrated the correlation between music and learning in an experiment in 1993. His experiments indicated that a 10-minute dose of Mozart could temporarily boost intelligence. Groups of students were given intelligence tests after listening to silence, relaxation tapes, or Mozart's *Sonata for Two Pianos in D Major* for a short time. He found that after silence, the average IQ score was 110, and after the relaxation tape, scores rose a point. After listening to Mozart, however, the scores jumped to 119 (Westley, 1998). Even students who did not like the music still had an increased score on the IQ test. Rauscher hypothesised that " listening to complex, non-repetitive music, like Mozart, may stimulate neural pathways that are important in thinking " (Castleman, 1994).

到，听音乐可能会对身体产生重大影响。治疗师注意到音乐有助于缓解焦虑，研究人员发现听音乐可以引起血压下降。除了这两个领域，音乐还被用于癌症化疗以减少恶心，用于手术以减少应激激素的产生，用于分娩和中风恢复（卡斯特曼，1994 和韦斯特利，1998）。它已被证明可以减轻疼痛并增强免疫系统的有效性。在日本，音乐汇编被用作药物，种类繁多。例如，如果你想治头痛或偏头痛，这张专辑推荐了门德尔松的《春之歌》、德沃夏克的《幽默曲》，或者乔治·格什温的《巴黎的美国人》的一部分（坎贝尔，1998）。音乐也被用来辅助学习，这种现象被称为"莫扎特效应"。

弗朗西斯·H. 劳舍尔博士在 1993 年的一项实验中首次证明了音乐与学习的相关性。他的实验表明，10 分钟剂量的莫扎特音乐可以暂时提高智力。两组学生分别在短时间内听默音、放松录音或莫扎特的《D 大调双钢琴奏鸣曲》后进行智力测验。他发现在沉默之后，平均智商分数为 110，而听放松录音之后，分数提高了 1 分。然而听了莫扎特的演奏之后，成绩却跃升到了 119（韦斯特利，1998）。即使是不喜欢音乐的学生，在智商测试中的得分也有所提高。劳舍尔假设"听复杂的、非重复的音乐，比如莫扎特音乐，可能会刺激对思维很重要的神经通路"（卡斯特曼，1994）。

The same experiment was repeated on rats by Rauscher and Hong Hua Li from Stanford. Rats also demonstrated enhancement in their intelligence performance. These new studies indicate that rats that were exposed to Mozart showed "increased gene expression of BDNF (a neural growth factor), CREB (a learning and memory compound), and Synapsin I (a synaptic growth protein)" in the brain's hippocampus, compared with rats in the control group, which heard only white noise (e.g. the whooshing sound of a radio tuned between stations).

How exactly does the Mozart Effect work? Researchers are still trying to determine the actual mechanisms for the formation of these enhanced learning pathways. Neuroscientists suspect that music can actually help build and strengthen connections between neurons in the cerebral cortex in a process similar to what occurs in brain development despite its type. When a baby is born, certain connections have already been made—like connections for heartbeat and breathing. As new information is learned and motor skills develop, new neural connections are formed. Neurons that are not used will eventually die while those used repeatedly will form strong connections. Although a large number of these neural connections require experience, they also must occur within a certain timeframe. For example, a child born with cataracts cannot develop connections within the visual cortex. If the cataracts are removed by surgery right away, the child's vision develops normally. However, after the age of 2, if the cataracts are removed, the child will remain blind because those pathways cannot establish themselves.

✎ 劳舍尔和斯坦福大学的李宏华在大鼠身上重复了同样的实验。大鼠的智力表现也有所提高。这些新的研究表明，与只听到白噪声（例如电台之间调谐的无线电的嗖嗖声）的对照组大鼠相比，接触莫扎特音乐的大鼠大脑海马体中"BDNF（一种神经生长因子）、CREB（一种学习记忆化合物）和突触生长蛋白I（一种突触生长蛋白）的基因表达有所增加"。

✎ 莫扎特效应到底是如何起作用的呢？研究者们仍在努力探索形成这些强化学习路径的实际机制。神经学家们怀疑，音乐实际上可以帮助建立和加强大脑皮层神经元之间的关联，其过程与大脑发育中发生的情况类似，尽管其类型不同。当婴儿出生时，已经建立了某些关联，比如心跳和呼吸的联系。随着新信息的学习和运动技能的发展，新的神经关联形成。未被利用的神经元最终会死亡，而被反复利用的神经元会形成强关联。虽然大量的神经关联需要经验，但它们也必须在一定的时间内发生。例如，患有白内障的孩子不能在视觉皮层内建立关联。若立即手术摘除白内障，孩子的视力就会正常发展。然而，在2岁以后，如果白内障被摘除，孩子仍将失明，因为这些通路无法自行建立。

Music seems to work in the same way. In October of 1997, researchers at the University of Konstanz in Germany found that music actually rewires neural circuits (Begley, 1996). Although some of these circuits are formed for physical skills needed to play an instrument, just listening to music strengthens connection used in higher-order thinking. Listening to music can then be thought of as "exercise" for the brain, improving concentration and enhancing intuition.

If you're a little skeptical about the claims made by supporters of the Mozart Effect, you're not alone. Many people accredit the advanced learning of some children who take music lessons to other personality traits, such as motivation and persistence, which is required in all types of learning. There have also been claims of that influencing the results of some experiments.

Furthermore, many people are critical of the role the media had in turning an isolated study into a trend for parents and music educators. After Mozart Effect was published to the public, the sales of Mozart CDs stayed on the top of the hit list for three weeks. In an article by Michael Linton, he wrote that the research that began this phenomenon (the study by researchers at the University of California Irvine) showed only a temporary boost in IQ, which was not significant enough to even last throughout the course of the experiment. Using music to influence intelligence was used in Confucian civilisation and Plato alluded to Pythagorean music when he described his ideal state in *The Republic*. In both of these examples, music did not have caused any

✎ 音乐似乎也是如此。1997 年 10 月，德国康斯坦茨大学的研究人员发现，音乐实际上重新连接了神经回路（贝格利，1996）。尽管其中一些回路是为演奏乐器所需的身体技能而形成的，但仅仅听音乐就可以强化高阶思维中的联系。听音乐可以被认为是大脑的"锻炼"，可以提高注意力和增强直觉。

✎ 如果你对"莫扎特效应"支持者提出的主张有点儿怀疑，你并不孤单。许多人将一些上过音乐课的孩子的超前学习归因于其他人格特质，如动机和毅力，这在所有类型的学习中都是必需的。也有人声称这会影响一些实验的结果。

✎ 此外，许多人对媒体在将孤立的研究转变为家长和音乐教育工作者的趋势中所起的作用持批评态度。"莫扎特效应"公之于众后，莫扎特音乐 CD 的销量连续三周稳居榜首。在迈克尔·林顿的一篇文章中，他写道，开始这一现象的研究（美国加州大学欧文分校研究人员的研究）只显示了智商的短暂提高，这并不显著，甚至不足以持续整个实验过程。用音乐来影响智力在儒家文化中被使用过，柏拉图在《理想国》中描述他的理想国时曾影射过毕达哥拉斯的音乐。在这两个例子中，音乐并没有引起任何压倒性的变化，这一理论最终消亡了。

overwhelming changes, and the theory eventually died out. Linton also asks, "If Mozart's Music were able to improve health, why was Mozart himself so frequently sick? If listening to Mozart's music increases intelligence and encourages spirituality, why aren't the world's smartest and most spiritual people Mozart specialists?" Linton raises an interesting point, if the Mozart Effect causes such significant changes, why isn't there more documented evidence?

The "trendiness" of the Mozart Effect may have died out somewhat, but there are still strong supporters (and opponents) of the claims made in 1993. Since that initial experiment, there has not been a surge of supporting evidence. However, many parents, after playing classical music while pregnant or when their children are young, will swear by the Mozart Effect. A classmate of mine once told me that listening to classical music while studying will help with memorisation. If we approach this controversy from a scientific aspect, although there has been some evidence that music does increase brain activity, actual improvements in learning and memory have not been adequately demonstrated.

林顿还问道："如果莫扎特的音乐能够增进健康，为什么莫扎特自己经常生病？如果听莫扎特的音乐可以提高智力，鼓舞精神，为什么世界上最聪明、最有灵性的人不是莫扎特专家呢？"林顿提出了一个有趣的观点，如果"莫扎特效应"导致了如此重大的变化，为什么没有更多的文献证据呢？

✎ "莫扎特效应"的"趋势性"可能在某种程度上已经消失，但1993年提出的论断仍有强有力的支持者（和反对者）。自最初的实验以来，没有大量的支持证据。然而，许多父母在怀孕期间或孩子年幼时播放古典音乐后，他们对"莫扎特效应"深信不疑。我的一个同学曾经告诉我，边学习边听古典音乐有助于记忆。如果我们从科学的角度来看待这一争议，尽管有一些证据表明音乐确实会增强大脑活动，但学习和记忆的实际改善还没有得到充分的证明。

核心词汇

physician *n.*	医生；内科医生
例句 Elderly people need time and compassion from their **physicians**. 老年人需要医生多花时间，还需要他们的关爱。	
ritual *n.*	仪式；典礼
例句 She objects to the **ritual** of organised religion. 她反对有组织的宗教仪规。	

stimulate *v.*　　　　　　　　　　　　　　　　　　　　　　刺激；激励；鼓舞；使兴奋

例句 The exhibition has **stimulated** interest in her works.
这次展览增进了人们对她的作品的兴趣。

phenomenon *n.*　　　　　　　　　　　　　　　　　　　　　　　　　　　　现象

例句 Globalisation is a **phenomenon** of the 21st century.　全球化是 21 世纪的现象。

neural *adj.*　　　　　　　　　　　　　　　　　　　　　　　　　　　　　神经的

例句 **Neural** networks are computer systems which mimic the workings of the brain.
神经网络是模拟大脑工作方式的计算机系统。

strengthen *v.*　　　　　　　　　　　　　　　　　　　　　　巩固；支持；壮大；加强

例句 The exercises are designed to **strengthen** your stomach muscles.
这些练习的目的在于增强你的腹部肌肉。

temporary *adj.*　　　　　　　　　　　　　　　　　　　　　　　　　暂时的；短暂的

例句 I'm looking for some **temporary** work.　我在找临时工作。

significant *adj.*　　　　　　　　　　　　　　　　　　　　重要的；显著的；意味深长的

例句 The results of the experiment are not statistically **significant**.
从统计学的观点看，实验结果意义不明显。

throughout *prep.*　　　　　　　　　　　　　　　　　　　　　　　　自始至终；遍及

例句 They export their products to markets **throughout** the world.
他们把产品出口到世界各地的市场。

aspect *n.*　　　　　　　　　　　　　　　　　　　　　　　　　　方面；样子；外观

例句 This was one **aspect** of her character he hadn't seen before.
这是他过去没有了解到的她的性格的一个方面。

7.17 真题同源文章17

Zimbabwe Find Illuminates Dawn of the Dinosaurs
津巴布韦的发现照亮了恐龙的黎明
Nearly complete specimen shows earliest dinosaurs needed temperate climate
几乎完整的标本显示最早的恐龙需要温和的气候

During the late Triassic period, when the terrestrial world was a single sprawling land mass called Pangaea, a dog-size plant-eating dinosaur perished near a river in the southern part of the continent. When the river flooded, its body was buried by sediment, with some bones still articulated as in life.

About 230 million years later, paleontologist Chris Griffin, then a doctoral student at the Virginia Polytechnic Institute and State University, spotted a thigh bone sticking out of a hill in the Cabora Bassa River Basin in what is now Zimbabwe. "I've got a dinosaur!" he called to his team.

"As soon as I dug that out, I knew that I was holding Africa's oldest dinosaur," says Griffin, now a postdoc at Yale University. "I had to sit down and breathe for a minute, because I thought, 'There could be a lot more [bones] in there.'"

In the weeks that followed, Griffin and paleontologists Darlington Munyikwa and Michel Zondo of the Natural History Museum of Zimbabwe in Bulawayo unearthed a nearly complete skeleton. It turned out to be a new species of early dinosaur:

在三叠纪晚期，当陆地世界是一个被称为盘古大陆的庞大陆地时，一种像狗一般大小的食草恐龙在该大陆南部的一条河流附近死亡。当河水泛滥时，它的尸体被沉积物掩埋，一些骨骼仍然像活着时一样铰接在一起。

大约2.3亿年后，当时是弗吉尼亚理工学院和州立大学博士生的古生物学家克里斯·格里芬在津巴布韦卡博拉·巴萨河流域的一个山丘上发现了一块大腿骨。他对他的团队喊道，"我得到了一只恐龙！"

"我一挖出来，我就知道我手中是非洲最古老的恐龙，"格里芬说，他现在是耶鲁大学的博士后。"我不得不坐下来呼吸一分钟，因为我认为，'里面可能还有更多的骨骼。'"

在随后的几周里，格里芬与津巴布韦自然历史博物馆的古生物学家达林顿·穆尼科瓦和迈克尔·宗多在布拉瓦约出土了一具近乎完整的骨骼。事实证明，这是一种新发现的早期恐

Mbiresaurus raathi, which they describe today in *Nature*.

Though small by dinosaur standards at 1.8 meters long, the find has outsize implications for the early spread of dinosaurs, says Stephen Brusatte, a vertebrate paleontologist at the University of Edinburgh who was not involved in the study. "We've known next to nothing about the earliest dinosaurs in Africa," Brusatte says. "It is one of the most important recent dinosaur discoveries anywhere in the world."

Until now, the earliest known dinosaurs, also dating to about 230 million years ago, were found in Argentina and Brazil, with a few partial specimens from India. When the continents were gathered together to form Pangaea, those sites all lay at about 50° south, explains Diego Pol, a paleontologist at the Egidio Feruglio Paleontology Museum in Argentina who was not part of the team. Earth was warmer at the time, lacking icecaps, and climate models suggest that latitude on Pangaea had a wet, temperate climate with hot summers and cool, rainy winters. Researchers have suspected the first dinosaurs needed this type of climate, and that this limited their spread across the supercontinent. But to confirm that idea, they needed dinosaur fossils from other parts of the same climate belt.

Griffin's team began its hunt with a geological map, tracing a Pangaean-era latitude line of 50°. They zeroed in on a shallow drainage in northern Zimbabwe where Munyikwa and Zondo knew other fossils had been found. "If dinosaurs are following

龙：拉希姆比龙。他们今天在《自然》杂志上对其进行了描述。

✎ 爱丁堡大学脊椎动物古生物学家斯蒂芬·布鲁萨特没有参与这项研究，他说，尽管按照恐龙的标准来看，这一发现很小，只有 1.8 米长，但对恐龙的早期扩散有着巨大的影响。布鲁萨特说："我们对非洲最早的恐龙几乎一无所知。这是世界上最近最重要的恐龙发现之一。"

✎ 迄今为止，在阿根廷和巴西发现了已知最早的恐龙，这些恐龙也可以追溯到约 2.3 亿年前，还有少数部分标本来自印度。阿根廷埃吉迪奥·费鲁格里奥古生物博物馆的古生物学家迭戈·波尔（他不是团队的一员）解释说，当大陆聚集在一起形成盘古大陆时，这些地点都位于南纬 50° 左右。当时地球更温暖，没有冰盖。气候模型表明，盘古大陆上的纬度是潮湿温和的气候，夏季炎热，冬季凉爽多雨。研究人员怀疑，最早期的恐龙需要这种气候，并认为这限制了它们在超级大陆上的扩散。但为了证实这一观点，他们需要来自同一气候带其他地区的恐龙化石。

✎ 格里芬的团队开始用地质图进行追捕，追踪了一条盘古大陆时代的 50° 纬度线。他们瞄准了津巴布韦北部的一个浅水流域，穆尼科瓦和宗多知道在那里还发现了其他化石。"如果恐

this climate, then we should be able to find some of the oldest dinosaurs right here in southern Africa," Griffin says they reasoned. "And we did. "

龙跟随这种气候，那么我们应该能够在南部非洲找到一些最古老的恐龙，"格里芬说他们是这么推测的。"而且我们做到了。"

The M. raathi find, which was almost complete save for portions of the skull and forelimbs, "was just very amazing and exciting," Munyikwa says. No bigger than a collie, M. raathi is named after Mbire, as the region was called during the 16th century Shona Empire, and a pioneering researcher who found fossils nearby. The dinosaur had a long tail, a smallish head, and small, triangular teeth, suggesting it favoured plants.

穆尼科瓦说，除了部分头骨和前肢外，发现的拉希姆比龙几乎是完整的，"这是非常惊奇和令人兴奋的"。拉希姆比龙并不比牧羊犬大，是以"姆比"命名的，因为该地区在16世纪的绍纳帝国时期被称作"姆比"，而一位先驱研究者在附近发现了这些化石。这只恐龙的尾巴较长，头部较小，牙齿较小，呈三角形，表明它喜欢植物。

The team also found fragments of bones from a large carnivorous dinosaur called a herrerasaurid, the first discovered in Africa. And it unearthed an array of other animal fossils, too: cynodonts, which are mammal relatives; armored crocodilian relatives called aetosaurs; and archaic reptiles called rhynchosaurs. Paleontologists have found similar creatures along the same climate band in South America and India.

该研究小组还发现了一只埃雷拉龙科大型食肉恐龙的骨骼碎片，这是在非洲首次发现。此外，还出土了一系列其他动物化石：犬齿龙类，这是哺乳动物的近亲；铠甲鳄的近亲，称为以太龙；以及被称为钩龙的古老爬行动物。古生物学家在南美洲和印度的同一气候带发现了类似的生物。

Taken together, the fossils are the strongest evidence yet that the earliest dinosaurs and their relatives were constrained to a temperate climate belt bordered by arid ones, Pol says. "The assemblage was very similar to that of South America," he says. Dinosaurs were restricted to their semihumid oasis for a few million years, until the arid regions to the north and south began to become wetter.

波尔指出，总的来说，这些化石是迄今为止最有力的证据，证明最早的恐龙和它们的亲属被限制在一个温带气候带，与干旱的气候带接壤。他说，"这种组合与南美洲的组合非常相似。"恐龙被限制在半湿润的绿洲中达数百万年之久，直到北部和南部的干旱地区开始变得更加潮湿。

The rare find provides a welcome boost to Zimbabwe's science that Munyikwa hopes will help attract more research funding. "This new species [shows] we have very important deposits," he says. The fossils are now on display at the Natural History Museum of Zimbabwe and are a point of pride for the community and nation, he says.

🖉 这一罕见的发现为津巴布韦的科学提供了可喜的助力，穆尼科瓦希望这将有助于吸引更多的研究资金。他说："这个新物种［表明］我们有非常重要的沉积物。"他说这些化石现在在津巴布韦自然历史博物馆展出，是社区和国家的骄傲。

"The study notes that other specimens likely await discovery across the same Pangaean climate belt, offering a road map of sorts for other paleontologists on the hunt for early dinosaurs," says Kristi Curry Rogers, a vertebrate paleontologist at Macalester College. "Now it's time for all the rest of us working in dinosaur paleobiology to get to work and discover some more early dinosaurs."

🖉 麦卡莱斯特学院脊椎动物古生物学家克里斯蒂·库里·罗杰斯说："研究发现，在同一盘古大陆气候带上，其他可能有待发现的标本，为其他古生物学家寻找早期恐龙提供了一份路线图。现在是我们所有在恐龙古生物学界工作的其他人开始工作和发现一些更早期恐龙的时候了。"

核心词汇

sprawling adj.	蔓延的；杂乱无序伸展的
例句 It is a modern **sprawling** town. 这是一座庞大的现代化城镇。	

paleontologist n.	古生物学者
例句 I did give up a career in basketball to become a **paleontologist**. 我确实放弃了篮球生涯，成了一名古生物学家。	

fossil n.	化石；僵化的事物
例句 The **fossils** had been chipped out of the rock. 那些化石已从岩石上被凿了下来。	

carnivorous adj.	（动物）食肉的；肉食的
例句 Snakes are **carnivorous**. 蛇是食肉动物。	

archaic adj.	古代的；过时的；陈旧的
例句 The system is **archaic** and unfair and needs changing. 这项制度陈旧且不公平，需要改变。	

fragment *n.*	碎片；片段

例句 Police found **fragments** of glass near the scene. 警方在现场附近发现了玻璃碎片。

vertebrate *n.*	脊椎动物

例句 A growing body of research shows that insects are declining about twice as fast as **vertebrates**.

越来越多的研究表明，昆虫数量的下降速度大约是脊椎动物的两倍。

armor *n.*	盔甲；装甲（部队）

例句 Knights of old times had to wear **armor** in battle. 从前的武士上战场时都穿盔甲。

reptile *n.*	爬行动物

例句 The archaic **reptile** is a living link with the ancestors of her people.

这种古老的爬行动物与她的祖先有着活生生的联系。

latitude *n.*	纬度；范围

例句 These forests cover a broad span of **latitudes**. 这些森林绵延在多个纬度上。

7.18 真题同源文章18

A Key Time for UK-Europe Science
英国与欧洲科学的关键时刻

The opening line of a recent *Financial Times* article put it best: "Relations between the UK and EU badly need a reset." Although the article was mostly about geopolitics, the disconnect also applies to science and the current uncertainty about whether the UK will remain an associated partner in European Union (EU) research programs such as

✎ 最近一篇《金融时报》的开篇最为贴切："英国与欧盟之间的关系迫切需要重启。"尽管该文章主要涉及地缘政治，但这种脱节也适用于科学领域，目前对于英国是否会继续作为欧盟地位关联伙伴参与"欧洲地平线"等欧盟研究计划仍不不确定。在后脱

Horizon Europe. In the post-Brexit era, and with a new UK Prime Minister to be named shortly, the UK and EU should be considering how best to maximise the potential of the numerous brilliant scientists, technicians, academics, and clinicians working in the universities and research institutes of all European countries, including the UK.

An unintended casualty of the UK's withdrawal from the EU was the country's ability to participate fully in the collaborative ecosystem of research and innovation that had evolved during the UK's 47-year membership in the organisation. British universities, and the staff and students working and studying in them, have been highly desired partners. These interactions, which could continue if the UK is an associated country, are currently at great risk because of the complexities of the post-Brexit negotiations. Hopefully, after last month's tumult surrounding the resignation of Boris Johnson and the uncertainty about who will be the next Prime Minister, there will be a calm reappraisal of the risks of going it alone for both the UK and the European continent. What could emerge is a renewed effort to find a negotiated solution that allows the UK to continue to maximise its potential as a fully engaged contributor to European research and innovation.

To its credit, the current UK government has worked to promote and enhance the country's own scientific endeavors by increasing current funding and pledging more in the future, and by enhancing visa schemes and other immigration rules to continue to attract and retain talented individuals from home and abroad.

欧时代，并且在不久后将任命新的英国首相之际，英国和欧盟应该考虑如何最大限度地发挥包括英国在内的所有欧洲国家大学和研究机构中众多杰出科学家、技术人员、学者和临床医生的潜力。

✎ 英国退出欧盟的一个意外后果是该国无法充分参与其于 47 年成员期间发展起来的研究与创新的合作生态系统。英国大学及其员工和学生一直是备受欢迎的合作伙伴。如果英国成为一个关联国家，可以继续这些互动，但由于脱欧后谈判的复杂性，这些互动会面临巨大的风险。希望在上个月鲍里斯·约翰逊辞职引发的动荡和下一任首相人选的不确定性之后，英国和欧洲大陆将冷静地重新评估独自行动的风险。可能出现的是寻求协商解决方案的新努力，使英国能够继续充分参与欧洲研究与创新。

✎ 值得称赞的是，目前的英国政府致力于通过增加当前的资金和承诺未来的更多资金，以及加强签证计划和其他移民规定，促进和加强该国自身的科学事业，以继续吸引和留住来自国内外的人才。

There has also been work on a so-called "Plan B" for the eventuality that the UK fails to associate with Horizon Europe, the EU's key research funding program with a budget of 95.5 billion euros. However, this would be a poor second best: Witness Switzerland's similar approach a few years ago, which left its researchers seriously isolated.

针对英国未能与"欧洲地平线"等欧盟重要研究资助计划建立联系的可能性,也提出了所谓的"B计划",该项目的预算为955亿欧元。然而,这将是次优选择。几年前,瑞士采取了类似的做法,结果导致其研究人员遭受严重孤立。

At the same time, the UK government recognises that some collaborations can pose national security risks, particularly with institutions in countries whose governments the UK disagrees with. This has led to a clamor among a subset of politicians for more legislation to "control" or "manage" the country's universities. I have been involved in some of these discussions and have been heartened by many experts in UK security agencies and in parts of the UK government who recognise the value of these partnerships and of keeping risk mitigation measures proportionate and balanced. The UK could learn from experiences in Australia and the United States where similar recent legislation related to national security has stymied research and innovation. For example, Australian universities expressed concern about their autonomy and about limitation of their abilities to deliver societal benefits.

同时,英国政府也意识到了一些合作可能带来国家安全风险,特别是与英国政府存在分歧的国家的机构合作时。这引发了一些政治人士的呼声,要求通过更多立法来"控制"或"管理"该国的大学。我参与了其中一些讨论,并对英国安全机构和部分英国政府的许多专家认识到这些合作伙伴关系的价值以及保持风险缓解措施的适度和平衡感到振奋。英国可以借鉴澳大利亚和美国的经验,在这些国家,最近类似的国家安全立法阻碍了研究和创新。例如,澳大利亚大学对其自主权以及实现社会效益能力的有限表示担忧。

The university sector in the UK has warmly welcomed the creation of the Research Collaboration Advice Team, which will provide a single point of contact with UK government and security agencies. I and others will continue to work with them and with the security services to understand risk, disseminate good practices, and provide an early warning system when real dangers are recognised.

英国大学部门热烈欢迎成立研究合作建议团队,该团队将与英国政府和安全机构建立一个单一联系点。我和大家将继续与他们及安全服务机构合作,一起了解风险、推广良好做法,并在发现真正的危险时提供预警系统。

A mature, two-way relationship between government and the university sector is in everyone's best interests. A similar maturity should be brought to finding solutions for the challenges posed by securing the UK's association with Horizon Europe and with other EU programs.

✎ 政府与大学部门之间成熟的双向关系符合每个人的最佳利益。在解决确保英国"欧洲地平线"和其他欧盟计划关联的挑战时，应该持有类似的成熟态度。

Without a "reset" of UK—EU scientific relations, the "brain drain" from the UK—which has already started, with at least 19 researchers funded by the European Research Council recently relocating to EU countries to keep their funding—will become an avalanche. The role of the UK in the cohesion and productivity of European science will be the victim, with serious implications for global science capability. There is an opportunity for the UK government and the European Commission to prevent this now. It's time to untangle science from post-Brexit geopolitics so that European science can thrive.

✎ 如果英国与欧盟科学关系不"重启"，已经在英国开始出现的"人才流失"将变成雪崩——欧洲研究委员会资助的至少 19 名研究人员最近迁移到了欧盟国家以保留资金。英国在欧洲科学凝聚力和生产力中的作用将受损，对全球科学能力将产生严重的影响。现在，英国政府和欧洲委员会有机会阻止这种情况发生。是时候将科学与脱欧后的地缘政治脱钩了，这样欧洲科学才能蓬勃发展。

核心词汇

institute *n.*	机构；协会；研究院；学院
例句 The National Cancer **Institute** now has a computerised system that can quickly provide information. 国家癌症研究所现在拥有一套能迅速提供信息的电脑化系统。	

disseminate *v.*	散布；传播
例句 It took years to **disseminate** information about Aids in Africa. 在非洲传播关于艾滋病方面的知识耗时数年。	

isolate *v.*	（使）隔离；孤立
例句 He was immediately **isolated** from the other prisoners. 他被立刻与其他囚犯隔离开了。	

collaboration *n.*   合作

例句 The government worked in close **collaboration** with teachers on the new curriculum.
政府和教师就新的课程进行了紧密的协作。

mitigation *n.*   减轻；缓解

例句 In **mitigation**, the defence lawyer said his client was seriously depressed at the time of the assault. 为了减轻罪行，辩护律师说他的当事人在袭击人的时候精神极度压抑。

legislation *n.*   法律；法规

例句 The new **legislation** concerns health and safety at work.
这项新法规涉及工作场所的健康与安全。

implication *n.*   可能引发的后果

例句 The Attorney General was aware of the political **implications** of his decision to prosecute.
司法部长很清楚他决定起诉可能引发的政治后果。

relocate *v.*   （使）迁移；（使）搬迁

例句 The firm may be forced to **relocate** from New York to Stanford.
这家公司也许会被迫从纽约迁移到斯坦福。

untangle *v.*   解开；松开

例句 Lawyers and accountants began trying to **untangle** the complex affairs of the bank.
律师和会计师开始着手梳理这家银行复杂的事务。

cohesion *n.*   团结；凝聚力

例句 By 1990, it was clear that the **cohesion** of the armed forces was rapidly breaking down.
显然，到1990年时，武装部队的凝聚力正在迅速瓦解。

7.19 真题同源文章19

Do American Consumers Need a Financial Protection Agency?
美国消费者需要一个金融保护机构吗?

According to the Federal Reserve System (Fed), the total debt outstanding of consumers during the second quarter of 2010 was $13.5 trillion, a total that was approximately equal to the gross public debt of the federal government and larger than the outstanding debt of the nonfinancial business sector ($10.9 trillion) or the combined outstanding debt of state and local governments ($2.4 trillion). The debt of the financial sector of the economy, which is largely used to finance the borrowings of consumers, government, and nonfinancial business, stood at $14.7 trillion.

The Fed disaggregates consumer total debt in into two large categories: home mortgages ($10.1 trillion) and consumer credit ($2.4 trillion). In accumulating debt, consumers borrow from a variety of different organisations including commercial banks, finance companies, mortgage companies, credit unions, the federal government, savings institutions, and insurance companies. And the act of borrowing or taking out a loan creates a variety of financial instruments or IOUs. For example, home mortgages include fixed interest rate mortgages and variable interest rate mortgages, and each of these mortgages has various maturities and other conditions. There is also the distinction between

根据联邦储备系统（美联储）的数据，2010年第二季度消费者的未偿债务总额为13.5万亿美元，这一总额约等于联邦政府的公共债务总额，高于非金融企业部门的未偿债务（10.9万亿美元）或州和地方政府未偿债务的总和（2.4万亿美元）。经济中金融部门的债务为14.7万亿美元，主要用于为消费者、政府和非金融企业的借款提供资金。

美联储将消费者总债务分为两大类：住房抵押贷款（10.1万亿美元）和消费信贷（2.4万亿美元）。在积累债务的过程中，消费者向各种不同的机构借款，包括商业银行、金融公司、抵押贷款公司、信用社、联邦政府、储蓄机构和保险公司。借款或贷款行为会产生各种各样的金融工具或借据。例如，住房抵押贷款包括固定利率抵押贷款和浮动利率抵押贷款，每种抵押贷款都有不同的期限和其他条件。此外，还有优质抵押贷款和次级抵押贷款之分。至于消费信贷，美

prime and subprime mortgages. As for consumer credit, the Fed also breaks this total down into two major categories: revolving and nonrevolving. One common definition of revolving credit is that it is an arrangement with a lender that allows the borrower access to funds up to a certain limit and repayment reestablishes the availability of funds. Credit cards are the best example of revolving credit. The Fed describes nonrevolving credit as "including automobile loans and all other loans not included in revolving credit, such as loans for mobile homes, education, boats, trailers, or vacations."

联储也将这一总额分为两大类：循环信贷和非循环信贷。循环信贷的一个常见定义是，它是与贷款人达成的一种约定，允许借款人在一定限额内使用资金，还款后可重新获得资金。信用卡就是循环信贷的最好例子。美联储将非循环信贷描述为"包括汽车贷款和未列入循环信贷的所有其他贷款，例如用于活动房屋、教育、船只、拖车或度假的贷款"。

Consider the situation of a representative family. It probably has a mortgage that it used to purchase its home, an outstanding car loan, unpaid balances on credit cards, and perhaps outstanding student loans. And during a lifetime, a consumer may take out several of each of these types of loans; for example, they may take out more than one mortgage because of the purchase of a different home or the refinancing of a mortgage.

✎ 考虑一个代表性家庭的情况。这个家庭可能有用于购房的按揭贷款、未偿还的汽车贷款、信用卡未偿还余额，或许还有未偿还的学生贷款。在消费者的一生中，他们可能会申请多笔此类贷款；例如，他们可能会因为购买不同的住房或重新贷款而申请多笔按揭贷款。

What underlies the concern about consumer borrowing and calls for a Consumer Financial Protection Agency is not just the magnitude of consumer debt. Rather, it is a concern that in the process of taking out a loan, the consumer does not have the knowledge or expertise of the lender. This is a problem that economists refer to as information asymmetry: a condition in which one party to a transaction has more information than the other party and creates the possibility that the party with the greater information will take advantage of the less well-informed counter party. If information asymmetry

✎ 人们对消费者借贷的担忧以及要求成立消费者金融保护局的呼声，并不仅仅是消费者债务的规模，而是担心在贷款过程中，消费者不具备贷款人的知识或专业技能。经济学家将这一问题称为信息不对称：交易一方比另一方掌握了更多的信息，从而使掌握更多信息的一方有可能利用信息较少的另一方。如果存在信息不对称，那么市场就不太可能产生有效的结果。

exists, then markets are less likely to produce efficient outcomes.

The financial crisis that began in the summer of 2007 revealed a number of problems with consumer credit arrangements. There were revelations about practices of various lenders that were although legal but considered inappropriate. For example, credit card companies did not indicate on credit card statements how long it would take the card holder to pay off their balance if the holder only made the required minimum payment. Another example was mortgage lenders making loans that exceeded the capacity of the borrower to repay or that mortgage lenders were steering borrowers into subprime (and higher interest rate mortgages) when they qualified for a prime loan.

Congress took up the issue of abuses by organisations that lent to consumers. The credit card industry was the first to be addressed (see Issue 10 in the 14th edition of this volume) and in 2009 *the Credit Card Accountability*, *Responsibility*, *and Disclosure Act* (*the Credit Card Act*) became law. Congress did eventually pass *the Wall Street Reform and Consumer Protection Act* (*Dodd-Frank*) in 2010. This legislation creates the Bureau of Consumer Financial Protection that is housed within the Fed. The two selections presented here are excerpted testimony in hearings held before the legislation was passed. They are representative of the controversy that still exists about the consumer protection part of the legislation.

✎ 始于 2007 年夏季的金融危机暴露了消费信贷合约中的许多问题。各种放款人的做法被揭露了，这些做法虽然合法，但被认为是不恰当的。例如，信用卡公司没有在信用卡对账单上注明，如果持卡人只支付规定的最低还款额，他们需要多长时间才能还清余额。另一个例子是，按揭贷款机构发放的贷款超出了借款人的偿还能力，或者按揭贷款机构在借款人有资格获得优质贷款的情况下，将其引导到次级贷款（以及利率更高的按揭贷款）中。

✎ 国会讨论了向消费者提供贷款的机构滥用权力的问题。信用卡行业是第一个受到关注的行业（参见本卷第 14 版第 10 期）。2009 年，《信用卡问责、责任和披露法》（《信用卡法》）成为法律。国会最终于 2010 年通过了《华尔街改革与消费者保护法案》（《多德 - 弗兰克法案》）。该法案设立了消费者金融保护局，隶属于美联储。这里介绍的两个选择案例是在立法通过前举行的听证会上的证词节选。它们代表了对该立法中消费者保护部分仍然存在的争议。

Janis Bowdler, the deputy director, Wealth-Building Policy Project, National Council of La Raza, supports the creation of a Consumer Financial Protection Agency (CFPA). She identifies three specific ways in which existing regulatory agencies have failed consumers, including the failure to create and promote tools that will allow consumers to make "true apples-to-apples comparisons" of credit products. She and her organisation believe a new agency is needed to redress these failures, and it would be a strong vehicle for improving the way financial markets serve their Latino clients.

詹尼斯·鲍德勒是拉扎全国委员会财富建设政策项目的副主任，她支持成立消费者金融保护局（CFPA）。她指出了现有监管机构辜负消费者的三种具体方式，包括未能创建和推广允许消费者对信贷产品进行"同类对比"的工具。她和所在机构认为，需要一个新的机构来纠正这些失误，这将是改善金融市场为拉丁裔客户服务方式的有力工具。

Bill Himpler, the executive vice president of the American Financial Services Association, opposes the creation of a CFPA. His argument takes several forms, including the fact that finance companies are already heavily regulated at the state level. He also believes that the creation of a CFPA is likely to mean "higher prices and reduced product choice for financial services customers."

美国金融服务协会执行副总裁比尔·希姆普勒反对成立美国金融监管局。他的论点有几种形式，包括金融公司已经在国家层面受到严格监管。他还认为，成立美国金融监管局很可能意味着"金融服务客户的价格上涨，产品选择减少"。

核心词汇

gross *adj.*	总的；整的
例句 **Gross** sales reached nearly $5 million a year. 全年销售总额达到近五百万美元。	
disaggregate *v.*	分解
例句 Experts have tried to **disaggregate** the influence of the harmful factors but in vain. 专家尝试过将这些有害因素的影响分离出来，但是徒劳无功。	
mortgage *n.*	抵押
例句 I paid off the **mortgage** within five years. 我用五年时间还清了抵押借款。	
variable interest	浮动利率
例句 The mortgage has a **variable interest** rate that can change over time. 这笔抵押贷款的利率是浮动的，随着时间的推移可能会变化。	

balance *n.* 余额

例句 The company's **balance** of accounts improved modestly last month.

这家公司上个月的账户余额有了小幅度的提升。

magnitude *n.* 规模；级别

例句 France and Spain do not face a problem of the same level of **magnitude** as Italy.

法国和西班牙没有面临与意大利同样的重要级别的问题。

asymmetry *n.* 不对称

例句 Alcohol can inhibit our ability to detect **asymmetry** in objects.

酒精能阻碍我们识别物体不对称性的能力。

transaction *n.* 交易

例句 We are not allowed to disclose details of the electronic **transaction**.

我们不被允许透露该电子交易的细节。

steer *v.* 引导；带领

例句 The method aims to **steer** you through the maze of business negations.

这个方法旨在引导你穿越商业谈判的迷宫。

excerpt *v.* 节选；摘录

例句 This sentence is **excerpted** from a famous speech.　这句话摘录自一篇著名的演讲。

7.20 真题同源文章20

New Technology Bill Aims to Strengthen the U. S. Semiconductor Industry
新科技法案旨在加强美国半导体产业

Most of the $280 billion in a new law to strengthen the U. S. semiconductor industry is a 5-year promise, not a reality. But along with the aspirational spending, the recently passed *CHIPS and Science Act* commits some $13 billion right

一项旨在加强美国半导体行业的新法律中的 2800 亿美元大部分是 5 年的承诺，而不是现实。但除了雄心勃勃的支出外，最近通过的《芯片与科学法案》目前承诺投入约 130 亿美元用

now for research and training in microelectronics. And U. S. universities are now forming large coalitions with companies and local governments in order to be ready to compete for the money as soon as a trio of federal agencies announces its plans.

"No sane university with a strong interest in microelectronics is sitting this out," says Jesús del Alamo, professor of electrical engineering at the Massachusetts Institute of Technology (MIT), which is involved with several such partnerships.

The act, signed into law on 9 August, funnels $11 billion over 5 years to the U.S. Department of Commerce to create a National Semiconductor Technology Center (NSTC) and a national advanced packaging manufacturing program. Another $2 billion will go to the Department of Defense (DOD) for a microelectronics commons, a national network of university laboratories to develop prototypes for the next generation of semiconductor technologies.

Both initiatives "are aimed at the dearth of lab-to-fab facilities," referring to university laboratories that develop new technologies to be incorporated into semiconductor fabrication plants, or fabs, says Philip Wong, an electrical engineer at Stanford University who heads its nanofabrication centre. In addition, the National Science Foundation (NSF) is getting $200 million over 5 years for education and workforce training in microelectronics.

"The [research and training] pipeline is just as important as the fabs, although it doesn't get nearly as much attention," says Lisa Su, CEO of chip

于微电子研究和培训。为了尽早获得这笔资金，美国大学目前正在与企业和地方政府结成大型联盟，以便在三个联邦机构宣布它们的计划之后立即准备好争夺资金。

✎ 麻省理工学院（MIT）电气工程教授热苏斯·德尔·阿拉莫表示：“任何对微电子有浓厚兴趣的明智的大学都不会置身事外。”麻省理工学院已参与多个此类的合作伙伴关系。

✎ 该法案于8月9日签署，将在未来5年内向美国商务部拨款110亿美元，用于创建国家半导体技术中心（NSTC）和国家先进封装制造计划。另外20亿美元将用于美国国防部创建微电子共享资源中心，这是一个由大学实验室组成的国家网络，致力于开发下一代半导体技术的原型。

✎ 斯坦福大学纳米制造中心负责人、电气工程师黄汉森表示，这两项举措“旨在填补实验室到工厂设施的不足”，指的是大学实验室开发新技术，然后将其纳入半导体制造工厂（即fabs）。此外，美国国家科学基金会（NSF）在未来5年内将获得2亿美元，用于微电子领域的教育和劳动力培训。

✎ 芯片制造商AMD的首席执行官兼总统科技顾问委员会（PCAST）成员苏姿丰表示：“[研究和培训]渠道与

maker AMD and a member of the President's Council of Advisors on Science and Technology (PCAST). She calls the new law "a once-in-a-generation…opportunity to fill the pipeline with the next generation of semiconductor technologies."

半导体制造工厂同样重要，尽管它没有得到足够的关注。"她将这项新法案称为"一次千载难逢的机会，能填补渠道，发展下一代半导体技术"。

A PCAST report due out this month will recommend NSTC spend 30% to 50% of its budget on fundamental research across a range of fields in microelectronics, from new materials and energy efficient computing to improved security and health care applications. And "a skilled workforce is a prerequisite for everything," says PCAST member Bill Dally, senior vice president for research at NVIDIA. "We need to do a lot of things to retain our leadership in semiconductors, and all of them require talented people."

✎ 本月即将发布的一份 PCAST 报告将建议 NSTC 在微电子领域的各个领域，从新材料和能效计算到改进的安全性和医疗保健应用，将其预算的 30% 至 50% 用于基础研究。PCAST 成员、NVIDIA 负责研发的高级副总裁比尔·达利表示："熟练劳动力是一切的前提。我们需要采取许多措施来保持我们在半导体领域的领导地位，而所有这些措施都需要有才华的人。"

Two large industry-academic-government partnerships are regarded as the leading contenders for NSTC: the American Semiconductor Innovation Coalition (ASIC), spearheaded by IBM and New York's Albany Nanotech Complex; and the Semiconductor Alliance, which features Intel, Micron, and the MITRE Corporation. Both groups boast a roster of academic heavyweights. MIT, the Georgia Institute of Technology, and Purdue University are members of ASIC, whereas Stanford and the University of California (UC), Berkeley, are closely aligned with the Alliance.

✎ 被视为 NSTC 主要竞争者的有两个大型"产－学－政"合作伙伴关系：由 IBM 和纽约奥尔巴尼纳米科技综合体主导的美国半导体创新联盟（ASIC），以及由英特尔、美光和 MITRE 公司组成的半导体联盟。这两个团体都拥有一批学术界重量级人物。麻省理工学院、佐治亚理工学院和普渡大学是 ASIC 的成员，而斯坦福大学和加州大学伯克利分校则与该联盟密切合作。

Although New York, Virginia, and Texas politicians have proposed their states as hosts, insiders say the centre is more likely to be a network of existing facilities spread across the country than a single edifice.

✎ 尽管纽约、弗吉尼亚和得克萨斯的政界人士提出将他们的州作为主办地，但知情人士表示，该中心更有可能是分布在全国各地的现有设施网络，而不是单一的地方。

The centre's to-do list includes funding multimillion-dollar upgrades to existing fab labs at dozens of universities and providing researchers access to a kind of standard workbench to lower the cost of testing and prototyping new chip technologies. NSTC would also support startup companies that want to commercialise those technologies. In addition, the centre would address the need for additional talent at all levels by funding hundreds of new faculty positions, thousands of scholarships, a uniform curriculum in microelectronics with hands-on training, and outreach to middle and high school students.

该中心的待办事项包括向数十所大学现有的制造实验室提供数百万美元的升级资金，并为研究人员提供一种标准工作台，以降低测试和原型制作新芯片技术的成本。NSTC 还将支持希望商业化这些技术的初创公司。此外，该中心将通过资助数百个新的教师职位、数千项奖学金、微电子统一课程及实践培训，以及面向中学和高中学生的宣传活动，以满足各个层次对额外人才的需求。

Only a small number of universities have the capacity to host that training. A white paper issued last year by Del Alamo and his colleagues estimates that upgrading a university fab lab to handle 200-millimeter wafers, the size that has become standard in advanced fabs, would cost $80 million. The university would then need $80 million a year in research grants to operate the lab, which could train some 500 graduate students and postdocs. That rules out many institutions, Del Alamo says. Even upgrading the select group of universities that remains would still leave the country far short of filling the 42, 000 new semi-conductor jobs that *the CHIPS Act* is expected to create, says Tsu-Jae King Liu, UC Berkeley's dean of engineering.

只有少数大学有能力承办这种培训。去年德尔·阿拉莫及其同事发布的一份白皮书估计，将一所大学的制造实验室升级以处理 200 毫米晶圆（在先进制造厂中为标准尺寸）将花费 8000 万美元。然后，该大学每年需要 8000 万美元的研究经费来运营实验室，该实验室可以培训约 500 名研究生和博士后。德尔·阿拉莫表示，这排除了许多机构。加州大学伯克利分校工程学院院长金智洁表示，即使对余下的部分大学进行升级，仍然无法填补《芯片法案》预计将创造的 4.2 万个新半导体工作岗位的差距。

So last year, King Liu spearheaded the formation of the American Semiconductor Academy (ASA), a national network for microelectronics education. She has teamed up with the SEMI Foundation, the nonprofit arm of the industry's trade association, to seek CHIPS funding from DOD and NSF to carry out that vision.

因此，去年，金智洁领导成立了美国半导体学院，这是一个全国性的微电子教育网络。她与该行业贸易协会的非营利机构 SEMI 基金会合作，寻求美国国防部和美国国家科学基金会《芯片法案》的资助，以实现这一愿景。

Attracting U. S. students into microelectronics has become a challenge over the past 30 years as semiconductor jobs moved overseas and Google and other U. S.-based companies threw money at recent graduates to write software rather than make devices, says Sanjay Banerjee, a professor of electrical and computer engineering and head of the microelectronic research centre at the University of Texas (UT), Austin. UT is part of a consortium that is seeking a slice of the DOD funding to reverse that trend.

Banerjee says the DOD proposal will build on a long-running NSF-funded program, called the National Nanotechnology Coordinated Infrastructure (NNCI), which provides $84 million over 5 years to 16 universities. A DOD grant would be like "putting NNCI on steroids," he says. "It will give us better tools, more staff, and facilities more relevant to industry."

The CHIPS legislation aims to spread research and education opportunities both geographically and by race/ethnicity. That will require participation by more institutions not on the nation's East and West coasts, as well as those serving large numbers of students from groups historically underrepresented in science and engineering. They include the country's historically Black colleges and universities (HBCUs), which as a group rank low on a list of institutions getting federal research dollars.

Consortia vying for the funds must make room for those institutions, says electrical engineer Michel Kornegay of Morgan State University, an HBCU in

✎ 来自得克萨斯大学奥斯汀分校电气与计算机工程系教授、微电子研究中心主任桑杰·班纳吉表示，在过去的30年里，随着半导体工作岗位转移到海外，以及谷歌和其他美国公司向应届毕业生提供编写软件而非制造设备的高薪，吸引美国学生进入微电子领域已经变得具有挑战性。得克萨斯大学是一个联盟的一部分，该联盟正在寻求从美国国防部的资金中分一杯羹，以扭转这一趋势。

✎ 班纳吉表示，美国国防部提案将建立在一个由美国国家科学基金会（NSF）资助的长期项目基础上，该项目名为国家纳米技术协调基础设施（NNCI），该基础设施在5年内为16所大学提供8400万美元。他说，美国国防部的资助就像"给NNCI服用类固醇"。"这将为我们提供更好的工具、更多的工作人员以及与行业更相关的设施。"

✎《芯片法案》旨在按照地理位置和种族/民族扩散研究和教育机会。这将需要更多不在美国东西海岸的机构的参与，以及为大量来自历史上在科学和工程领域代表少数群体的学生提供服务的机构的参与。这些机构包括该国历史上的黑人学院和大学，它们在获得联邦研究资金的机构名单上排名靠后。

✎ 巴尔的摩市摩根州立大学电气工程师米歇尔·科恩盖表示，争夺资金的联盟必须为这些机构腾出位置。这所

Baltimore. "Folks talk in general terms about equity and inclusion," says Kornegay, a member of the ASA network. "But they don't spell out how they plan to do that, and whether the people who are going to implement those plans have a track record of success."

The influx of CHIPS money could even widen the gap between the haves and the have-nots if those problems aren't addressed, warns Patricia Mead, dean of engineering at Norfolk State University, an HBCU. "In America, the rich will always get richer," she says. "So you need strong leadership that is going to make a real commitment to broaden the footprint of microelectronics training in this country."

大学是该国历史上的一所黑人大学。科恩盖是美国半导体学校网络的成员之一，他说："人们谈论的是平等和包容，但他们没有具体说明他们计划如何做到这一点，以及负责执行这些计划的人是否有成功的案例。"

✎ 诺福克州立大学（该国一所传统黑人大学）工程学院院长帕特里夏·米德警告说，如果不解决这些问题，《芯片法案》资金的涌入甚至可能加大贫富差距。"在美国，富人总是会变得更富，"她说，"因此，你需要强有力的领导层承诺在这个国家扩大微电子培训的范围。"

核心词汇

aspirational *adj.*	有雄心壮志的；有抱负的
例句 You have to set an **aspirational** path and be impatient to achieve it. 你必须确立一个远大的目标，然后迫不及待地去实现它。	
coalition *n.*	联合体；联盟
例句 His policy risks fracturing the **coalition**. 他的政策有分裂联盟的危险。	
prototype *n.*	原型；雏形；最初形态
例句 Chris Retzler has built a **prototype** of a machine called the wave rotor. 克里斯·雷兹勒制造出了一台叫作波转子的样机。	
initiative *n.*	倡议；新方案
例句 He proposed a new diplomatic **initiative** to try to stop the war. 他提出了一项新的试图阻止战争的外交倡议。	
boast *v.*	自夸；自吹自擂
例句 She is always **boasting** about how wonderful her children are. 她总是夸耀她的孩子们多么出色。	

edifice *n.* 大厦；宏伟建筑

例句 A group of men are erecting a monstrous copper **edifice**.
一群人正在建造一座巨大的铜制建筑。

workbench *n.* 工作台

例句 The device client provides a customised embedded **workbench**.
设备客户机提供一个定制的嵌入式工作台。

outreach *n.* 外展服务

例句 Agency **outreach** activity needs to be expanded. 需要扩大机构的拓展活动。

reverse *v.* 颠倒；彻底转变；使完全相反

例句 The company had to do something to **reverse** its sliding fortunes.
该公司不得不采取措施来逆转其下滑的运势。

implement *v.* 使生效；贯彻；执行；实施

例句 Leadership is about the ability to **implement** change.
领导才能是一种实行变革的能力。

附录 1　雅思阅读高频核心学术词汇

List 1

词汇	词性和释义	词汇	词性和释义
analyse	*v.* 分析	estimate	*v.* 估计
approach	*n.* 方法 *v.* 接近	evidence	*n.* 证据
area	*n.* 区域	export	*n. /v.* 出口
assess	*v.* 评估	factor	*n.* 因素
assume	*v.* 假设	financial	*adj.* 金融的
authority	*n.* 权力；当局	formula	*n.* 公式；配方
available	*adj.* 可得的	function	*n.* 功能 *v.* 起作用
benefit	*n.* 利益	identified	*adj.* 被识别的
concept	*n.* 概念	income	*n.* 收入
consist	*v.* 组成；在于	indicate	*v.* 表明；指出
constitutional	*adj.* 体制的	individual	*n.* 个人
context	*n.* 环境；上下文	interpretation	*n.* 翻译
contract	*n.* 合同	involved	*adj.* 有关的
create	*v.* 创造	issue	*n.* 议题
data	*n.* 数据	labour	*n.* 劳动力
definition	*n.* 定义	legal	*adj.* 合法的
derived	*adj.* 衍生的	legislation	*n.* 立法
distribution	*n.* 分布；分配	major	*adj.* 主要的 *n.* 专业
economic	*adj.* 经济的	occur	*v.* 发生
environment	*n.* 环境	percent	*n.* 百分比
established	*adj.* 已确立的	period	*n.* 时期；周期

（续）

词汇	词性和释义	词汇	词性和释义
policy	*n.* 政策	sector	*n.* 部门
principle	*n.* 原则	significant	*adj.* 重要的
procedure	*n.* 步骤	similar	*adj.* 相似的
process	*v.* 加工 *n.* 过程	source	*n.* 来源
required	*adj.* 必需的；必修的	specific	*adj.* 特定的
research	*n. /v.* 研究	structure	*n.* 结构
response	*n.* 反应；回答	theory	*n.* 理论
role	*n.* 角色	variable	*adj.* 可变的
section	*n.* 部分；章节		

List 2

词汇	词性和释义	词汇	词性和释义
achieve	*v.* 达成	construction	*n.* 建设
acquisition	*n.* 获得	consumer	*n.* 消费者
administration	*n.* 管理	credit	*n.* 信用
affect	*v.* 影响；感动	cultural	*adj.* 文化的
appropriate	*adj.* 适当的	design	*n. /v.* 设计
aspect	*n.* 方面	distinction	*n.* 区别
assistance	*n.* 辅助	element	*n.* 基础；原理
category	*n.* 类别	equation	*n.* 等式；方程式
chapter	*n.* 章；回	evaluation	*n.* 评价
commission	*n.* 委员会	feature	*n.* 特点
community	*n.* 社区；团体	final	*adj.* 最终的
complex	*adj.* 复杂的	focus	*n.* 焦点；中心
computer	*n.* 计算机	impact	*n. /v.* 影响
conclusion	*n.* 结论	injury	*n.* 损伤
conduct	*v.* 带领；引导	institute	*v.* 制定；创立
consequence	*n.* 结果	invest	*v.* 投资

（续）

词汇	词性和释义	词汇	词性和释义
item	*n.* 物件；项目	regulation	*n.* 规则；章程
journal	*n.* 杂志；日记	relevant	*adj.* 有关的
maintain	*v.* 维持；主张	resident	*n.* 居民
normal	*adj.* 正常的	resource	*n.* 资源
obtain	*v.* 获得	restrict	*v.* 限制；约束
participate	*v.* 参与	secure	*v.* 保护 *adj.* 安全的
perceive	*v.* 察觉；理解	seek	*v.* 寻求
positive	*adj.* 积极的	select	*v.* 挑选
potential	*adj.* 潜在的 *n.* 潜力	site	*n.* 地点
previous	*adj.* 以前的	strategy	*n.* 战略
primary	*adj.* 初级的；主要的	survey	*n./v.* 调查
purchase	*v.* 购买	text	*n.* 文本
range	*n.* 范围	tradition	*n.* 传统
region	*n.* 地区	transfer	*v.* 转移；转让

List 3

词汇	词性和释义	词汇	词性和释义
alternative	*adj.* 供选择的	coordinate	*v.* 协调
circumstance	*n.* 环境；情况	core	*n.* 核心
comment	*n./v.* 评论	corporate	*adj.* 公司的；法人的
compensate	*v.* 补偿；赔偿	correspond	*v.* 一致
component	*n.* 成分	criterion	*n.* 标准（*pl.* criteria）
consent	*v.* 同意	deduce	*v.* 推断
considerable	*adj.* 相当多(大、重要)的	demonstrate	*v.* 展示
constant	*adj.* 不变的	document	*n.* 文件
contain	*v.* 包含	dominate	*v.* 支配；控制
contribute	*v.* 贡献	emphasis	*n.* 强调
convene	*v.* 召集；召开；集合	ensure	*v.* 确保

（续）

词汇	词性和释义	词汇	词性和释义
exclude	v. 排除	physical	adj. 物理的；身体的
framework	n. 框架	proportion	n. 比例
fund	n. 基金	publish	v. 发表；公布
illustrate	v. 阐明；举例	react	v. 反应
immigrate	v. （从外国）移民；移居	register	v. 注册；登记
imply	v. 意味；暗示	rely	v. 依靠
initial	adj. 最初的	remove	v. 移动；去除
instance	n. 实例；情况	scheme	n. 计划
interact	v. 相互影响	sequence	n. 顺序
justify	v. 证明……合法/合理	sex	n. 性别
layer	n. 层	shift	n./v. 转变
link	n. 连接；联系 v. 把……连接起来	specify	v. 详细说明
locate	v. 定位	sufficient	adj. 充分的
maximise	v. 增至最大	task	n. 任务
minor	adj. 次要的；较小的	technical	adj. 技术的
negate	v. 否定	technique	n. 技巧；技艺；工艺
outcome	n. 结果	technology	n. 技术
partner	n. 合伙人；同伴	valid	adj. 有效的
philosophy	n. 哲学	volume	n. 量；卷

List 4

词汇	词性和释义	词汇	词性和释义
access	n./v. 进入；接近	attitude	n. 态度
adequate	adj. 充足的	attribute	n. 特质 v. 把……归因于
annual	adj. 年度的	civil	adj. 公民的
apparent	adj. 显然的	code	n. 密码 v. 编码
approximate	v. 近似；接近	commit	v. 犯（罪）；做出（错事）

（续）

词汇	词性和释义	词汇	词性和释义
communicate	*v.* 交流；传达	obvious	*adj.* 明显的
concentrate	*v.* 集中；浓缩	occupy	*v.* 占据；占领
confer	*v.* 授予；协商	option	*n.* 选项；选择
contrast	*n. /v.* 对比；对照	output	*n.* 输出；产量
cycle	*n.* 循环；自行车	overall	*adj.* 全部的
debate	*n. /v.* 争论	parallel	*n.* 相似的人；相似特征
despite	*prep.* 尽管	parameter	*n.* 参数；系数
dimension	*n.* 尺寸；维度	phase	*n.* 阶段
domestic	*adj.* 国内的；家庭的	predict	*v.* 预言
emerge	*v.* 出现；露面	principal	*adj.* 主要的 *n.* 校长
error	*n.* 误差；错误	prior	*adj.* 优先的
ethnic	*adj.* 种族的；人种的	professional	*adj.* 专业的
goal	*n.* 目标	project	*n.* 计划；项目
grant	*v.* 授予；允许	promote	*v.* 促进；提升
hence	*adv.* 因此；以后	regime	*n.* 政权；管理体制
hypothesis	*n.* 假设	resolve	*v.* 解决；分解
implement	*v.* 实施；执行	retain	*v.* 保持；记住
implicate	*v.* 暗示	series	*n.* 系列
impose	*v.* 强加；利用	statistic	*adj.* 统计的
integrate	*v.* 整合；结合	status	*n.* 地位；情形
internal	*adj.* 内部的	stress	*n.* 压力 *v.* 强调
investigate	*v.* 调查	subsequent	*adj.* 后来的
job	*n.* 工作；职业	sum	*n.* 总数；总结
label	*n.* 标签 *v.* 标注	summary	*n.* 概要；总结
mechanism	*n.* 机制；原理	undertake	*v.* 从事；承担

List 5

词汇	词性和释义	词汇	词性和释义
academy	*n.* 学院；学会	generate	*v.* 使形成；发生
adjust	*v.* 调整	generation	*n.* 一代人
alter	*v.* 改变；修改	imagine	*v.* 想象；描绘
amend	*v.* 修正；改善	liberal	*adj.* 开明的
aware	*adj.* 意识到的	license	*n.* 执照；许可证
capacity	*n.* 能力；容量	logic	*n.* 逻辑；逻辑学
challenge	*n.* 挑战	margin	*n.* 边缘；利润
clause	*n.* 条款	medical	*adj.* 医学的；医疗的
compound	*v.* 合成；混合	mental	*adj.* 精神的；脑力的
conflict	*n.* 冲突；矛盾	modify	*v.* 修改；修饰
consult	*v.* 请教；咨询	monitor	*n.* 监视器；班长
contact	*v.* 接触；联系	network	*n.* 网络；网状物
decline	*v.* 下降；减少	notion	*n.* 概念；见解
discrete	*adj.* 不连续的；离散的	objective	*adj.* 客观的 *n.* 目标
draft	*n.* 起草；草稿	orient	*v.* 使适应；使朝向
enable	*v.* 使能够	perspective	*n.* 观点；透视法
energy	*n.* 能源；精力	precise	*adj.* 精确的
enforce	*v.* 强迫；执行	prime	*adj.* 主要的；基本的
entity	*n.* 实体；存在	psychology	*n.* 心理学
equivalent	*adj.* 等价的；相等的	pursue	*v.* 继续；追赶
evolve	*v.* 发展；进化	ratio	*n.* 比率；比例
expand	*v.* 膨胀；扩张	reject	*v.* 拒绝；排斥
expose	*v.* 揭发；显示；暴露	revenue	*n.* 税收；收益
external	*adj.* 外部的	stable	*adj.* 稳定的；牢固的
facilitate	*v.* 促进；使便利	style	*n.* 风格；类型
fundamental	*adj.* 基本的	substitute	*n./v.* 代替

（续）

词汇	词性和释义	词汇	词性和释义
sustain	*v.* 保持；支撑	trend	*n.* 趋势；走向
symbol	*n.* 符号；象征	version	*n.* 版本；描述
target	*n.* 目标	welfare	*n.* 福利；幸福
transit	*n.* 运输 *v.* 穿过；经过	whereas	*conj.* 然而；但是

List 6

词汇	词性和释义	词汇	词性和释义
abstract	*n.* 摘要 *adj.* 抽象的	exceed	*v.* 超过；胜过
accurate	*adj.* 准确的	expert	*n.* 专家 *adj.* 内行的
acknowledge	*v.* 承认；答谢	explicit	*adj.* 明确的；直率的
aggregate	*v.* 集合；合计	federal	*adj.* 联邦的
allocate	*v.* 分配；拨出	fee	*n.* 费用
assign	*v.* 分配；指派	flexible	*adj.* 灵活的
attach	*v.* 使依附；贴上	furthermore	*adv.* 此外
author	*n.* 作者	gender	*n.* 性别
bond	*n.* 债券；纽带	ignorant	*adj.* 无知的；愚昧的
brief	*adj.* 简洁的；短暂的	incentive	*n.* 动机；激励
capable	*adj.* 能干的	incidence	*n.* 发生率
cite	*v.* 引用	incorporate	*v.* 包含；合并
cooperate	*v.* 合作	index	*n.* 指数；索引
discriminate	*v.* 歧视	inhibit	*v.* 抑制；禁止
display	*v.* 显示	initiate	*v.* 开始；发起
diverse	*adj.* 不同的；多变的	input	*n.* 投入；输入
domain	*n.* 领域；产业	instruct	*v.* 指导；命令
edit	*v.* 编辑；校订	intelligence	*n.* 智力
enhance	*v.* 提高；加强	interval	*n.* 间隔；间距
estate	*n.* 个人财产	lecture	*n.* 讲座

（续）

词汇	词性和释义	词汇	词性和释义
migrate	*v.* 迁移；移居	recover	*v.* 恢复
minimum	*n.* 最小值	reveal	*v.* 显示；揭露
ministry	*n.* （政府）部门	scope	*n.* 范围；视野
motive	*n.* 动机；目的	subsidy	*n.* 补贴；津贴
neutral	*adj.* 中立的	tape	*n.* 胶带；磁带
nevertheless	*adv.* 然而；不过	trace	*n.* 追溯；追踪
overseas	*adj.* 国外的	transform	*v.* 改变；转换
precede	*v.* 领先；优于	transport	*v.* 运输
presume	*v.* 假定；推测	underlie	*v.* 成为……的基础
rational	*adj.* 合理的	utilise	*v.* 利用

List 7

词汇	词性和释义	词汇	词性和释义
adapt	*v.* 适应；改编	decade	*n.* 十年
adult	*n.* 成年人	definite	*adj.* 肯定的；确定的
advocate	*v.* 提倡；主张	deny	*v.* 否认；拒绝
aid	*n.* 援助；帮助	differentiate	*v.* 区分；区别
channel	*n.* 频道；渠道	dispose	*v.* 处理；安排
chemical	*adj. /n.* 化学的（制品）	dynamic	*adj.* 动态的；有活力的
classic	*adj.* 典型的；最优秀的	eliminate	*v.* 消除；排除
comprehensive	*adj.* 全面的	empirical	*adj.* 经验主义的
comprise	*v.* 包含；由……组成	equip	*v.* 装备；配备
confirm	*v.* 确认；批准	extract	*v.* 提取；摘录
contrary	*adj.* 相反的；对立的	file	*n.* 文件；档案
convert	*v.* 使转换；转变	finite	*adj.* 有限的；限定的
couple	*n.* 对；夫妇	foundation	*n.* 基础；基金会

（续）

词汇	词性和释义	词汇	词性和释义
globe	*n.* 地球；球体	publication	*n.* 出版；出版物
grade	*n.* 等级；成绩	quote	*v.* 引述；举证
guarantee	*v.* 保证；担保	release	*v.* 释放；发射
hierarchy	*n.* 层级；等级制度	reverse	*v.* 反转 *n.* 相反的情况
identical	*adj.* 完全相同的	simulate	*v.* 模仿；假装
ideology	*n.* 意识形态	sole	*adj.* 唯一的；仅有的
infer	*v.* 推断；推论	somewhat	*adv.* 多少；有点儿
innovate	*v.* 创新；革新	submit	*v.* 屈从；呈递
insert	*v.* 插入；嵌入	successor	*n.* 继承者
intervene	*v.* 干涉；调停	survive	*v.* 幸存；生还
isolate	*v.* 使隔离；使孤立	thesis	*n.* 论文
media	*n.* 媒体	topic	*n.* 主题；题目
mode	*n.* 模式；风格	transmit	*v.* 传输；传播
paradigm	*n.* 范例；范式	ultimate	*adj.* 最终的；根本的
phenomenon	*n.* 现象	unique	*adj.* 独特的
priority	*n.* 优先；优先权	visible	*adj.* 可见的
prohibit	*v.* 阻止；禁止	voluntary	*adj.* 自愿的；自发的

List 8

词汇	词性和释义	词汇	词性和释义
abandon	*v.* 放弃；放纵	appreciate	*v.* 欣赏；感激
accompany	*v.* 陪伴；伴随	arbitrary	*adj.* 任意的；武断的
accumulate	*v.* 积累	automate	*v.* 使自动化
ambiguous	*adj.* 模糊不清的	bias	*n.* 偏见
append	*v.* 附加；增补	chart	*n.* 图表；图纸

（续）

词汇	词性和释义	词汇	词性和释义
clarify	v. 澄清；阐明	manipulate	v. 操纵；操作
commodity	n. 商品；货物	minimise	v. 最小化
complement	n. 补足物	nuclear	adj. 原子能的
conform	v. 符合；遵照	offset	v. 抵消；补偿
contemporary	adj. 当代的	paragraph	n. 段落
contradict	v. 反驳；与……矛盾	plus	adj. 正的 prep. 加上
crucial	adj. 至关重要的	practitioner	n. 从业者
currency	n. 货币；通货	predominant	adj. 主要的；卓越的
denote	v. 表示；指示	prospect	n. 前景
detect	v. 觉察；发现	radical	adj. 重大的；激进的
deviate	v. 脱离；越轨	random	adj. 随机的；胡乱的
displace	v. 取代；置换	reinforce	v. 加强；补充
drama	n. 戏剧	restore	v. 恢复；归还
eventual	adj. 最后的；结果的	revise	v. 修正；复习
exhibit	v. 展览；显示	schedule	n. 安排；时间表
exploit	v. 开发；利用	tense	adj. 紧张的；拉紧的
fluctuate	v. 波动；动摇	terminate	v. 使终止；结束
guideline	n. 指导方针	theme	n. 主题
highlight	v. 突出；强调	thereby	adv. 从而；因此
implicit	adj. 含蓄的；暗示的	uniform	adj. 统一的 n. 制服
induce	v. 诱导；引起	vehicle	n. 车辆
inevitable	adj. 不可避免的	via	prep. 取道；经由
infrastructure	n. 基础设施	virtual	adj. 虚拟的；事实上的
inspect	v. 检阅；视察	visual	adj. 视觉的；栩栩如生的
intense	adj. 强烈的；激烈的	widespread	adj. 普遍的；广泛的

List 9

词汇	词性和释义	词汇	词性和释义
accommodate	v. 容纳；供应	insight	n. 洞察力；洞悉
analogy	n. 类比	integral	adj. 完整的；必需的
anticipate	v. 预期	intermediate	adj. 中间的
assure	v. 保证；担保	manual	adj. 手工的；体力的
attain	v. 达到；实现	mature	adj. 成熟的
behalf	n. 代表；利益	mediate	v. 调解 adj. 中间的
bulk	n. 大块；大部分	medium	adj. 中间的 n. 媒体
cease	n. 停止	military	adj. 军事的
coherent	adj. 连贯的；一致的	minimal	adj. 最小的
coincide	v. 一致；同时发生	mutual	adj. 共同的；相互的
commence	v. 开始；着手	norm	n. 准则；规范
compatible	adj. 兼容的	overlap	v. 重叠；重复
concurrent	adj. 同时发生的	passive	adj. 被动的；消极的
confine	v. 界限；限制	portion	n. 部分
controversy	n. 争论；辩论	preliminary	n. 准备工作；预赛
converse	adj. 相反的；颠倒的	protocol	n. 协议；礼节
device	n. 仪器；装置	qualitative	adj. 质量的
devote	v. 致力于；奉献	refine	v. 提炼；完善
diminish	v. 减少；缩小	relax	v. 放松；休息
distort	v. 扭曲；曲解	restrain	v. 抑制；控制
duration	n. 持续；期间	revolution	n. 革命；变革
erode	v. 腐蚀；侵蚀	rigid	adj. 严格的；死板的
ethic	adj. 伦理的	route	n. 路线；航线
format	n. 格式；形式	scenario	n. 方案；剧情梗概
founded	adj. 以……为基础的	sphere	n. 范围；球体
inherent	adj. 固有的；内在的	subordinate	n. 下属；下级

（续）

词汇	词性和释义	词汇	词性和释义
supplement	*n.* 补充	trigger	*v.* 引发；触发
suspend	*v.* 推迟；暂停	unify	*v.* 统一；使相同
team	*n.* 队；组	violate	*v.* 违反；侵犯
temporary	*adj.* 暂时的；临时的	vision	*n.* 视力；视野

List 10

词汇	词性和释义	词汇	词性和释义
adjacent	*adj.* 邻近的	invoke	*v.* 引起；使人想起
albeit	*conj.* 虽然；尽管	levy	*v.* 征收（税）
assemble	*v.* 集合；聚集	likewise	*adv.* 同样的；也
collapse	*v.* 倒塌；瓦解	nonetheless	*adv.* 尽管如此
colleague	*n.* 同事；同僚	notwithstanding	*conj./prep.* 尽管
compile	*v.* 汇编	odd	*adj.* 古怪的；奇数的
conceive	*v.* 怀孕；构思	ongoing	*adj.* 不间断的；前进的
convince	*v.* 说服；使信服	panel	*n.* 仪表盘；专门小组
depress	*v.* 使沮丧	persist	*v.* 坚持
encounter	*v.* 遭遇；邂逅	pose	*v.* 造成；形成
enormous	*adj.* 巨大的	reluctance	*n.* 勉强
forthcoming	*adj.* 即将来临的	so-called	*adj.* 所谓的
incline	*v.* 倾斜；倾向	straightforward	*adj.* 简单的；坦率的
integrity	*n.* 完整；正直	undergo	*v.* 经历；经受
intrinsic	*adj.* 本质的；固有的	whereby	*adv.* 凭借

附录 2　雅思阅读必备学科分类词汇

1. 自然景观

1.1 自然环境

词汇	词性和释义	词汇	词性和释义
natural	*adj.* 自然的；天然的	toxic	*adj.* 有毒的；引起中毒的
scenery	*n.* 景色；风景	pollute	*v.* 污染；弄脏
canyon	*n.* 峡谷	pollution	*n.* 污染；玷污；污染物；垃圾
limpid	*adj.* 清澈的	pollutant	*n.* 污染物
gorge	*n.* 峡；谷	contaminate	*v.* 污染
spectacle	*n.* 奇观；景象	sewage	*n.* （下水道的）污水；污物
shade	*n.* 树荫	waste	*n.* 废物；荒地 *adj.* 废弃的；荒芜的
jungle	*n.* 丛林	fume	*n.* 烟气；烟雾
meadow	*n.* 草地；牧场	fauna	*n.* 动物群
shrub	*n.* 灌木；灌木丛	ozonosphere	*n.* 臭氧层
luxuriant	*adj.* 繁茂的；茂盛的	balmy	*adj.* 温和的
habitat	*n.* （动、植物的）栖息地	humid	*adj.* 潮湿的
ecosystem	*n.* 生态系统	humidity	*n.* 潮湿
decibel	*n.* 分贝	damp	*n.* 湿气；潮气 *adj.* 潮湿的；有湿气的
noxious	*adj.* 有害的；有毒的	dank	*adj.* 阴湿的

（续）

词汇	词性和释义	词汇	词性和释义
deforestation	*n.* 森林采伐	smog	*n.* 烟雾
desertification	*n.* 沙漠化	fog	*n.* 雾；烟雾
radiation	*n.* 辐射	haze	*n.* 烟雾；雾霾
deterioration	*n.* 恶化	rainfall	*n.* 降雨；降雨量
meteorology	*n.* 气象（学）	drizzle	*n.* 毛毛细雨
climate	*n.* 气候	shower	*n.* 阵雨
atmosphere	*n.* 大气；空气	blizzard	*n.* 暴风雪
hurricane	*n.* 飓风	downpour	*n.* 倾盆大雨
gale	*n.* 大风	frost	*n.* 霜；霜冻
breeze	*n.* 微风	vapour	*n.* 水蒸气
blast	*n.* 疾风	tempest	*n.* 暴风雨
whirlwind	*n.* 旋风	dew	*n.* 露水
typhoon	*n.* 台风	tropical rainforest	热带雨林
tornado	*n.* 旋风；龙卷风	acid rain	酸雨
renewable	*adj.* 可再生的	waste disposal	废物处理
serene	*adj.* 平静的；安详的	waste water	废水
chilly	*adj.* 寒冷的	waste gas	废气
drought	*n.* 干旱	water shortage	水资源短缺
sterile	*adj.* 贫瘠的	disposable product	一次性产品
arid	*adj.* 干燥的；干旱的；贫瘠的；荒芜的	wind energy	风能
barometer	*n.* 气压计	rapid rain	急雨
troposphere	*n.* 对流层	thunder rain	雷雨
current	*n.* 气流	periodical rain	间歇雨
funnel	*n.* 漏斗云		

1.2 地 理

词汇	词性和释义	词汇	词性和释义
Alpine	*adj.* 高山的；阿尔卑斯山的	lowland	*n.* 低地
Arctic	*adj.* 北极的	islet	*n.* 小岛
Antarctic	*adj.* 南极的	offshore	*adj.* 离岸的 *adv.* （风）向海地；离岸地
climatic	*adj.* 气候的	bay	*n.* 海湾
windward	*adj.* 上风的；迎风的	erosion	*n.* 侵蚀
avalanche	*n.* 雪崩	groundwater	*n.* 地下水
catastrophe	*n.* 大灾难	insular	*adj.* 海岛的
crevasse	*n.* 裂缝；冰隙	peninsula	*n.* 半岛
friction	*n.* 摩擦；摩擦力	ledge	*n.* 岩架
geochron	*n.* 地质年代	oasis	*n.* （沙漠中的）绿洲
glacier	*n.* 冰川	tide	*n.* 潮汐
gravity	*n.* 重力；万有引力	ebb	*n.* 退潮 *v.* （潮水）退去
clockwise	*adj.* 顺时针方向的 *adv.* 顺时针方向转动地	continent	*n.* 大陆
nocturnal	*adj.* 夜间的	terrestrial	*adj.* 领土的
periodic	*adj.* 周期的；定期的	outskirt	*n.* 市郊；郊区
thermal	*adj.* 热的；热量的	region	*n.* 地区，地域
torrential	*adj.* 奔流的；如急流的	endemic	*adj.* 地方性的
torrid	*adj.* 灼热的；炎热的	cosmopolitan	*adj.* 世界性的
ablation	*n.* 消融	subterrane	*n.* 地下
advection	*n.* 平流；对流	subterranean	*adj.* 地下的
agglomeration	*n.* 聚集	cavern	*n.* 大山洞；大洞穴
cyclone	*n.* 气旋；旋风	cleft	*n.* （自然的）裂缝
highland	*n.* 高地；高原	crevice	*n.* （岩石的）裂缝；裂口

（续）

词汇	词性和释义	词汇	词性和释义
chasm	*n.* 裂缝；裂口	iceberg	*n.* 冰山
equator	*n.* 赤道	plate	*n.* 板块
longitude	*n.* 经度	tremor	*n.* （轻微）震动；颤动
altitude	*n.* （尤指海拔）高度；高处	seismic	*adj.* 地震的；地震引起的
latitude	*n.* 纬度	seismology	*n.* 地震学
meridian	*n.* 子午线；经线	magnitude	*n.* 震级
subsidiary	*n.* 支流	stratum	*n.* 地层
coastland	*n.* 沿海岸地区	mantle	*n.* 地幔
contour	*n.* 轮廓，海岸线	crust	*n.* 地壳
geography	*n.* 地理学；地理	core	*n.* 地核
horizon	*n.* 地平线	lithogenous	*adj.* 造岩的；岩成的
plain	*n.* 平原；草原	lithosphere	*n.* 岩石圈
strait	*n.* 海峡	layer	*n.* 层；表层
channel	*n.* 海峡；水道	fault	*n.* 断层
valley	*n.* 山谷	magma	*n.* 岩浆
plateau	*n.* 高原	squirt	*v.* 喷出；喷射
basin	*n.* 盆地	erupt	*v.* 爆发
salinity	*n.* 盐分；盐度	outburst	*n.* 爆发；喷出
sediment	*n.* 沉淀物；沉积物	volcanic	*adj.* 火山的
elevation	*n.* 高度；海拔	the Arctic Circle	北极圈
formation	*n.* 形成；构成	the Antarctic Circle	南极圈
geothermy	*n.* 地热	the northern hemisphere	北半球
terrain	*n.* 地形	the southern hemisphere	南半球
topography	*n.* 地形学	the Tropic of Cancer	北回归线
tropics	*n.* 热带；热带地区	the Tropic of Capricorn	南回归线
crater	*n.* 火山口		

2. 动植物

2.1 动物

词汇	词性和释义	词汇	词性和释义
carnivore	n. 食肉动物	dicky bird	鸟儿；小鸟
carnivorous	adj. 食肉的	dinosaur	n. 恐龙
herbivore	n. 食草动物	dolphin	n. 海豚
herbivorous	adj. 食草的	elasmobranch	n. 软骨鱼；板鳃类鱼
omnivorous	adj.（动物）杂食性的	embryo	n. 胚胎
amphibian	n. 两栖动物	fin	n. 鱼翅；鱼鳍
mammal	n. 哺乳动物	gorilla	n. 大猩猩
hatch	v. 孵化	imago	n. 成虫
hereditary	adj. 遗传的	jellyfish	n. 水母；海蜇
Mesozoic	adj. 中生代的	larva	n. 幼虫；幼体
webbed	adj. 有蹼的	locust	n. 蝗虫
ape	n. 猿猴	malaria	n. 疟疾
beak	n. 鸟喙	marsupial	n. 有袋动物
beeswax	n. 蜂蜡	otter	n. 水獭
branchia	n. 鳃	primate	n. 灵长类
carrion	n.（动物尸体的）腐肉	pupa	n. 蛹
caste	n. 等级	termite	n. 白蚁
corpse	n. 尸体	tortoise	n. 龟；陆龟
crow	n. 乌鸦	turtle	n. 鳖；海龟；陆龟
cub	n. 幼小的兽	wasp	n. 黄蜂
den	n. 兽窝	conch	n. 海螺

（续）

词汇	词性和释义	词汇	词性和释义
mussel	n. 珠蚌；河蚌	migrate	v.（鸟类等）迁徙
gregarious	adj. 群居的	graze	v. 放牧
swarm	n.（蜜蜂、蚂蚁等的）群	peck	v. 啄；啄食
flock	n.（禽、畜等的）群	offspring	n.（动物的）崽
herd	n. 兽群；牧群	spawn	n.（鱼、蛙等的）卵 v.（鱼、蛙等）大量产卵
appetite	n. 食欲	domesticate	v. 驯养
predator	n. 捕食者；食肉动物	fertilise	v. 使受精
predatory	adj. 捕食的；食肉的	reproduce	v. 繁殖；再生
prey	n. 被捕食者	squeak	n.（老鼠等的）吱吱声 v.（老鼠等）吱吱叫
poikilotherm	n. 变温动物；冷血动物	hibernate	v. 冬眠
rodent	n. 啮齿动物	extinction	n. 灭绝
scavenger	n. 食腐动物	monogamous	adj. 一雌一雄的
microbe	n. 微生物；细菌	polyandrous	adj. 一雌多雄的
reptile	n. 爬行动物	polygamous	adj. 一雄多雌的
homotherm	n. 恒温动物	nest	n. 巢；窝
mollusk	n. 软体动物	niche	n. 小生态环境
coelenterate	n. 腔肠动物	pest	n. 害虫
vertebrate	n. 脊椎动物	rhinoceros	n. 犀牛
invertebrate	n. 无脊椎动物	chimpanzee	n. 黑猩猩
finch	n. 雀类	baboon	n. 狒狒
fowl	n. 家禽	lizard	n. 蜥蜴
monster	n. 怪物；巨兽	moth	n. 蛾
worm	n. 虫；蠕虫	canary	n. 金丝雀
beast	n. 兽	caterpillar	n. 毛虫
aquatic	adj. 水生的；水栖的	chameleon	n. 变色龙

（续）

词汇	词性和释义	词汇	词性和释义
bat	*n.* 蝙蝠	prawn	*n.* 对虾；大虾
family	*n.* 科	shrimp	*n.* 小虾
class	*n.* 纲	lobster	*n.* 龙虾
suborder	*n.* 亚目	sponge	*n.* 海绵；海绵体
order	*n.* 目	plankton	*n.* 浮游生物
genus	*n.* （动、植物等分类的）属	oyster	*n.* 牡蛎；蚝
antenna	*n.* 触须；触角	clam	*n.* 蛤
tentacle	*n.* 触须；触角	coral	*n.* 珊瑚；珊瑚虫
brain	*n.* 大脑	crab	*n.* 螃蟹
spleen	*n.* 脾脏	Darwinism	*n.* 达尔文学说；进化论
hide	*n.* 兽皮	evolve	*v.* 进化
spine	*n.* 脊柱；脊椎	reproduction	*n.* 繁殖
spineless	*adj.* 无脊椎的	proliferate	*v.* 繁衍
toe	*n.* 脚趾	propagate	*v.* 繁殖
bill	*n.* 鸟嘴	subsist	*v.* 生存；存在
fuzzy	*adj.* 有绒毛的	parasite	*n.* 寄生虫；寄生植物
hump	*n.* 驼峰	mimicry	*n.* 模仿；拟态
scale	*n.* 鳞片	symbiosis	*n.* 共生（现象）
wing	*n.* 翅膀；翼	organism	*n.* 生物；有机物
fluffy	*adj.* 绒毛的	strain	*n.* （动、植物的）品种
carnal	*adj.* 肉体的	vital	*adj.* 生命的；与生命有关的
nervous	*adj.* 神经系统的	respiratory	*adj.* 呼吸的
grease	*n.* 动物油脂；油脂	stodgy	*adj.* 难消化的
beaver	*n.* 海狸	secrete	*v.* 分泌
starfish	*n.* 海星	secretion	*n.* 分泌（物）
whale	*n.* 鲸	assimilate	*v.* 吸收；消化
porpoise	*n.* 鼠海豚	metabolism	*n.* 新陈代谢

（续）

词汇	词性和释义
morphology	*n.* 形态学
microscope	*n.* 显微镜
origin of species	物种起源
unfertilised egg	未受精卵
animal rights activist	动物权益保护主义者
endangered animal	濒危动物
perform experiments on animals	在动物身上做实验
test animal	用于实验的动物
be subjected to experiments	被迫接受实验
live and let live	活着就是与万物共存
dominant species	优势物种

2.2 植 物

词汇	词性和释义	词汇	词性和释义
botany	*n.* 植物学	archesporial	*adj.* 孢子细胞的
botanical	*adj.* 植物学的	cauline	*adj.* 茎（上）的
chlorophyll	*n.* 叶绿素	rhodospermous	*adj.* 红藻科的
deciduous	*adj.* 每年落叶的	venomous	*adj.* 分泌毒液的
inorganic	*adj.* 无机的	angiosperm	*n.* 被子植物
organic	*adj.* 有机的	coconut	*n.* 椰子
plantation	*n.* 种植园	fermentation	*n.* 发酵
photosynthesis	*n.* 光合作用	fern	*n.* 蕨类植物
reed	*n.* 芦苇	gymnosperm	*n.* 裸子植物
pollinate	*v.* 传粉；授粉	hormone	*n.* 激素
sprout	*v.* 发芽	monad	*n.* 单孢体；单细胞生物

（续）

词汇	词性和释义	词汇	词性和释义
polymer	*n.* 聚合物	cluster	*n.* 簇；团
powder	*n.* 粉；粉末	timber	*n.* 木材；木料
rosin	*n.* 松香；树脂	germinate	*v.* 发芽
rubber	*n.* 橡胶；合成橡胶	rosette	*n.* 玫瑰形饰物
seedling	*n.* 幼苗	orchid	*n.* 兰花
spore	*n.* 孢子	petal	*n.* 花瓣
vermin	*n.* 害虫	husk	*n.* （果类或谷物的）外壳；皮
shrub	*n.* 灌木丛	pollen	*n.* 花粉 *v.* 传授花粉给……
sequoia	*n.* 红杉	root	*n.* 根；根部
herb	*n.* 药草；香草	log	*n.* 圆木
foliage	*n.* 树叶；枝叶	flora	*n.* 植物界
bud	*n.* 芽	necrosis	*n.* （组织细胞的）坏死
leaflet	*n.* 小叶	peel	*n.* （水果、蔬菜等的）外皮；果皮 *v.* 剥（皮）；削（皮）
leafstalk	*n.* 叶柄	shell	*n.* （坚果等的）壳 *v.* 给……去壳
trunk	*n.* 树干	shoot	*n.* 幼苗；嫩芽
stalk	*n.* 茎；柄；梗；秆	starch	*n.* 淀粉
stem	*n.* 茎；干	vitamin	*n.* 维生素
branch	*n.* 枝；树枝	carbohydrate	*n.* 碳水化合物；糖类
bough	*n.* 大树枝；主枝	glucose	*n.* 葡萄糖
twig	*n.* 小树枝	artificial flower	人造花
bark	*n.* 树皮	deciduous tree	落叶树
bunch	*n.* 串；束	evergreen tree	常绿树

3. 交通与建筑

3.1 交　通

词汇	词性和释义	词汇	词性和释义
reverse	v. 倒（车）	cyclist	n. 骑自行车的人
overtake	v. 超（车）	motorcyclist	n. 骑摩托车的人
skid	v.（车辆）打滑	energy-saving	adj. 节能的
suspension	n.（车辆的）悬架；减震装置	modernisation	n. 现代化
traction	n.（车辆的）牵引力	bottleneck	n. 交通拥堵地区
windscreen	n. 汽车挡风玻璃	overcrowded	adj. 过度拥挤的
accelerate	v. 加速	violator	n. 违规者
brake	n. 车闸；刹车 v. 刹（车）	start up　启动	
decelerate	v. 减速	speed limit　限速	
park	v. 停（车）；泊（车）	highway code　交通法规	
bearing	n. 方位	traffic sign　交通标志	
highway	n. 公路	change gear　变速	
T-junction	n. 丁字路口	top speed　最高速度	
pedestrian	n. 行人	switch off the motor　熄火	
pavement	n. 人行道	guard rail　护栏	
intersection	n. 交叉路口	pedestrians' street　步行街	
motorcycle	n. 摩托车	inside lane　慢车道	
coach	n. 大客车	outside lane　快车道	
express	n. 快车	single carriageway　单行道	
helicopter	n. 直升机	ring road　环路	
electromobile	n. 电动车	overtaking lane　超车道	

（续）

词汇	词性和释义	词汇	词性和释义
makeshift road 临时道路		break traffic regulations 违反交通规则	
tarred road 柏油路		get struck in traffic 遇上堵车	
elevated highroad 高速公路		road networks 公路网	
dual carriageway 双行道		rush hour 高峰时间	
the number of car ownership 汽车拥有量		ease the traffic pressure 缓解交通压力	
pollution-free fuel 无污染燃料		chronic lead poisoning 慢性铅中毒	
observe traffic regulations 遵守交通规则		automobile industry 汽车工业	

3.2 建 筑

词汇	词性和释义	词汇	词性和释义
architecture	n. 建筑	eave	n. 屋檐
skyscraper	n. 摩天大楼	column	n. 柱；支柱
monument	n. 纪念碑	brace	n. 支架
palace	n. 宫殿	concrete	n. 混凝土
temple	n. 庙宇	clay	n. 黏土
basilica	n. 大殿；大教堂	elasticity	n. 弹性
cathedral	n. 大教堂	excavation	n. 挖掘；发掘
tower	n. 塔；塔楼	thatch	n. 茅草；草屋顶
cottage	n. 村舍；小别墅	wickerwork	n. 柳条编制品
landmark	n. 地标	camp	n. 露营地；阵营 v. 露营；扎营
external	adj. 外部的	shelter	n. 居所；住处；遮蔽；庇护 v. 掩蔽；保护
well-preserved	adj. 保护良好的	greensward	n. 草地；草坪
beam	n. 梁	pier	n. 桥墩

（续）

词汇	词性和释义	词汇	词性和释义
resonance	*n.* 共振	civil architecture　民用建筑	
spire	*n.* 教堂的塔尖	classical architecture　古典建筑	
tomb	*n.* 坟墓	conventional architecture　寺院建筑	
ventilation	*n.* 通风	decorated architecture　尖拱式建筑	
cosmic	*adj.* 宇宙的；极广阔的	domestic architecture　民用建筑	
basso-relievo	*n.* 浮雕	garden architecture　庭院建筑	
block of flats　公寓楼		duplex apartment　双层式建筑	
delicate design　巧妙的设计		ten-storey office block　十层办公大楼	
structural botany　植物建造学		old-fashioned house　老式房屋	
ancient architecture　古代建筑		landscape architecture　园林建筑	

4. 社会生活

4.1 经　济

词汇	词性和释义	词汇	词性和释义
prosperous	*adj.* 繁荣的	indigent	*adj.* 贫穷的
prosperity	*n.* 繁荣；成功	depression	*n.* 萧条
compensation	*n.* 补偿	deficit	*n.* 赤字
lease	*v.* 出租	levy	*n.* 税款 *v.* 征收
exponent	*n.* 指数	rebate	*n.* 返回款；折扣
drawback	*n.* 退款	ration	*n.* 定量；配给量 *v.* 配给；分发
rare	*adj.* 稀罕的；珍贵的	merchandise	*n.* 商品 *v.* 推销；销售
asset	*n.* 财产；财富	currency	*n.* 通货
fortune	*n.* 财富	disburse	*v.* 支付；支出；分配

（续）

词汇	词性和释义	词汇	词性和释义
consume	*v.* 消费；消耗	transaction	*n.* 交易
cause	*n.* 事业 *v.* 导致；引起	assess	*v.* 评价；估算
quota	*n.* 限额	consolidate	*v.* 合并
inflation	*n.* 通货膨胀	contract	*n.* 契约
deflation	*n.* 通货紧缩	loan	*n.* 贷款
deal	*n.* （一笔）交易 *v.* 交易	benefit	*n.* 利益
yen	*n.* 日元	refund	*n.* 退款；返还款
acting	*adj.* 代理的	output	*n.* 产量；输出量
discount	*n.* 折扣 *v.* 打折	revenue	*n.* 收入
audit	*n.* 审计；稽核 *v.* 审查；审计	fund	*n.* 资金；基金 *v.* 为……提供资金
residue	*n.* 剩余财产	debt	*n.* 债务
account	*n.* 账户；账目	budget	*n.* 预算 *v.* 做预算
bankruptcy	*n.* 破产	patronage	*n.* 赞助；资助
savings	*n.* 储蓄金；存款	means	*n.* 财富；钱财
reimburse	*v.* 偿还	interest	*n.* 利息
merge	*v.* 合并	bonus	*n.* 红利；奖金
depreciate	*v.* 贬值；跌价	customs	*n.* 进口税；关税
appreciate	*v.* 升值；增值	purchase	*n.* 购买；采购；购买的东西 *v.* 购买
revalue	*v.* 升值；增值	commission	*n.* 佣金
cheque	*n.* 支票	ransom	*n.* 赎金 *v.* 交付赎金
bill	*n.* 钞票；账单	charge	*n.* 费用；收费 *v.* 收（费）；要价
collateral	*n.* 抵押品	bond	*n.* 公债；按揭贷款
exchange	*v.* 兑换	economic prosperity	经济繁荣

（续）

词汇	词性和释义	词汇	词性和释义
purchasing power 购买力		levy the tax 征税	
explicit cost 显性成本		enhance the quality of life 提高生活质量	
implicit cost 隐形成本		marketable product 畅销产品	
money market 金融市场		potential market 潜在市场	
quantity demanded 需求量		perfect services 完善服务	
quantity supplied 供给量		in all walks of life 在各行各业	
boost economic development 促进经济发展		fake and exaggerated information 虚假信息	
promote relative industries 促进相关产业发展		be deceptive and misleading 具有欺骗性和误导性	

4.2 法 律

词汇	词性和释义	词汇	词性和释义
penal	*adj.* 刑罚的；惩罚的	domineering	*adj.* 专横的；盛气凌人的
illicit	*adj.* 违法的	mandatory	*adj.* 命令的；强制的
unruly	*adj.* 不守法的	licensed	*adj.* 被许可的
illegitimate	*adj.* 非法的；私生的	heir	*n.* 继承人
default	*n.* 不履行责任 *v.* 不履行（责任）	arbitration	*n.* 调停；仲裁
violate	*v.* 违反；违背	fine	*n.* 罚金
bound	*adj.* 有义务的	confiscate	*v.* 没收；把……充公
compulsory	*adj.* 义务的	convict	*v.* 宣判……有罪；定罪
obligatory	*adj.* 义务的；强制的	verdict	*v.* 判决
enlightened	*adj.* 开明的	judgment	*n.* 判决
humane	*adj.* 仁慈的	indemnity	*n.* 赔偿；赔偿金

（续）

词汇	词性和释义	词汇	词性和释义
pickpocket	*n.* 扒手	stipulate	*v.* 约定；规定
imprisonment	*n.* 监禁	testify	*v.* 证明；证实
invalidate	*v.* 使作废	testimony	*n.* 证言
captivity	*n.* 囚禁；拘留	justify	*v.* 证明……是正当的
trial	*n.* 审判；审讯	substantiate	*v.* 证实
detain	*v.* 拘留；扣留	confirm	*v.* 证实；确认
extenuate	*v.* 使（罪过等）显得轻微	affirm	*v.* 证实
court	*n.* 法庭	assure	*v.* 使确信
bar	*n.* 法庭	evidence	*n.* 证据
authorise	*v.* 授权	follow	*v.* 跟随；遵循
empower	*v.* 授权	observe	*v.* 遵守
oath	*n.* 誓言；誓约	observance	*n.* 遵守
pledge	*v.* 使发誓	abide	*v.* 遵守
plead	*v.* 为……辩护	accuse	*v.* 指责；指控
flee	*v.* 逃跑；逃离	accusation	*n.* 控告
defend	*v.* 辩护	complaint	*n.* 控告
proscribe	*v.* 禁止	impeach	*v.* 弹劾
forbid	*v.* 禁止	indictment	*n.* 起诉
abstinence	*n.* 戒绝；节制	incriminate	*v.* 使负罪；连累
ban	*n.* 禁令，禁止	prosecute	*v.* 起诉；检举
veto	*n.* 否决；否决权 *v.* 行使否决权	denounce	*v.* 指责；谴责；弹劾；告发；指控
revise	*v.* 修订；修正	lawsuit	*n.* 诉讼
verify	*v.* 验证	query	*n.* 质问；询问 *v.* 质疑；提问
deserve	*v.* 应得；应受（惩罚等）	interrogate	*v.* 审问；询问

（续）

词汇	词性和释义	词汇	词性和释义
impunity	n. 免于惩罚	counsel	n. 律师
exemptɪ	v. 免除 adj. 被免除的	burglary	n. 入室盗窃
condone	v. 宽恕；赦免	pornoshop	n. 色情商店
liberate	v. 释放	rapist	n. 强奸犯
remit	v. 赦免	counterfeit	v. 伪造
release	n. 释放；豁免	blackmail	v. 敲诈勒索
absolve	v. 赦免；解除	rehabilitate	v. 改造
acquit	v. 无罪释放	deterrent	n. 威慑力
abolish	v. 废除；取消	commit a crime	犯罪
term	n. 条款	break the law	违反法律
clause	n. 条款	life prisonment	无期徒刑
bill	n. 法案	death penalty	死刑
constitution	n. 宪法	death sentence	死刑
decree	n. 法令；规定 v. 颁布	abide by the law	守法
legislate	v. 立法；制定法律	settle down effective laws 制定积极有效的法律	
legislation	n. 立法；法律的制定	abuse of law	滥用法律
legalise	v. 使合法化	career criminal	职业罪犯
prescribe	v. 指示	organised crime	集团犯罪
credential	n. 凭证；证书	child abuse	虐待儿童
enact	v. 制定法律；颁布；规定	tax evasion	逃税

4.3 军 事

词汇	词性和释义	词汇	词性和释义
enlist	v. 征召；招募	invade	v. 侵入；侵略
array	n. 队列；排列	military	n. 军队；军人 adj. 军事的；军用的
raid	n. 袭击；突袭 v. 突然袭击	destroyer	n. 驱逐舰
charge	v. 攻击；突击	frigate	n. 护卫舰
encroach	v. 侵犯	submarine	n. 潜艇
despoil	v. 掠夺；抢劫	naval	adj. 海军的
confidential	adj. 机密的	repulse	v. 击退
cipher	n. 暗号；密码	expedition	n. 远征
disarm	v. 缴……的械；解除…… 的武装	siege	n. 围攻；包围 v. 围困；围攻
clandestine	adj. 秘密的；暗中的	besiege	v. 围攻
dissimulate	v. 掩盖；掩饰（动机）	beset	v. 包围
scout	v. 侦察	envelop	v. 包围
fort	n. 要塞；堡垒	tactics	n. 战术
hatchet	n. 短柄小斧	morale	n. 民心；士气
dagger	n. 短剑	maneuver	n. 机动；调遣；策略 v. 调遣
armor	n. 装甲；盔甲	bomber	n. 轰炸机
armament	n. 军备；武装	freighter	n. 运输机
corps	n. 军团；兵团	hardware	n. 装备
absorb	v. 吞并	strategic missile	战略导弹

（续）

词汇	词性和释义	词汇	词性和释义
anti-sub torpedo　反潜鱼雷		naval fleet　海上舰队	
depth charge　深水炸弹		marine corp　海军陆战队	
amphibious force　海陆空军		naval blockade　海上封锁	
amphibious tank　水陆坦克		submarine hunter　猎潜艇	
ground attack　地面进攻		anti-submarine vessel　反潜艇	
special taskforce　特种部队		armed robbery　武装抢劫	
joint military drill　联合军事演习		battle plane　战斗机	
military vessel　战舰		armed helicopter　武装直升机	
landing ship　登陆艇		battle plane　战斗机	

4.4　政　治

词汇	词性和释义	词汇	词性和释义
partisan	*adj.* 党派的；派系感强的	unconventional	*adj.*（行为等）不遵循传统的；（做事方式）非传统的
Senate	*n.* 参议院；上院	dictatorial	*adj.* 独裁的；专断的；霸道的；专横的
Congress	*n.* 代表大会；国会	authoritative	*adj.* 权威的；官方的
diplomacy	*n.* 外交；外交技巧；策略	influential	*adj.* 有影响的；有权势的
confederate	*n.* 同盟国；同盟者 *adj.* 同盟的；联合的	centralise	*v.* 把……集中起来
league	*n.* 联盟；社团 *v.* 使结盟；使结合	authority	*n.* 权威
affiliate	*n.* 附属机构；分支机构 *v.* 使隶属；使并入（较大的团体等）	privilege	*n.* 特权

（续）

词汇	词性和释义	词汇	词性和释义
democracy	*n.* 民主	immigrate	*v.* （从外国）移入
nationality	*n.* 国籍	immigrant	*n.* （外来）移民 *adj.* （从外国）移来的；移民的；移居的
kingdom	*n.* 王国	enslave	*v.* 奴役
realm	*n.* 王国；领域	enslavement	*n.* 强制；奴役
regime	*n.* 政权；政体	hustle	*v.* 驱赶
sovereignty	*n.* 主权	impel	*v.* 驱使
autonomy	*n.* 自治；自治权	anarchism	*n.* 无政府主义
commission	*n.* 委员会	republican	*adj.* 共和国的；共和政体的；共和主义的
committee	*n.* 委员会	monarchy	*n.* 君主政体；君主政治
election	*n.* 选举	colonise	*v.* 开拓殖民地
ballot	*n.* 选票	amendment	*n.* 修正案；修订
ideology	*n.* 意识形态	deport	*v.* 驱逐出境；放逐
parade	*n.* 游行；（部队的）检阅 *v.* 游行；列队行进；（使）集合接受检阅	reign	*n.* 王权；君权；统治时期 *v.* 统治；称王
govern	*v.* 支配；控制	tyrannical	*adj.* 暴政的；暴君的；专制的
confer	*v.* 协商	ultimatum	*n.* 最后通牒
entitle	*v.* 赋予……权利	domination	*n.* 控制；统治
exploit	*v.* 剥削	abdicate	*v.* 退位；放弃权力
reformation	*n.* 改革；变革	administer	*v.* 管理
emigrate	*v.* 移居（外国或他乡）	administration	*n.* 行政
emigrant	*n.* 移民；移居外国的人 *adj.* 移民的；移居的	institute	*v.* 建立
inspect	*v.* 视察	welfare	*n.* 福利；幸福

（续）

词汇	词性和释义	词汇	词性和释义
vote	*v.* 投票	creed	*n.* 信仰；信条
strike	*n.* 罢工 *v.* 罢工	doomed	*adj.* 命中注定的
municipal	*adj.* 市政的	destine	*v.* 命运注定
urban	*adj.* 城市的	destiny	*n.* 命运
rustic	*adj.* 乡村的	fatalism	*n.* 宿命论
community	*n.* 社区；社会；团体	blessed	*adj.* 受祝福的
metropolitan	*adj.* 大都市的	invocation	*n.* 祈祷
conventional	*adj.* 传统的	devout	*adj.* 虔诚的
exotic	*adj.* 外来的；有异国风味的	cult	*n.* 崇拜
patriarchal	*adj.* 男性主宰的；家长的；族长的	consecrate	*v.* 奉献于；献身
institutionalise	*v.* 使制度化；使习俗化	sacred	*adj.* 神圣的
status	*n.* 地位	Christian	*n.* 基督教徒 *adj.* 基督教的
clan	*n.* 部落；氏族	doctrine	*n.* 教义
household	*n.* 一家人；家庭 *adj.* 家庭的；日常的	dogma	*n.* 教义；教条
marital	*adj.* 婚姻的；夫妻间的	rite	*n.* 宗教仪式
ethic	*n.* 伦理学；道德标准	religion	*n.* 宗教
taboo	*n.* 禁忌；避讳	atheism	*n.* 无神论
Buddhism	*n.* 佛教	heresy	*n.* 异端；异端邪说
Taoism	*n.* 道教	invoke	*v.* 恳求；祈求
Christianity	*n.* 基督教	preach	*v.* 说教；布道
Islam	*n.* 伊斯兰教	enchant	*v.* 施魔法于

4.5 娱 乐

词汇	词性和释义	词汇	词性和释义
movement	*n.* 乐章	mold	*v.* 塑造
note	*n.* 音符	embroider	*v.* 绣花
score	*n.* 乐谱	tragedy	*n.* 悲剧
euphonious	*adj.* 悦耳的	opera	*n.* 歌剧
harsh	*adj.* 刺耳的	enact	*v.* 扮演
lyric	*n.* 歌词	rehearse	*v.* 预演；排练
conservatory	*n.* 音乐学院	character	*n.* 角色
episode	*n.* 插曲	design	*n.* 设计；图案 *v.* 设计
orchestra	*n.* 管弦乐队	profile	*n.* 外形；轮廓
chorus	*n.* 合唱团	aesthetic	*adj.* 审美的；美学的
concert	*n.* 音乐会	crosstalk	*n.* 相声
band	*n.* 乐队	chess	*n.* 国际象棋
record	*n.* 唱片	hiking	*n.* 徒步旅行
percussion	*n.* 打击乐器	hitch-hike	*n.* 搭便车旅行
string	*n.* 弦乐	surfing	*n.* 冲浪
wind	*n.* 管乐	stopover	*n.* 中途停留
picturesque	*adj.* 如画般的；生动的	handicraft	*n.* 手工艺
vivid	*adj.* 生动的	talk show　脱口秀	
gallery	*n.* 画廊	music appreciation　音乐欣赏	
museum	*n.* 博物馆	art gallery　画廊	
portrait	*n.* 肖像；画像	scenery spot　景点	
impressionism	*n.* 印象派	mineral bath　矿泉浴	
portray	*v.* 绘制	pleasure ground　游乐场	

（续）

词汇	词性和释义	词汇	词性和释义
amusement park　游乐园		first come, first serve　"先到先服务"原则	
round/return trip　往返		saver ticket　优惠票；打折票	
make a reservation　预订		airport tax　机场税	
cancel one's reservation　取消预订			

5. 综合学科

5.1 教育

词汇	词性和释义	词汇	词性和释义
ethical	*adj.* 道德的；伦理的	instruct	*v.* 教；命令
audition	*n.* 试听	instil	*v.* 灌输
credit	*n.* 学分	initiate	*v.* 启蒙；传授
nursery	*n.* 托儿所	sermon	*n.* 说教
syllabus	*n.* 课程大纲	self-discipline	*n.* 自律；自我约束
absenteeism	*n.* 旷课	anthropologist	*n.* 人类学者；人类学家
discipline	*n.* 学科	intelligence	*n.* 智力
curriculum	*n.* 课程	intellectual	*adj.* 智力的
didactic	*adj.* 教诲的；说教的	principal	*n.* 校长
leading	*adj.* 指导的	apprentice	*n.* 学徒
edify	*v.* 陶冶；教化	orator	*n.* 演讲者
lead	*v.* 引导；领导	illiterate	*n.* 文盲
direct	*v.* 引导	bachelor	*n.* 学士
conduct	*v.* 引导	inferior	*n.* 下级；晚辈
enlighten	*v.* 启发；开导	juvenile	*adj.* 青少年的

（续）

词汇	词性和释义
psychology	*n.* 心理学
science	*n.* 理科
humanities	*n.* 人文学科
social sciences	社会科学
liberal studies	人文学科
basic sciences	基础科学
applied sciences	应用科学
primary-level education	小学教育
secondary-level education	中学教育
tertiary-level education	大学教育
vocational education	职业教育
compulsory education	义务教育
compulsory subjects	必修课程
ethical standard	道德规范
boarding nursery	全托幼儿所
breeding nursery	育儿托儿所
motivate the students to do sth.	鼓励学生做某事
give the students inspiration	给学生灵感
psychological soundness	心理健康
a sense of obligation	责任感
following…blindly	盲从……
adverse circumstances	逆境
team spirit	团队精神
learn things through understanding	在理解的基础上学习
extra-curricular activity	课外活动
theoretical knowledge	理论知识
employable skill	就业技能

5.2 语　言

词汇	词性和释义	词汇	词性和释义
linguistics	*n.* 语言学	term	*n.* 术语
phonetics	*n.* 语音学	maxim	*n.* 格言；箴言
phonology	*n.* 音位学	satire	*n.* 讽刺作品
tense	*n.* 时态	farce	*n.* 闹剧
genre	*n.* 体裁；风格	adage	*n.* 格言；谚语
clause	*n.* 分句；从句	synopsis	*n.* 大纲；梗概
dialect	*n.* 方言；土话	compile	*v.* 收集；编纂
glossary	*n.* 术语汇编；词汇表	emend	*v.* 修订
character	*n.* 文字；字母	paraphrase	*v.* 解释；释义；改写
cogent	*adj.* 强有力的；有说服力的	adapt	*v.* 改编
fluent	*adj.* 流利的；流畅的	adaptable	*adj.* 可改编的
persuasive	*adj.* 有说服力的	adaption	*n.* 改写；修改
concise	*adj.* 简明的	excerpt	*n.* 摘录
implicit	*adj.* 含蓄的；隐含的	abstract	*n.* 摘要；概要
tag	*n.* 附加语	abstraction	*n.* 摘要
lyric	*n.* 歌词	abridge	*v.* 缩短；删节
verse	*n.* 诗；韵文	coin	*v.* 创造（新词语）
fiction	*n.* 小说	semantics	*n.* 语义学
byword	*n.* 谚语；俗语	syntax	*n.* 句法；句法规则
fable	*n.* 寓言；传说	pictograph	*n.* 象形文字

5.3 医　学

词汇	词性和释义	词汇	词性和释义
diagnose	*v.* 诊断	acute	*adj.* 急性的
diagnosis	*n.* 诊断	feverish	*adj.* 发烧的
inject	*v.* 注射；注入	morbid	*adj.* 病态的；不正常的
heal	*v.* 治愈；痊愈	numb	*adj.* 麻木的
remedy	*n.* 治疗法；药物	unconscious	*adj.* 失去知觉的； 未察觉的
treat	*v.* 治疗；医治	fragile	*adj.* 体质弱的
prescription	*n.* 药方	suscept	*n.* 感病体
dissect	*v.* 解剖	malady	*n.* 疾病
clinic	*n.* 诊所	symptom	*n.* 症状；征兆
anatomy	*n.* 剖析；解剖学	bleed	*v.* 流血
condition	*n.* 健康状况	relapse	*v.* （疾病）复发
hygiene	*n.* 卫生	bruise	*n.* 瘀伤 *v.* 擦伤
physical	*adj.* 身体的；物质的	fester	*v.* 使化脓
malnourished	*adj.* 营养失调的； 营养不良的	intoxicate	*v.* 使中毒
mental	*adj.* 精神的；智力的	bandage	*v.* 扎上绷带
spiritual	*adj.* 心灵的	thermometer	*n.* 体温计
subject	*n.* 实验对象	ointment	*n.* 药膏
contagious	*adj.* 传染的	non-drowsy	*adj.* 不致困的
infect	*v.* 传染；感染	recuperate	*v.* 康复；恢复
infectious	*adj.* 传染的；感染的	medication	*n.* 药物
contract	*v.* 感染	syrup	*n.* 糖浆

（续）

词汇	词性和释义
pad	*n.* 药棉块
transplant	*v.* 移植
syndrome	*n.* 综合征
handicap	*n.* 缺陷
physician	*n.* 内科医生
facial mask	口罩
mean deviation	均差
mean error	平均偏差
mechanical stage	机械台
medical apparatuses and instruments	医疗器械
medical data processor	医用数据处理机
medical laser system	医用激光系统
medical laser therapy equipment	医用激光治疗设备
medical rubber glove	医用橡胶手套
microscope illuminator	显微照明器
microscope lamp	显微镜灯
microscope micrometer	显微镜测微计
microscope objective	显微镜物镜
microscope photometer	显微镜光度计
microscope projector	显微镜投影仪
microscope slide	显微镜载玻片；显微镜载物架
microscope stage	显微镜载物台
microscope tube	显微镜筒
microtome blade	显微切片机
microtome knife	显微切片刀

（续）

词汇	词性和释义
microwave accelerator	微波加速器
microwave amplifier	微波放大器
microwave diathermy	微波透热疗法
microwave diathermy unit	微波透热治疗机
microwave filter	微波滤波器

5.4 化　学

词汇	词性和释义	词汇	词性和释义
chemistry	*n.* 化学	intermediary	*n.* 媒介物
hackneyed	*adj.* 陈腐的	catalyst	*n.* 催化剂
caustic	*adj.* 腐蚀性的	scorch	*v.* （因化学品的作用）（使）变色；烧焦；烧糊 *n.* 烧焦处；焦痕
erode	*v.* 腐蚀	tint	*v.* 上色；染色
stale	*adj.* 陈腐的	hydronic	*adj.* 循环加热（或冷却）的
rot	*v.* 腐烂	artificial	*adj.* 人造的；假的
rotten	*adj.* 腐烂的	molecule	*n.* 分子
corrode	*v.* 腐蚀	solution	*n.* 溶解；溶液
gasoline	*n.* 汽油	impurity	*n.* 杂质
silica	*n.* 二氧化硅	compound	*n.* 混合物；化合物
petroleum	*n.* 石油	sodium	*n.* 钠
hydrocarbon	*n.* 碳氢化合物	zinc	*n.* 锌
methane	*n.* 甲烷；沼气	helium	*n.* 氦
decomposition	*n.* 分解；腐烂	ammonia	*n.* 氨；氨水
limestone	*n.* 石灰石	iodine	*n.* 碘；碘酒

（续）

词汇	词性和释义	词汇	词性和释义
oxygen	*n.* 氧气	ignite	*v.* （使）燃烧；点燃
tin	*n.* 锡	combination	*n.* 化合；组合
calcium	*n.* 钙	polymerisation	*n.* 聚合
silicon	*n.* 硅；硅元素	catalysis	*n.* 催化作用
sulfur	*n.* 硫黄	adhesive	*n.* 黏合剂；黏着剂 *adj.* 黏性的
nitrogen	*n.* 氮	bleach	*n.* 漂白剂 *v.* 漂白
silver	*n.* 银	dye	*n.* 染料；染液 *v.* 给……染色
nickel	*n.* 镍	biochemistry	*n.* 生物化学
lead	*n.* 铅	alchemy	*n.* 炼金术
copper	*n.* 铜	ion	*n.* 离子
platinum	*n.* 白金；铂	solubility	*n.* 可溶性；溶解性
functional	*adj.* 起作用的	solvent	*adj.* 可溶解的；有溶解能力的
neutralise	*v.* 中和	element	*n.* 元素
action	*n.* 作用	blend	*v.* 使混合；（和某物）混合；融合 *n.* 混合物；混合品
sear	*v.* 烧灼	vein	*n.* 矿脉；矿层
burning	*adj.* 燃烧的	pit	*n.* 坑；地坑；煤矿
blast	*v.* 爆破	borehole	*n.* 钻孔；地上凿洞
particle	*n.* 颗粒	quartz	*n.* 石英
substance	*n.* 物质	marble	*n.* 大理石
explosive	*adj.* 爆炸的	gem	*n.* 宝石
explode	*v.* 爆炸	fieldstone	*n.* 散石；大卵石
kindle	*v.* 燃起；点燃	emerald	*n.* 祖母绿；翡翠；绿宝石

（续）

词汇	词性和释义	词汇	词性和释义
granite	*n.* 花岗岩	mineral	*n.* 矿物；矿石
lava	*n.* 熔岩；火山岩	ore	*n.* 矿石
ruby	*n.* 红宝石	aluminum	*n.* 铝
bonanza	*n.* 富矿带	nuclear	*adj.* 原子能的；原子核的

5.5 物　理

词汇	词性和释义	词汇	词性和释义
physics	*n.* 物理学	boundary	*n.* 边界
electron	*n.* 电子	boundless	*adj.* 无限的
neutron	*n.* 中子	endless	*adj.* 无止境的
nucleus	*n.* 核；原子核	cohesive	*adj.* 有凝聚力的
proton	*n.* 质子	horizontal	*n.* 水平线；水平面 *adj.* 水平的；地平线的
atom	*n.* 原子	bulk	*n.* 容积
fusion	*n.* 熔解；熔化	brim	*n.* （浅底容器的）边缘 *v.* 注满；溢出
temperature	*n.* 温度	edge	*n.* 边
centigrade	*n.* 摄氏 *adj.* 摄氏的	rim	*n.* 边缘
clot	*v.* （使）凝结 *n.* 凝块	brink	*n.* 边缘
sublimate	*v.* 升华	constituent	*n.* 成分
distillation	*n.* 蒸馏	dimension	*n.* 维（构成空间的因素）；规模；范围
radiation	*n.* 辐射	elasticity	*n.* 弹性
eject	*v.* 喷出	cohesion	*n.* 内聚力

（续）

词汇	词性和释义	词汇	词性和释义
mechanics	*n.* 机械学	resonance	*n.* 回声；回响
impetus	*n.* 推动力	echo	*n.* 回声；回音 *v.* 回响；回荡
decelerate	*v.* （使）减速	ultrasonic	*n.* 超声波
expedite	*v.* 加速；加快	sonar	*n.* 声呐装置；声呐系统
quiver	*v.* 振动；颤抖 *n.* （微微）颤抖	acoustic	*adj.* 音响的；听觉的
jar	*v.* 使震动 *n.* 猛然震动	band	*n.* 波段；频带
vibration	*n.* 震动	charge	*n.* 电荷；充电量 *v.* 充电
transpire	*v.* 发散；排出	electricity	*n.* 电流；电；电学
constitute	*v.* 构成；组成	voltage	*n.* 电压；伏特数
density	*n.* 密度	magnet	*n.* 磁体；磁铁
liquid	*n.* 液体 *adj.* 液体的；清澈的	magnetism	*n.* 磁力；磁学
dilute	*v.* 稀释；冲淡	electromagnet	*n.* 电磁铁；电磁体
dehydrate	*v.* （使）脱水	electromagnetism	*n.* 电磁；电磁学
declivity	*n.* 斜坡；坡度	electronic	*adj.* 电子的
foam	*n.* 泡沫 *v.* （使）起泡沫	electronics	*n.* 电子学
ventilation	*n.* 通风；空气流通	amplifier	*n.* 扩音器；放大器
evaporate	*v.* 蒸发	battery	*n.* 电池
evaporation	*n.* 蒸发（作用）	chip	*n.* 芯片
thermodynamics	*n.* 热力学	conductor	*n.* 导体
friction	*n.* 摩擦	insulator	*n.* 绝缘体；绝热器
attrition	*n.* 磨损	semiconductor	*n.* 半导体
chafe	*n.* 擦伤 *v.* 擦热；擦伤；擦痛	transistor	*n.* 晶体管

（续）

词汇	词性和释义	词汇	词性和释义
ultraviolet	*adj.* 紫外线的；紫外线辐射的	wavelength	*n.* 波长
microwave	*n.* 微波；微波炉	spectrum	*n.* 光；光谱；频谱
gravitation	*n.* 引力	ray	*n.* 光线
statics	*n.* 静力学	optics	*n.* 光学
relativity	*n.* 相对性；相对论	optical	*adj.* 光学的；眼的；视力的
velocity	*n.* 速度；速率	translucent	*adj.* 半透明的
dynamics	*n.* 动力学	opaque	*adj.* 不透明的；不透光的
force	*n.* 力	transparent	*adj.* 透明的
lens	*n.* 透镜；镜头	acceleration	*n.* 加速度
magnifier	*n.* 放大镜；放大器	current	*n.* （液体、气体的）流

5.6 天 文

词汇	词性和释义	词汇	词性和释义
astronomy	*n.* 天文学	ion	*n.* 离子
astronomical	*adj.* 天文学的；天文的	Earth	*n.* 地球
synchronous	*adj.* 同步的	Uranus	*n.* 天王星
terrestrial	*adj.* 类地行星的；陆地的	Pluto	*n.* 冥王星
asteroid	*n.* 小行星	Neptune	*n.* 海王星
collapsar	*n.* 坍缩星；黑洞	Mars	*n.* 火星
comet	*n.* 彗星	Mercury	*n.* 水星
constellation	*n.* 星座	Saturn	*n.* 土星
galaxy	*n.* 星系	Venus	*n.* 金星
electron	*n.* 电子	Jupiter	*n.* 木星

（续）

词汇	词性和释义	词汇	词性和释义
probe	*n.* 太空探测器；探测飞船	planetoid	*n.* 小行星
diffract	*v.* 使衍射	intergalactic	*adj.* 星系间的
atomic	*adj.* 原子的；原子能的	interplanetary	*adj.* 行星间的
hydrophilic	*adj.* 吸湿的	interstellar	*adj.* 星际的
nautical	*adj.* 船舶的；航海的	corona	*n.* 日冕
universe	*n.* 宇宙	chromosphere	*n.* 色球层
universal	*adj.* 宇宙的	solar	*adj.* 太阳的
celestial	*adj.* 天空的	photosphere	*n.* 光球
orbit	*n.* 轨道	pseudoscience	*n.* 伪科学
planet	*n.* 行星	astrology	*n.* 占星术；占星学
chondrite	*n.* 球粒陨石	astrophysics	*n.* 天体物理学
cluster	*n.* 星团	lunar	*adj.* 月球的；月亮的
meteor	*n.* 流星	revolve	*v.* （使）旋转
dwarf	*n.* 矮星	land	*v.* 着陆；降落
cosmos	*n.* 宇宙	spaceship	*n.* 宇宙飞船
cosmology	*n.* 宇宙学；宇宙论	spacecraft	*n.* 宇宙飞船；航天器
nebula	*n.* 星云；星云状的星系	telescope	*n.* 望远镜
quasar	*n.* 类星体	meteor shower	流星雨
space	*n.* 空间		

5.7 数 学

词汇	词性和释义	词汇	词性和释义
mathematics	*n.* 数学	subtract	*v.* 减去
arithmetic	*n.* 算术	deduction	*n.* 减去；扣除
geometry	*n.* 几何学	addition	*n.* 加法
statistics	*n.* 统计学；统计表	plus	*n.* 正号；加号 *adj.* 正的；加的
even	*adj.* 偶数的	minus	*n.* 负数；减号；负号 *adj.* 减的；负的
odd	*adj.* 奇数的	multiply	*v.* 乘；乘以
decimal	*n.* 小数 *adj.* 十进位的；小数的	divide	*v.* 除；除以
ratio	*n.* 比率	numeral	*n.* 数字；数码
calculate	*v.* 计算；估计	percentage	*n.* 百分数；百分比
enumerate	*v.* 列举；枚举	equation	*n.* 方程式；等式
constant	*n.* 常数；常量	quarter	*n.* 四分之一
variant	*n.* 变体；变形	fraction	*n.* 分数
variable	*n.* 变量	rank	*n.* 矩阵的秩
abacus	*n.* 算盘	discrete	*adj.* 离散的；离散变量的
aggregate	*n.* 合计；总数	symmetry	*n.* 对称（性）
sum	*n.* 总数	sequence	*n.* 序列
calculator	*n.* 计算机；计算器	induction	*n.* 归纳法；归纳
degree	*n.* 度数；度	inference	*n.* 推论；推理
calculus	*n.* 微积分（学）	circulate	*v.* （使）循环
digit	*n.* 数字；数位	circular	*adj.* 循环的；圆形的
function	*n.* 函数	probability	*n.* 概率

（续）

词汇	词性和释义	词汇	词性和释义
dispersion	*n.* 离差；差量	column	*n.* 圆柱
vertical	*adj.* 垂直的	cylinder	*n.* 圆柱体
plumb	*adj.* 垂直的	angle	*n.* 角
cube	*n.* 立方体；立方形	plane	*n.* 平面
facet	*n.* 平面	ellipse	*n.* 椭圆；椭圆形
sphere	*n.* 球体	diagram	*n.* 图表
loop	*n.* 圈；环	polygon	*n.* 多角形；多边形
triangle	*n.* 三角形	intersect	*v.* 相交
circumference	*n.* 圆周	radius	*n.* 半径
cone	*n.* 圆锥体	rectangle	*n.* 长方形；矩形
caliber	*n.* 口径	square	*n.* 正方形；平方
diameter	*n.* 直径	parallel	*adj.* 平行的；并行的
circle	*n.* 圆周		

5.8 农 学

词汇	词性和释义	词汇	词性和释义
agriculture	*n.* 农业；农艺；农学	hay	*n.* 干草；草料
irrigate	*v.* 灌溉	haystack	*n.* 干草堆
tractor	*n.* 拖拉机	weed	*n.* 野草；杂草 *v.* 除杂草
cotton	*n.* 棉花	sorghum	*n.* 高粱
garlic	*n.* 大蒜；蒜头	livestock	*n.* 家畜；牲畜
eggplant	*n.* 茄子	poultry	*n.* 家禽
fodder	*n.* 饲料；草料	fowl	*n.* 家禽

（续）

词汇	词性和释义	词汇	词性和释义
conservatory	*n.* 温室；暖房	horticulture	*n.* 园艺（学）
cowshed	*n.* 牛棚；牛舍	hydroponics	*n.* 水培；溶液栽培
granary	*n.* 谷仓	insecticide	*n.* 杀虫剂
greenhouse	*n.* 温室；花房	trough	*n.* 饲料槽；饮水槽
seedbed	*n.* 苗床	ranch	*n.* 大农场；大牧场
orchard	*n.* 果园	plantation	*n.* 种植场；种植园
prolific	*adj.* 多产的	pasture	*n.* 草地；牧场
rich	*adj.*（土壤）肥沃的	pigpen	*n.* 猪舍
ripe	*adj.*（庄稼）成熟的	accumulated temperature of cultivation 栽培积温	
harvest	*n.* 收获 *v.* 收割	accumulated temperature of daytime　昼积温	
agrobiology	*n.* 农业生物学	accumulated temperature of growth　生育积温	
agrochemistry	*n.* 农业化学	acellular organism　非细胞生物	
agroecology	*n.* 农业生态学	acid base equilibrium　酸碱平衡	
agroeconomics	*n.* 农业经济学	acid soil improvement　酸性土壤改良	
arable	*adj.* 适于耕种的	agricultural implement　农具	
indigenous	*adj.* 土产的；当地的	agricultural insect　农业昆虫	
fertiliser	*n.* 肥料	agricultural machinery　农业机械	
husbandry	*n.*（尤指精心经营的）农牧业	agricultural pollution　农业污染	
graze	*v.* 放牧；吃草	agricultural problem　农业问题	
cultivate	*v.* 耕种	agricultural produce　农产品	
manure	*n.* 肥料；粪肥 *v.* 施肥于	agricultural product　农产品	

5.9 考 古

词汇	词性和释义	词汇	词性和释义
archaeology	*n.* 考古学	skull	*n.* 头盖骨
anthropologist	*n.* 人类学家	archaic	*adj.* 古代的
paleoanthropologist	*n.* 古人类学家	ascend	*v.* 上升；升高
unearth	*v.* 发掘；发现	originate	*v.* 发源于
fossil	*n.* 化石	hominid	*n.* 人科（包括人及其祖先）
petrify	*v.* 使石化；变为化石	homogeneous	*adj.* 同一种族（种类）的
exhume	*v.* 发掘；掘出	morphology	*n.* 形态学
excavate	*v.* 发掘；挖出	primitive	*adj.* 原始的；最初的
invaluable	*adj.* 无价的	remnant	*n.* 残余；遗迹
Neolithic	*adj.* 新石器时代的	Stone Age　石器时代	
Mesolithic	*adj.* 中石器时代的	Bronze Age　青铜器时代	
Paleolithic	*adj.* 旧石器时代的	Iron Age　铁器时代	
origin	*n.* 起源；由来	ancient civilisation　古代文明	
chronological	*adj.* 按时间顺序排列的	cultural relics　文物	
artefact	*n.* 人造制品	archaeological specimen　考古学样品	
antiquity	*n.* 古迹；古物	archaeological site　考古遗址	
antique	*n.* 古物；古董		